IT Career JumpStart

IT Career JumpStart

An Introduction to PC Hardware, Software, and Networking

Naomi J. Alpern

Joey Alpern

Randy Muller

WILEY

John Wiley & Sons, Inc.

Senior Acquisitions Editor: Jeff Kellum
Development Editor: Susan Herman
Technical Editor: Rodney Fournier
Production Editor: Liz Britten
Copy Editor: Rebecca Rider
Editorial Manager: Pete Gaughan
Production Manager: Tim Tate
Vice President and Executive Group Publisher: Richard Swadley
Vice President and Publisher: Neil Edde
Book Designer: Judy Fung
Compositor: Craig Johnson, Happenstance Type-O-Rama
Proofreader: Louise Watson, Word One, New York
Indexer: Ted Laux
Project Coordinator, Cover: Katherine Crocker
Cover Designer: Ryan Sneed
Cover Image: © Comstock Images / Getty Images

Copyright © 2012 by John Wiley & Sons, Inc., Indianapolis, Indiana
Published simultaneously in Canada

ISBN: 978-1-118-20615-7
ISBN: 978-1-118-22859-3 (ebk.)
ISBN: 978-1-118-23299-6 (ebk.)
ISBN: 978-1-118-26572-7 (ebk.)

For general information on our other products and services or to obtain technical support, please contact our Customer Care Department within the U.S. at (877) 762-2974, outside the U.S. at (317) 572-3993 or fax (317) 572-4002.

Wiley publishes in a variety of print and electronic formats and by print-on-demand. Some material included with standard print versions of this book may not be included in e-books or in print-on-demand. If this book refers to media such as a CD or DVD that is not included in the version you purchased, you may download this material at http://booksupport.wiley.com. For more information about Wiley products, visit www.wiley.com.

Library of Congress Control Number: 2011941732

10 9 8 7 6 5 4 3 2 1

Dear Reader,

Thank you for choosing *IT Career JumpStart*. This book is part of a family of premium-quality Sybex books, all of which are written by outstanding authors who combine practical experience with a gift for teaching.

Sybex was founded in 1976. More than 30 years later, we're still committed to producing consistently exceptional books. With each of our titles, we're working hard to set a new standard for the industry. From the paper we print on to the authors we work with, our goal is to bring you the best books available.

I hope you see all that reflected in these pages. I'd be very interested to hear your comments and get your feedback on how we're doing. Feel free to let me know what you think about this or any other Sybex book by sending me an email at nedde@wiley.com. If you think you've found a technical error in this book, please visit http://sybex.custhelp.com. Customer feedback is critical to our efforts at Sybex.

Best regards,

Neil Edde
Vice President and Publisher
Sybex, an Imprint of Wiley

To our bears, the work that went into this book was always for you.

—*Naomi and Joey Alpern*

To Penny—Your patience, love, and understanding made this possible.

—*Randy Muller*

Acknowledgments

We would like to thank our superb Acquisitions Editor, Jeff Kellum, without whose determination and follow-through this book would never have come to fruition. He was a steady force throughout all the ups and downs during the roller coaster ride this book took before taking shape and becoming a reality—even if he did originally ask if we could write two chapters a week and be done in six to eight weeks. Huge thanks, also, to our co-author, Randy, for working through chapters in parallel, allowing us to meet Jeff's new set of more down-to-earth timelines and also helping to lighten the load. Randy: We're looking forward to the next chance meeting!

Many thanks go out to Susan Herman, our Developmental Editor, and Liz Britten, our Production Editor, for pushing hard to get drafts turned in on time and reviewed and returned promptly, even when the universe decided not to cooperate and continued to throw obstacle after obstacle in the way.

Thanks also to the rest of the team and all the rest of the editorial staff at Wiley for all the work behind the scenes that is required to bring a book to print. Finally, we want to thank our kids, Darien and Justin, for putting up with long weekend afternoons spent with mommy and daddy clicking away on keyboards. In the end it's all for them.

—Naomi and Joey Alpern

About the Authors

Naomi J. Alpern currently works for Microsoft Consulting Services as a Senior Consultant specializing in Unified Communications and IT Architecture and Planning. Since the start of her technical career, she has worked in many facets of the technology world, including IT administration, technical training, and most recently, full-time consulting. Naomi holds a Bachelor of Science in Leisure Services Management from Florida International University. Additionally, she holds many Microsoft certifications, including an MCSE and MCT, as well as other industry certifications such as Citrix Certified Enterprise Administrator, Security+, Network+, and A+. Naomi lives in Charlotte, NC, where she spends her spare time, along with her husband, Joey, chasing after their two young sons, Darien, 8, and Justin, 4. On the odd occasion that she runs into some alone time, she enjoys curling up with a cheesy horror or mystery novel for company.

Joey Alpern currently works as an independent consultant specializing in web development and database component integration. Since the start of his technical career, he has worked in various industries, ranging from the creation of internal systems for technical staffing agencies to dotcom startups; his most recent adventure occurred in the luxury cruise industry. Joey holds a Bachelor of Science in Computer Science from Florida International University. With over 13 years of development and coding experience, he is comfortable with multiple languages, including C++, Java, Visual Basic, .Net, and even Pascal. Additionally, he is Java certified and often finds working with computers easier than working with people.

Randy Muller is an independent trainer and consultant specializing in Unified Communications and Security. Randy was an army officer stationed in Germany where he began his IT career. Since then he has been an IT consultant, author, and a technical trainer. Randy holds degrees from Indiana University in History and Geography and has numerous Microsoft certifications including MCT, and also has certifications in Security+, CEH, and CHFI. Randy lives in Stevensville, Montana, with his wife, Penny and her three sons, Jack, Andy, and Chris. When he is not travelling to his training assignments, Randy enjoys planning his next house.

Contents

Chapter 8   A Communications Framework   161

Introduction

Computers are very common today, and just about any computer is connected to a network. People with the knowledge and expertise to configure and maintain networks are needed in any organization. Networking can be a complex topic, especially for those new to the field of Internet technology (IT). Having a basic understanding of the various hardware and software components used in a computer network is key for any IT professional. By stripping down a network to its bare essentials and discussing this complex topic in a clear and concise manner, we hope to help the beginner understand fundamental IT concepts, and thus create a base knowledge for more advanced topics and technologies.

This book covers all the prerequisites for anybody looking for a career in IT. It is designed for the novice user who wants to become familiar with how computers work and eventually wants a career in IT.

What This Book Covers

Before you begin pursuing a career in IT, you should have certain prerequisite information:

- ◆ A working knowledge of an operating system such as Unix, Windows 7, Windows Server 2008, or Windows Server 2008 R2
- ◆ Proficiency with the Windows interface and a working knowledge of Windows Explorer
- ◆ An understanding of networking concepts such as networks, servers, clients, network adapter cards and hardware, protocols, network operating systems, and drivers
- ◆ An understanding of computer hardware, including processors, memory, hard disks, communication ports, and peripheral devices

This book covers these prerequisites in easy-to-understand language with graphics to illustrate the concepts. Information is presented in small chunks so that it won't be overwhelming.

Based on the knowledge you need to begin your certification preparations, this book is organized as follows:

Chapters 1–4   These chapters deal with computer hardware. They cover computer processors, data storage, input/output devices, and hardware configuration issues.

Chapters 5–7   These chapters cover software. You will learn about the different local operating systems, get a good overview of the command line, and learn the basics of the Windows 7 interface.

Chapters 8–11 These chapters cover common networking concepts such as the Open Systems Interconnection (OSI) model, peer-to-peer and client-server network models, network topologies, networking hardware, network protocols, and common network operating systems.

Chapters 12–15 These chapters focus on Windows 7 and Windows Server 2008 R2, covering their history, the platforms, user and group management, and file and print resource management.

Making the Most of This Book

At the beginning of each chapter of *IT Career JumpStart*, you'll find a list of topics that you can expect to learn about within that chapter.

To help you soak up new material easily, we've highlighted *new terms* in italics and defined them in the margins of the pages. In addition, several special elements highlight important information:

_____
NOTE
_____

Notes provide extra information and references to related information.

_____
TIP
_____

Tips are insights that help you perform tasks more easily and effectively.

_____
WARNING
_____

Warnings let you know about things you should do—or shouldn't do—as you learn more.

At the end of each chapter, you can test your knowledge of the topics covered by answering the chapter's Review Questions. (You'll find the answers to the Review Questions in Appendix A.)

There's also some special material for your reference. If you'd like to quickly look up the meaning of a term, the Glossary contains terms that have been introduced throughout the book. If you are wondering what acronyms stand for, refer to Appendix B, which shows the acronyms in this book spelled out.

Chapter 1

The Computer's Brain: Processors and Memory

pro•cess *v*: to complete a series of actions

Every computer consists of a microprocessor and memory. Without the two, the computer would not function. The microprocessor, commonly referred to as the central processing unit (CPU), is the brain of the computer. Like the human brain, the CPU is responsible for managing the timing of each operation and carrying out the instructions or commands from an application or the operating system.

The CPU uses memory as a place to store or retrieve information. Memory comes in several forms, such as random access memory (RAM) and read-only memory (ROM). Memory provides a temporary location for storing information and contains more permanent system configuration information.

Introduction to Processors

The most central component to the computer is the processor. It is responsible for executing the instructions that are given to the computer. The processor determines the operating systems you can use, the software applications you can run on the computer, and the computer's ability and performance. It is also typically one of the major factors in computer cost. Computers that contain newer and more powerful processors are more expensive than computers with less complex processors. This has led processor manufacturers to offer several different lines of processors for the home user, business workstation, and server markets.

Processor Performance

The goal of processor performance is to make applications run faster. Performance is commonly defined by how long it takes for a specific task to be executed. Traditionally, processor performance has been defined as how many instructions can be completed in each clock cycle, or instructions per clock (IPC), times the number of clock cycles. Thus, performance is measured as

$$IPC \times Frequency$$

Processor Types: A First Look

motherboard
The main board in a computer that manages communication between devices internally and externally.

central processing unit (CPU)
The microprocessor, or brain, of the computer. It uses logic to perform mathematical operations that are used to manipulate data.

Complex Instruction Set Computing (CISC)
A full complement of instructions used by a processor to complete tasks such as mathematical calculations. Used in the most common type of processor produced; Intel processors are currently based on this standard.

Reduced Instruction Set Computing (RISC)
A reduced set of instructions used by a processor. PowerPC and Alpha processors are manufactured using this standard. The reduced instruction set enables a microprocessor to operate at higher speeds.

So many types of computer processors, also referred to as microprocessors, are on the market today that it can be quite confusing to wade through them all. All processors are not created equal, and each processor has its own characteristics that make it unique. For instance, a processor that is built around an architecture common to other processors of the same time period may actually operate at double or triple the speed. Fierce competition among the various chip makers lays the groundwork for new technological innovations and constant improvements.

The most obvious difference among processors is the physical appearance of the chips, meaning that many processors differ noticeably from one another in size and shape. The first processor that Intel released was packaged in a small chip that contained two rows of 20 pins each. As processor technology improved, the shape and packaging scheme of the processor also changed. Modern processors, such as the Intel Core i7 class processors, use the same socket as the Xeon processors and can only be placed on the *motherboard*, which has the appropriate socket. This design also reduces the cost involved in producing the *CPU*.

Another noticeable difference among processors is the type of instruction set they use. The instruction sets that are most common to processors are either *Complex Instruction Set Computing (CISC)* or *Reduced Instruction Set Computing (RISC)*.

CISC has been a common method of processing operations, especially in Intel CPUs. CISC uses a set of commands, which include subcommands that require additional CPU memory and time to process. Each command must go through a decode unit, located inside the CPU, to be broken down into *microcode*. The microcode is then processed one command at a time, which slows computing.

RISC, on the other hand, uses smaller commands that enable it to operate at higher speeds. The smaller commands work directly with microcode, so there is no need for a decode unit. This factor—along with a RISC chip's capability to execute multiple commands simultaneously—dramatically increases the processing power.

Finally, different manufacturers design processors to varying specifications. You should be sure that the processor type and model you choose are compatible with the operating system that you want to use. If the processor is not 100-percent compatible with the operating system, the computer will not operate at its best or might not work at all.

microcode
The smallest form of an instruction in a CPU.

The terms processor, microprocessor, chip, and CPU are used interchangeably.

NOTE

Deciphering Processor Terminology

For most computer novices, terms such as *microcode efficiency* and *internal cache RAM* can sound like part of a foreign language. To help you keep things straight, here are some common terms and their definitions:

Clock cycles   The internal speed of a computer or processor expressed in *megahertz (MHz)* or *gigahertz (GHz)*. The faster the clock speed, the faster the computer performs a specific operation.

CPU speed   The number of operations that are processed in one second.

Data path   The number of *bits* that can be transported into the processor chip during one operation.

Floating-point unit (FPU), or math coprocessor   A secondary processor that speeds operations by taking over math calculations of decimal numbers. Also called a numeric processor.

Level 1 (L1), or internal, cache   Memory in the CPU that is used to temporarily store instructions and data while they are waiting to be processed. One of the distinguishing features of different processors is the amount of internal cache that is supported.

Level 2 (L2), or backside, cache   Memory that is used by the CPU to temporarily store data that is waiting to be processed. Originally located on the motherboard, CPU architectures such as the Pentium II, III, and 4 have incorporated L2 cache directly on the same board as the CPU. This holds true in today's i5 and i7 processors with L2 and L3 cache on board. The CPU can access the on-board L2 cache two to four times faster than it can access the L2 cache on the motherboard.

Level 3 (L3), or backside, cache   Memory that is used by the CPU to temporarily store data that is waiting to be processed and is used in

megahertz (MHz)
One million cycles per second. The internal clock speed of a microprocessor is expressed in MHz.

gigahertz (GHz)
One billion cycles per second. The internal clock speed of a microprocessor is expressed in GHz.

bit
A binary digit. The digit is the smallest unit of information and represents either an off state (zero) or an on state (one).

conjunction with the L2 cache. The L3 cache is used to hold memory feeds to the L2 cache, and its memory is typically slower than the L2 memory but faster than main memory.

Microcode efficiency   The capability of a CPU to process microcode in a manner that uses the least amount of time and completes the greatest number of operations.

Word size   The largest number in bits that can be processed during one operation.

NOTE   **All the computer's components, including the processor, are installed on the motherboard. This fiberglass sheet is designed for a specific type of CPU. When purchasing a motherboard, you should check with the motherboard manufacturer to determine which types of CPUs are supported.**

The Intel Processor Lineup

Over time, Intel has introduced several generations of microprocessors. Each processor type is referred to as a generation; each is based on the new technological enhancements of the day. With each product release come new software and hardware products to take advantage of the new technology.

Several generations of Intel processors are available today. Since the arrival of the first Intel chip in the IBM PC, Intel has dominated the market. It seems that every time you turn around, a new chip promises greater performance and processing capabilities than the previous one.

What makes Intel the market leader is its ability to bring the newest innovations in chip technology to the public, usually before its competitors, who are not far behind. Competition is fierce, and each manufacturer attempts to improve on the designs of the others, releasing similar chips that promise better performance.

The following table shows the specifications for some of the newer Intel processors issued to date. You should read the specifications and reviews for each processor to understand its capabilities and reliability.

Model	Clock Speed	Number of Cores	Cache Size
Core i3-530	2.93 GHz	2	4 MB
Core i3-550	3.20 GHz	2	4 MB
Core i3-330M*	2.13 GHz	2	3 MB
Core i3-370M	2.40 GHz	2	3 MB
Core i3-37M	2.40 GHz	2	3 MB
Core i5-750	2.66GHz	4	8 MB

Model	Clock Speed	Number of Cores	Cache Size
Core i5-760	2.8 GHz	4	8 MB
Core i5-430M	2.26 GHz	2	3 MB
Core i5-540M	2.53GHz	2	3 MB
Core i7-975	3.33 GHz	4	8 MB
Core i7-980X	3.33 GHz	6	12 MB
Core i7-920XM	2.00 GHz	4	8 MB
Core i7-940XM	2.13 GHz	4	8 MB

* Mobile Processor

Factors Affecting Performance

Many factors come together to determine the performance of any computer. All other factors being equal, faster components will give better performance, but any computer will be limited by its "weakest links." As an analogy, consider that putting a larger engine in a standard automobile will make it faster, but only if the automobile is going in a straight line. As soon as you try to make the car follow a twisting road, other components such as the drivetrain and the tires can limit the performance of the larger engine.

Within a processor family, faster processors will outperform slower processors. But when we're comparing processors from different families, that rule does not apply. For example, the rating of 400 MHz for a processor from one family does not indicate that it will run significantly faster than a 333 MHz processor from a more advanced processor family.

As you learned earlier, clock cycles and data path are two factors that can influence the performance of your computer. Other factors are

Cache memory   Very fast memory that sits between the CPU and the main RAM. Cache memory can be as fast as 5 to 10 nanoseconds, whereas main RAM is usually not faster than 60 to 70 nanoseconds. (Yes, a lower number is better here because it indicates that the memory takes less time to move data.)

Bus speed   The rate at which data can be transferred between the CPU and the rest of the motherboard. Typical bus speeds are 1 GHz and higher with the current standard for motherboards entering the market.

The type of peripherals on your computer can affect system performance. If your application spends a lot of time accessing your hard disk, selecting a better-performing disk system would improve CPU efficiency. Storage systems are covered in detail in Chapter 2, "Storing Your Files: Data Storage."   *NOTE*

History of Intel Chips

Intel released the world's first microprocessor, the Intel 4004, in 1971. It was a 4-bit microprocessor containing a programmable controller chip that could process 45 instructions. The 4 bits meant that the chip had four lines for data to travel on, much like a four-lane highway. Because of its limitations, it was implemented only in a few early video games and some other devices. The following year, Intel released the 8008, an 8-bit microprocessor with enhanced memory storage and the capability to process 48 instructions.

Intel then began to research and develop faster, more capable processors. From that research emerged the 8080, which could process instructions 10 times faster than its predecessors. Although the speed had dramatically improved, it was still limited by the number of instructions it could process. Finally, in 1978, Intel broke many barriers by releasing the first of many computer-ready microprocessors, the 8086. The 8086 was a breakthrough technology with a bus speed of 16 bits and the capability to support and use 1 MB of RAM. Unfortunately, the cost of manufacturing such a chip and compatible 16-bit components made the chip unaffordable. Intel responded the following year with the production of an 8-bit chip, the 8088.

Intel continued to break new ground as the release of each new generation of processor offered improved functions and processing capabilities. The most dramatic improvement was the number of instructions, based on a scale of millions, that the processor could process in one second. This rate, referred to as *millions of instructions per second (MIPS)*, ranges from 0.75 MIPS for the 8088 to over 159,000 MIPS for the Core i7 990X.

The second most dramatic improvement was the speed of the internal clock, measured in gigahertz. All processors are driven by an internal clock mechanism that keeps the rhythm of the chip, much like the rhythm of a heartbeat. The faster the speed of the internal clock, the faster the processor can process instructions. Intel continued to increase the speed of the internal clock from 4.77 MHz for the original 8088 to more than 3.6 GHz for the newest generation of Core i7 Intel microprocessors.

The Pentium Family

Intel released the Pentium chip to take advantage of *Peripheral Component Interconnect (PCI) bus architecture*. This processor consisted of 3.1 million *transistors* and a new 64-bit data path. The chip was originally designed to operate at 66 MHz but was scaled down to 60 MHz to support the new transistor design, which was experiencing heat and power problems. The first chips deployed also suffered from a bug in the microcode that hampered the processor's capability to calculate complex mathematical equations with precision. This problem was immediately fixed through a new batch of chips.

millions of instructions per second (MIPS)
A measurement of the number of microcode instructions that a CPU or microprocessor can complete in one second, or cycle.

bus architecture
Any linear pathway on which electrical signals travel and carry data from a source to a destination.

transistor
A microscopic electronic device that uses positive electrons to create the binary value of one, or "on," and negative electrons to create the binary value of zero, or "off." Modern CPUs have millions of transistors.

Peripheral Component Interconnect (PCI)
A bus standard for the transfer of data between the CPU, expansion cards, and RAM. PCI communicates at 33 MHz.

The most significant development in the Pentium was the use of two parallel 32-bit *pipeline*s that enabled it to execute twice the number of instructions as previous Intel processors—a technological advancement that Intel named superscalar technology. Almost all processors today use this technology.

Released with the Pentium family of processors was *Multimedia Extension (MMX)* technology. MMX technology is often referred to as multimedia-enhanced technology, but this is not completely accurate. MMX-equipped processors contained additional instruction code sets that increased the processing speed for audio, video, and graphical data by up to 60 percent as compared to traditional Pentium processors. The MMX chips dramatically improved the response time of games and multimedia-based applications.

The types of Pentium processors include

- Pentium
- Pentium MMX
- Pentium Pro
- Pentium II (PII)
- Celeron
- Pentium II Xeon
- Pentium III (PIII)
- Pentium III Xeon
- Itanium/Itanium 2
- Pentium 4
- Tualatin
- Core i3
- Core i5
- Core i7

pipeline

A place in the processor where operations occur in a series of stages. The operation is not complete until it has passed through all stages.

Multimedia Extension (MMX)

A processor technology that dramatically improves the response time of games and multimedia-based applications. The technology was introduced through the MMX-equipped line of Intel Pentium chips.

Pentium

The Pentium chip introduced the world to the first parallel 32-bit data path, which enabled the Pentium to process 64 bits—twice as much data as before. The Pentium was the first microprocessor chip designed to work with the PCI bus specification and had internal clock speeds ranging from 60 MHz to 200 MHz.

Pentium MMX

The Pentium with MMX technology included an expanded instruction code set with 57 new MMX microcode instructions. MMX enabled the microprocessor to increase the processing speed of audio, video, and graphics by up to 60 percent.

Pentium Pro

The Pentium Pro was the successor to Intel's Pentium processor. One of the unique features of this microprocessor was its internal RISC architecture with CISC-RISC translator service. The translator service was able to use the CISC set of instructions, common to all Intel chips, convert them to the RISC set, the faster of the two, and then complete the tasks as necessary using RISC.

The architectural enhancement that really distinguished the Pro from the original Pentium would influence how most microprocessors would later be developed. The Pro was two chips in one: On the bottom of the Pentium was the actual processor. Connected directly overhead of the processor was an L2 cache. By placing the L2 cache close to the processor, Intel was able to greatly increase the performance of the Pentium Pro.

Pentium II (PII)

The Intel Pentium II, or PII, processor was essentially an enhanced Pentium Pro processor with MMX extensions, cache memory, and a new interface design. The PII was designed to fit into a *single-edge cartridge (SEC)* that plugs into a 242-pin slot.

single-edge cartridge (SEC)
An advanced packaging scheme that the Intel Pentium II and later models used. The processor was encased in a cartridge module with a single edge that plugged into a 242-pin slot on the system board, much as an expansion card plugged into the system board.

Celeron

The only noticeable difference between the Celeron and regular Pentium II processors is the lack of cache memory within its cartridge. Later models of the Celeron include cache memory on the same chip as the processor.

Pentium II Xeon

One of the major enhancements in the Pentium II Xeon was a larger on-board cache. This processor was available with either 1 MB or 2 MB of L2 cache and a clock rate of 450 MHz.

Pentium III (PIII)

With its faster clock rates (up to 733 MHz), the Pentium III supported demanding applications such as full-screen, full-motion video and realistic graphics. Seventy new instructions had been added to make technologies such as 3D graphics, video, speech, and imaging faster and more affordable for mainstream users. Each Pentium III also contained a unique processor serial number. Intel's intent behind this feature was to enhance system security and asset tracking. However, many individuals object to the serial number as infringement on their privacy because it could be used to identify computers on the Internet.

Pentium III Xeon

The Pentium III Xeon processor challenged RISC-based servers in both price/performance and raw performance. It's available in speeds of up to 550 MHz and supports configurations that have more than one processor in the same box.

Itanium/Itanium 2

The Itanium processor employs a 64-bit architecture and enhanced instruction handling to greatly increase the performance of computational and multimedia operations and supports clock speeds of up to 800 MHz. The Itanium 2 processor uses a 128-bit architecture and supports speeds of 900 MHz and 1 GHz.

Pentium 4

The Pentium 4 introduced architectural changes that allowed the processor to increase performance by processing more instructions per clock cycle. This technology is referred to as Hyper Pipeline and allows for 20 pipeline stages as opposed to the 10 pipeline stages used in the Pentium III family. Other enhancements were added through NetBurst technology, which includes such features as improved L1 and L2 caches and the Rapid Execution Engine. Current Pentium 4 processors can support speeds of up to 2.53 GHz.

Tualatin

The Tualatin processor was originally designed to be a logical next step in the Pentium III family. However, as the schedule for this processor slipped, Intel shifted focus to the Pentium 4 processor family. As a result, the Tualatin processor was not released until mid-2001. The Tualatin processors support speeds of up to 1.2 GHz.

Core i3 Series

The Core i3 is one of Intel's newer baseline processors. There are two categories for the Core i3: the 300 series, which contains all laptop products, and the 500 series, which contains all desktop products. All Core i3 processors have dual cores and all have Intel Hyper-Threading, which allows each CPU core to execute two processing threads. One thing that the Core i3s do not have is Intel's dynamic clock speed technology called Turbo Boost, which can result in more significant performance increases. The Core i3 has an integrated graphics processor.

Core i5 Series

The Core i5 is a mid-range line processor from Intel and has either dual or quad cores. There are four categories for the Core i5. The 400 and 500 series processors are designed for mobile computing and have dual cores. The 600 and 700 are desktop processors: The 600 has dual cores and the 700 has quad cores. All Core i5 processors have Turbo Boost, which is one of the primary differences separating the Core i3 series from the Core i5. The Core i5 700 series is the only one in the Core i5 family that does not have an integrated graphics processor.

Core i7 Series

The Core i7 is the high-end line from Intel and it has dual, quad, and hex core processors. All Core i7 processors have Hyper-Threading and Turbo Boost. The i7 (as well as the i3 and i5) processor supports 32-bit or 64-bit versions of an operating system. The drawback to a 32-bit system is that it supports only up to 3.3 GB of RAM, so you do not get the benefit of any additional RAM installed on the system.

NOTE   Although most of us would like to get our hands on the new high-speed processors, the reality is that it will be a while before they are affordable. Also, to really reap the benefits of those high-speed CPUs, computers need to have equivalently high-powered hardware. That is why you will see the first high-speed high CPUs only in expensive servers.

Stacking Up the Competition

Many manufacturers have attempted to compete with Intel to produce microprocessor chips. For many years, Intel's competitors produced clone copies of its chips, often slightly altering the original design to allow for faster processing speeds. A good example of this was the release by Advanced Micro Devices (AMD) of a 40 MHz version of the 386 processor to rival the 33 MHz version that Intel was producing. Non-Intel, or clone, chips became popular because of their cheaper price and improved features.

In addition to clone chips, other manufacturers produced powerful processors that were not based on Intel architecture. Digital Equipment Corporation (DEC), Sun Microsystems, IBM, and Motorola all produced powerful CPUs. Most of these chips were RISC-based CPUs designed to meet two needs: First, RISC-type chips can meet the powerful speed demands of Unix workstations; second, companies want to differentiate themselves from Intel to increase sales.

When Intel released the Pentium generation of processors, the clone manufacturers adopted their own unique naming conventions that diverged from the path that Intel laid with a new release. At the same time, Intel was experiencing a problem with the early release of its Pentium line—a high-level mathematical division problem. Intel's competitors took advantage of the opportunity by releasing their chips to compete with the Pentium processor.

The subsections that follow provide an overview of these processors:

◆ AMD

◆ Cyrix

◆ PowerPC

◆ Alpha

Be sure to check the Microsoft *Hardware Compatibility List (HCL)* before you attempt to buy non-Intel processors. Many of these processors may be obsolete, or no longer widely used. We are including discussion here for historical purposes.

Advanced Micro Devices (AMD)

In 1996, AMD introduced the K5 to compete with the already-released Intel Pentium processor. The K5 was released in a 64-bit version as a follow-up to the earlier K5x86, which resembled a higher-performance 486-based processor. The performance of the K5 equaled that of the Pentium at a reduced cost to the consumer.

AMD soon followed the K5 generation with the release of the K6 processor. The K6 offered a boost by accelerating the audio, video, and 3D capabilities of the chip in processing software, and adding MMX technology to compete with the Celeron, Pentium II, and Pentium III.

In addition to competing with the latest PC processors equipped with MMX technology, the AMD K6 offered a bigger "bang for the buck." The AMD K6 processors still plugged into standard motherboards by using current technology with chipset and *Basic Input/Output System (BIOS)* support, without needing special motherboards required by processors such as the Intel Pentium Pro and Pentium II models.

The next-generation processors were the Athlon (formerly the K7) and the Duron. Unlike earlier AMD processors, these processors could not be used with standard motherboards. Instead, they required a special Athlon- or Duron-compatible motherboard. One factor that set these chips apart from their Intel and Cyrix counterparts is that they used RISC technology. By using the reduced instruction set, they were able to process instructions at a more

Hardware Compatibility List (HCL)
Provided by Microsoft, the HCL lists all hardware that has been tested by Microsoft and has proved to work with a particular operating system. Hardware not on the HCL might work, but it is not certain to.

Basic Input/Output System (BIOS)
Software located in a ROM chip that is responsible for communicating directly between the computer hardware and the operating system.

rapid rate. This capability and other improved implementations in design enabled these chips to often outperform their Intel counterparts.

The Athlon family of processors is geared toward workstations and servers, while the Duron family of processors is geared toward lower-end business and home users.

AMD's latest processors are the Phenom and Phenom II. The original Phenom was released in 2007 and is considered the first true quad core processor. The Phenom II was released in 2008 and supports dual through hex core processors. The Phenom II offers an L3 cache size of 6 MB, which leads to increased performance.

Cyrix

Cyrix introduced a rival to the Intel Pentium processor in 1995. The first generation of its non-clone processor was named the MI 6x86 series. Although early releases of the MI encountered heat-related issues, Cyrix resolved the issues and produced a model that did not suffer from the initial design problem. The improved chip offered lower power consumption requirements that enabled the chip to operate at cooler temperatures.

Although the chip was originally designed to rival the Pentium, it included additional features found in the Intel Pentium Pro. One of the important features of the MI processor was that it could predict the next instruction to process before encountering it, thereby considerably boosting processor performance.

A follow-up to the MI series of processors was the MII series, a direct competitor with the Celeron and Pentium II CPUs. The improved design included additional optimization, enabling instructions to be processed faster than by other processors. The MII processors' improved capabilities were overshadowed by software incompatibilities that made them unable to take full advantage of the improved timing. Cyrix later released software utilities and patches to address the timing issues. The MII featured a set of 57 new instructions that were fully compatible with what was the industry-standard MMX software.

PowerPC

Apple, IBM, and Motorola developed the PowerPC as a new microprocessor technology. The PowerPC microprocessor used RISC technology to produce a high processing rate. The innovative design of the PowerPC chip enabled it to deliver high-performance computing power with lower power consumption than its counterparts.

The IBM RS/6000 Unix-based workstation and Apple Macintosh computers used the PowerPC chip. Its design was much different from the traditional design of the Intel microprocessors. The term *PowerPC* referred to more than just a type of processor; it was also an architecture standard that outlined specifications by which manufacturers could design processors. The resulting designs that followed the specifications offered performance advantages and innovative manufacturing techniques such as those IBM created.

IBM developed one of the most significant changes in processor manufacturing, which it called *Silicon-on-Insulator (SOI)* technology. The PowerPC 750, marketed by Apple Computer as the G3, was the first chip released that used this new manufacturing method. SOI technology provided increased processor performance while it offered low power consumption. Low power consumption is the key to producing products such as handheld devices, which operate for long periods of time powered by a battery. Since the PowerPC 750, Motorola has released the PowerPC MPC 7400, which is more commonly known in Apple circles as the G4.

Silicon-on-Insulator (SOI)
The microchip manufacturing innovation that IBM invented. It is based on the capability to enhance silicon technology by reducing the time it takes to move electricity through a conductor.

Alpha

The Alpha was a high-speed microprocessor that DEC developed. The Alpha processor was typically found in workstations and servers that needed more processing power than that found in Intel-based servers.

One of the Alpha chip's selling points was that it was the only other chip besides the Intel x86 generations of processors that could run the Microsoft Windows NT operating system. Alpha-equipped workstations were often characterized as the fastest NT workstations on the planet. NT took advantage of the Alpha's capability to produce or generate graphics up to eight times faster than Intel Pentium–based systems. Alpha chips were also commonly found in Unix workstations.

Although Microsoft and DEC did not support Windows 2000, Windows XP, or Windows Server 2003 on the Alpha platform, other operating systems, including HP's version of Unix and Linux, were supported. Other manufacturers, such as Samsung, produced servers and workstations that ran Alpha processors.

NOTE

Using Multiprocessor and Multicore Computers

Desktop and laptop computers can have multiple processors and multiple cores within a processor. Computers that contain more than one processor and/or core can scale to meet the needs of more demanding application programs. Microsoft server and desktop operating systems can all take advantage of the increased computing power of multiple processors and cores. The following graphics show the difference between Symmetrical Multiprocessing and Asymmetrical Multiprocessing.

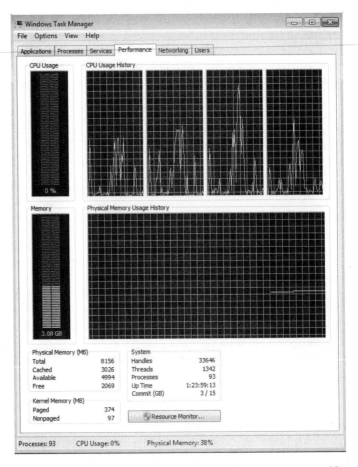

If you have a multi-CPU computer you can implement processor affinity. With processor affinity, you can configure applications to establish a relationship between worker process and one or more CPUs to more efficiently use CPU caches. Processor affinity is used in conjunction with the processor affinity mask setting to specify CPUs.

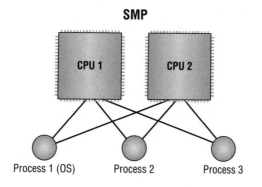

CPUs in a multiprocessing system may all be treated as equals, or they may be reserved for special purposes. *Symmetric multiprocessing (SMP)* occurs when all processors are treated as equals. In SMP, all tasks are shared equally. The tasks are split among the processors.

symmetric multiprocessing (SMP)
A computer architecture that uses multiple CPUs to improve a computer's performance. As performance demands increase on an SMP-capable computer, additional CPUs can be added to boost performance. During operation, if one CPU is idle, it can be given any task to perform. In the following graphic, you can see how tasks are assigned.

SMP

In computers where all CPUs are not equal, system resources may be divided in several ways, including *asymmetric multiprocessing (ASMP)* and *non-uniform memory access (NUMA) multiprocessing.*

In ASMP, one processor is reserved to run the operating system and the *input/output (I/O) devices.* The second ASMP processor runs the application, including the other miscellaneous tasks that the first processor does not handle. This method is often inefficient, because one processor can become busier than the other.

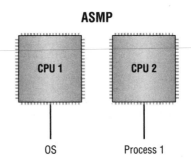

When using NUMA, access time to system memory depends on where the memory is located relative to a specific processor. Also, it is faster to access the system's local memory than it is to access non-local memory. Remote memory (local to another processor) or memory that is shared between processors could present performance issues.

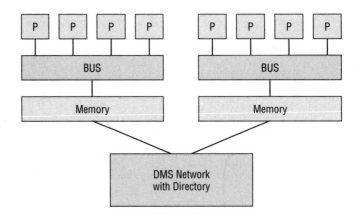

Cooling a System

As with all computers, cooling is paramount. Rarely is a computer too cool in normal circumstances. By ensuring your computer has adequate airflow with intake/exhaust fans, you will assist tremendously. Also, regularly clean the internal case. How dirty your system gets will depend on its location (office, home, or factory) as well as its physical environment (dust, dirt, rodents, snakes, and insects). In some extreme cases, you can use a liquid-cooled system to chill your computer, but if you do, you must always be concerned with leakage and resultant damage to the electronics in the case.

Physical Memory

Memory is an important part of any computer's system. Memory is used in every function of a computer, and it can have a major effect on computer performance. If you are going to get the most out of your computer, you must understand the types of physical memory and how to select the type that is best suited to your computing needs.

NOTE

Memory has always been a consideration with computers and that still holds true with today's computers. In Windows 7 and Windows Server 2008 R2, memory is more important than ever. The minimum requirement for Windows 7 (32-bit) is 1 GB, and 2 GB is recommended. Windows Server 2008 R2 has a minimum requirement of 512 MB.

Memory is basically a series of cells with an address. Each memory cell stores a small piece of information, and each memory cell is identified by a unique address so the processor knows where the cell resides and can easily access it. Computers use several types of memory, each serving a different purpose.

Random Access Memory (RAM)

Random access memory (RAM), often referred to as main memory, is a temporary type of memory that the computer uses as a work area. This type of memory is dynamic (sometimes it is also referred to as volatile memory), meaning that it is constantly changing because of the activity of the processor. When you shut off the power to the computer, RAM loses everything stored in it. RAM stores program instructions and related data for the CPU to quickly access without having to extract data from a slower type of storage device, such as the hard disk or a USB storage device.

Hard disks and USB storage devices are more permanent forms of data storage. Programs and their output data are stored on disks or chips for future use. When you shut off the power to the computer, the data on the storage media is intact. However, accessing data and program instructions from storage media can take over a 100 times longer than from RAM.

random access memory (RAM)
A temporary memory location that stores the operating system, applications, and files that are currently in use. The content of this type of memory is constantly changing. When you shut down the computer, all information in this type of memory is lost.

RAM Types

Every computer needs RAM, but which type? Not all types of RAM will work on a computer. Some physically won't fit in the RAM socket, and others will fit but won't work, preventing the computer from passing the *power-on self-test (POST)*.

power-on self-test (POST)
A set of diagnostic tests that are used to determine the state of hardware installed in the computer. Some components that fail the POST, such as bad RAM or a disconnected keyboard, will prevent the computer from booting up properly.

To select the right type of RAM, you need to know your CPU type and motherboard. Some CPUs, such as the Intel i5 and i7, work only with motherboards designed for their specific chips' make. The motherboard is typically designed to meet the highest performance levels of a particular CPU and, therefore, it determines which types of physical RAM can be used. RAM comes in one of two types: Single Inline Memory Modules (SIMMs), an older specification, and Dual Inline Memory Modules (DIMMs), the current standard.

SIMMs

SIMMs are physically different from DIMMs. Older SIMMs were designed with 30 pins that connected to a slot in the motherboard. These modules were slow and typically had to be added in groups of two or four identical SIMMs to be recognized by the BIOS. The current model is a 72-pin SIMM. On motherboards designed for the Pentium processor, the SIMMs must be added in pairs.

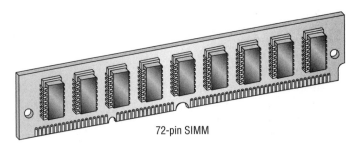

72-pin SIMM

DIMMs

parity
An extra bit found on some memory modules. Non-parity memory has 8 bits. Parity adds an extra bit that is used to keep track of the other 8 bits. This can help prevent memory errors and is recommended for use in servers.

DIMMs have 240 pins with a data path of either 64 bits for non-parity memory or 72 bits for *parity* memory. DIMMs have the largest data path of any memory module. The wider data path makes the chip as fast as the data path on the CPU. This means that the DIMMs can be added one at a time and in varying sizes. It is because of this improved performance and flexibility that DIMMs have become popular in today's personal computers. A variant of the DIMM module is the SO-DIMM (Small Outline DIMM), which is used in laptops.

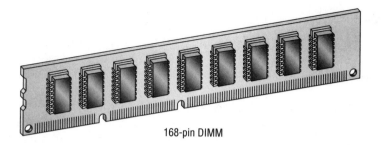

168-pin DIMM

RAM Speed

Identifying the type of RAM that will physically fit into your computer is only one part of the selection process. Also consider the performance of the RAM you select. Two types of RAM to choose from include Extended Data Out (EDO) and Synchronous Dynamic RAM (SDRAM). Each offers improved performance over older models. Check with your computer manufacturer to see which type of RAM is supported on your computer.

EDO RAM

EDO RAM uses dual-pipeline architecture that enables the unit to store data (write) at the same time it sends it out (reads). EDO RAM is limited to a bus speed of 66 MHz due to its non-parity design. EDO RAM can be purchased in 72-pin SIMMs or 168-pin DIMMs.

SDRAM

SDRAM is similar in design to EDO RAM in that it writes at the same time that it reads, vastly accelerating data along. SDRAM is a popular choice over EDO RAM due to its high bus speed of 100 MHz and its low cost.

DDR SDRAM

This was the first Double Data Rate (DDR) design. The benefit of this design was that the reading and writing of information was done on both cycles, meaning a greater effective data rate (twice the actual speed of the clock and address lines). DDR RAM speeds ranged from 200 to 400 MHz. DDR RAM was used in older computers from the Athlon 64 and Pentium 4 era. DDR RAM capacities typically ranged from 128 MB to 1 GB.

DDR2 SDRAM

DDR2 (DDR type 2) is an improvement on the interface specification with a higher bandwidth interface than DDR, making for improved performance. It is not compatible with DDR because of voltage and timing differences. DDR2 has a lower voltage requirement of 1.8 V compared to 2.5 V in DDR. DDR2 has data rates of 400–1066 MHz. DDR2 RAM capacities typically range from 512 MB to 4 GB.

DDR3 SDRAM

The DDR3 specification has a higher bandwidth interface compared with that of the DDR2, which allows for improved performance. As with DDR, it is not compatible with earlier versions of DDR due to voltage and timing differences. Two main benefits of DDR3 over DDR2 are that it can transfer data at twice the rate (800–2133 MHz) and it has a lower voltage rate of 1.5 V (nearly 30 percent lower than DDR2). DDR3 RAM supports chip sizes of up to 8 GB.

Read-Only Memory (ROM)

read-only memory (ROM)
A type of memory that has data precopied onto it. The data can only be read from and cannot be overwritten. ROM is used to store the BIOS software.

Read-only memory (ROM) is a special type of memory in which data is written onto a chip during manufacturing. Information stored in ROM is permanent and can only be changed in special circumstances. ROM stores the BIOS, the set of instructions a computer uses during the first stages of initialization. Without the BIOS, the computer would not have a mechanism to verify that the main hardware components are installed and functioning properly.

ROM can also hold other, non-volatile instruction sets to include updates for firmware (for computers and computer components), updates for networking devices (Cisco routers and switches), and updates for voice over Internet protocol (VOIP) components (e.g., audio gateways). In many newer systems and devices, ROM chips have been replaced with Flash memory cards. These devices can include various audio/video devices, household appliances, and industrial equipment.

Other ROM Types

Besides the basic ROM chip discussed earlier, other ROM chips are used in computers and small computing devices. The ROM chips described next are programmable, meaning that information can be recorded onto them. These types of chips are important because they enable software that is critical to the computer start-up process to be updated.

PROM

Programmable read-only memory (PROM) is a special type of chip that is manufactured without any configuration. Manufacturers can then *burn in*, or program, the chip to contain whatever configuration is needed.

EPROM

Erasable programmable read-only memory (EPROM) maintains its contents without using electrical power. The stored contents of an EPROM chip are erased and reprogrammed by removing the protective cover and using special equipment to reprogram the chip.

EEPROM

Electrically erasable programmable ROM (EEPROM) typically maintains the BIOS code, which can be updated either with a downloadable file or with a disk that the BIOS manufacturer supplies.

Bus Architecture

When configuring the hardware for a new computer, you have to consider the CPU and motherboard, as discussed earlier in this chapter. In addition, you need to decide which *expansion cards* to install. Expansion cards include sound cards, video adapters, and *network interface cards (NICs)*.

The expansion cards fit into expansion slots that are built into the motherboard. The most common exceptions are special types of computers such as laptop computers. Expansion cards and the slots they fit into can have several different connector types. The connector types are physically different from one another and have varying performance characteristics.

Some reasons why expansion slots are useful are

◆ The earliest motherboards didn't have room for all the necessary components.

◆ The expansion slots add flexibility in the event that you need to replace a failed expansion card without having to buy a complete new motherboard.

◆ Most motherboards have several types of expansion slots. The older type of expansion slots, described in the next section, are available to support older expansion cards, protecting consumers' original investment in their hardware.

In most modern computers, you insert a new add-in, or expansion, card as follows:

Before opening any electronic device, make sure that the power is turned off and that you are grounded. To ground yourself, use a special tool called an electrostatic discharge wrist strap. One end of the wrist strap attaches to you, and the

expansion card
An add-on device, such as a sound or video card, that is installed directly into an expansion slot built into a motherboard. The card must be of the same bus architecture as the slot on the motherboard.

network interface card (NIC)
A device that connects a computer to the physical cable media and produces signals for transferring data.

WARNING

other end clips to the metal case of the computer. Using the strap prevents you from shocking the computer and possibly causing irreversible damage.

1. Turn the power off and disconnect the power cord from the case.
2. Open the case.
3. Make sure the card that you are trying to install is the proper type for an open expansion slot.
4. Insert the card and fasten it down.
5. Close the case.
6. Turn the power back on.

Bus Types

Many types of buses have been introduced since the personal computer was created. Some, such as Industry Standard Architecture (ISA), have had long histories. Others, such as IBM's Micro Channel Architecture (MCA), were never widely adopted for one reason or another. PCI was one of the most widely used (described earlier in the section, "The Pentium Family"), though it is rapidly being phased out in favor of PCIe. Not long ago, PCI was seen as adding better performance to emerging high-speed computers. Now, even the once-sought-after PCI is considered sluggish.

Accelerated Graphics Port (AGP)

megabytes per second (MBps)
A measurement of the transfer speed of a device in terms of millions of bytes per second.

AGP was developed as a replacement for PCI. AGP uses the Intel two-chip 440LX AGP set. This set of chips sits directly on the motherboard and provides similar functionality to PCI. The new chips are responsible for handling the transfer of data between memory, the processor, and the ISA cards all at the same time. Transfer of data to and from PCI cards still occurs at 132 *megabytes per second (MBps)* at 33 MHz. The significant change from PCI is in the speed of transfers to RAM and to the accelerated graphics port. Both have transfer speeds of 528 MBps. This fourfold performance increase provides a significant boost, speeding data along to high-speed CPUs and RAM.

Enhanced Industry Standard Architecture (EISA)

In response to IBM's proprietary MCA bus, the other major hardware vendors (led primarily by Compaq) developed this enhanced bus design.

FireWire (IEEE 1394)

FireWire or IEEE 1394 is a specification for a high-speed serial bus interface standard. FireWire is used for high-speed communications and isochronous real-time data transfer; it is frequently used by personal computers, as well as in digital audio, digital video, automotive, and aeronautics applications. The interface is variously known by the brand names of FireWire (Apple), i.LINK (Sony), and Lynx (Texas Instruments). The IEEE 1394 replaced parallel SCSI in many applications, because of lower implementation costs and a simplified, more adaptable cabling system. FireWire is also available in wireless, fiber-optic, and coaxial versions using the isochronous protocols.

Nearly all digital still and video cameras have a four-circuit IEEE 1394 interface. The Firewire connection is the primary transfer mechanism for high-end professional audio and video equipment. Most computers built since 2003 have built-in FireWire/i.LINK ports.

HDMI

HDMI (High-Definition Multimedia Interface) is a compact audio/video interface for transmitting uncompressed digital data. Typically this is found on devices that are connected to digital audio/video sources such as DVD players/Blu-ray Disc players, camcorders, personal computers and laptops, video game consoles such as the PlayStation 3 and Xbox 360, and AV receivers. HDMI is also used to hook up your laptop or other device to an HDTV, HD monitors, or other projectors.

IBM Micro Channel Architecture (MCA)

IBM's third version of a motherboard expansion bus increased the width of the bus (to 32 bits) and increased the speed. However, unlike with the two original bus designs, IBM didn't freely allow all the other hardware vendors to build cards that were compatible with the MCA specifications and as a result, it was not widely adopted and was eventually discontinued.

IBM PC

The original IBM PC supported 8-bit expansion cards that ran at the same speed as its Intel 8088 processor, 4.77 MHz.

IBM PC-AT, or Industry Standard Architecture (ISA)

The IBM PC-AT introduced two major enhancements: The data path was increased (by the use of a second connector) to 16 bits, and the speed of the expansion cards, usually fixed at 8.33 MHz, was made independent of the processor speed.

Peripheral Component Interconnect (PCI)

The PCI architecture is a 32-bit-wide local bus design that runs at 33 MHz. Due to their local bus design, PCI devices have direct access to the CPU local bus. The PCI local bus is connected to the CPU local bus and system memory bus via a PCI-Host bridge. This is a caching device that provides the interface between the CPU, memory, and PCI local bus. The cache enables the CPU to hand off executions to the PCI bus in order to free up valuable CPU resources. The CPU can continue to fetch information from the caching bridge while the cache controller provides an expansion device with access to system memory.

More than one communication on more than one bus can occur at the same time. This concurrent bus operation could not happen with previous architectures (such as VESA). Additionally, PCI expansion devices are fully independent of the CPU local bus; there is no CPU dependency at all. This design enables the CPU to be upgraded without requiring new designs for devices on the CPU or expansion buses.

Peripheral Component Interconnect Express (PCIe)

PCIe is a new computer expansion card standard that will eventually replace PCI and AGP bus standards. The new PCIe standard offers a faster bus throughput and a smaller physical connector footprint and supports hardware I/O virtualization. The latest version of PCIe is 3.0 with availability of devices announced in June 2011. Work on PCIe 4.0 has started. The latest version of PCIe supports a sustained transfer rate in excess of 500 MBps.

Universal Serial Bus (USB)

The original USB specification was released in 1996, followed by USB 1.1, 2.0, and 3.0 (which was adopted in 2008, with the first device released in January 2010). The USB port is an expected and standard port on computers, networking devices, and elsewhere (some airlines have USB ports available for passengers, and they can be found on some televisions, monitors, keyboards, and elsewhere).

A specific standard is applied to USB ports that is used to establish communication between USB devices and a host controller (usually a personal computer). Though the USB effectively replaced earlier ports, it is in turn being replaced with newer and faster buses, including FireWire, eSATA, PCIe and USB 3. You can use a USB port to connect a wide array of devices including mice, keyboards, digital cameras, printers, and more. In fact, USB devices can be daisy-chained (up to 127 devices), where one port may have several devices connected to it through a USB hub.

One key fact about USB is that, in almost all cases, it is a Plug and Play device. The drivers for the devices are included on the devices (for instance, some mass storage devices) or are on companion media (CD-ROM). The first widely used 1.1 USB devices had a speed of 12 MBps; USB 2.0 followed with an accepted speed of up to 480 MBps. USB 3.0 has speeds of up to 5 GBps (as well as backward compatibility with USB 2.0 and reduced power consumption).

USB ports have a distinct advantage over older port standards such as RS-232 or parallel ports; they can provide power to devices that are connected to them. As a result, USB devices do need a separate external power source (such as a small external hard drive).

Video Electronics Standards Association (VESA) Local Bus (VL-Bus)

The VL-Bus was not a replacement for the other bus types but was instead usually used as an auxiliary bus. The primary devices that supported the VL-Bus were, as you might expect because of its name, video cards. However, some high-performance disk controllers were released that used this standard. Using VL-Bus technology, especially over the long term, had limitations. Major limitations of the VL-Bus included a restriction in the number of VL-Bus devices, a maximum 32-bit data path (preventing expansion to the new Intel Pentium 64-bit systems), and a clock-speed limit of only 33 MHz.

Terms to Know

asymmetric multiprocessing (ASMP)

Basic Input/Output (BIOS)

bit

bus architecture

Complex Instruction Set Computing (CISC)

central processing unit (CPU)

expansion card

gigahertz (GHz)

Hardware Compatibility List (HCL)

input/output (I/O) devices

megabytes per second (MBps)

megahertz (MHz)

microcode

millions of instructions per second (MIPS)

Multimedia Extension (MMX)

motherboard

network interface card (NIC)

non-uniform memory access (NUMA) multiprocessing

parity

Peripheral Component Interconnect (PCI)

pipeline

power-on self-test (POST)

random access memory (RAM)

Reduced Instruction Set Computing (RISC)

read-only memory (ROM)

single-edge cartridge (SEC)

symmetric multiprocessing (SMP)

Silicon-on-Insulator (SOI)

transistor

Review Questions

1. Which processor was released in the first IBM PC?
2. How did the 8086 differ from the 8088?
3. What does *CPU speed* refer to?
4. What is a DIMM and where is it used?
5. How does real mode differ from protected mode?
6. What does *clock cycles* refer to?
7. What is EEPROM?
8. What does PROM stand for, and where is it used?
9. What is a PCIe?
10. How many transistors made up the original Pentium processor?
11. How does asymmetrical multiprocessing differ from symmetrical?
12. What is a math coprocessor?
13. What is the recommended amount of RAM for Windows 7?
14. What is the primary difference between RAM and ROM?
15. What performance gains does PCI have over the EISA bus architecture?

Chapter 2

Storing Your Files: Data Storage

store v : to place something in a location for later use

Every computer has a collection of files. This collection includes the files that run the operating system, the files the computer needs to use applications, and the data files you create. All these files have to be saved somewhere, and that somewhere is called data storage.

Keys to Data Storage

You can store data in a variety of formats. The format you choose depends on your needs, the cost, and the form the data takes. Here are some factors to consider when you choose your media or types of storage devices:

◆ Should the media be fixed or removable? Fixed media stays with the computer and offers the best performance. Removable media adds the benefits of being mobile; you can use it with another computer or for *backup* purposes, but it is slower.

◆ What capacity do you need now and in the future? Are you storing a small amount of data or a large amount of data?

◆ How common is the storage media? If the storage media is not commonly used, it might be incompatible with other computer types. For example, if you received a 3.5-inch floppy disk, would it work on your computer? Would it work on some computers that are sold today or would you need specialized hardware?

◆ What is the cost of the storage media? Cost is often a primary concern and is measured in cost per megabyte. When read/write compact discs (DVDs) first became available, most users considered them to be too expensive. Because prices have dropped so significantly, DVDs are now a common storage media. Another media to consider is USB thumb drives, which can hold up to 256GB and have a much faster read time than DVDs.

Here are some storage quantities and their equivalents:

1,024 kilobytes (KB)	= 1 megabyte (MB)
1,024 MB	= 1 gigabyte (GB)
1,024 GB	= 1 terabyte (TB)
1,024 TB	= 1 petabyte (PB)
1,024 PB	= 1 exabyte (EB)

backup
The copying of all your data to a secondary storage option. If your primary storage option becomes unavailable, you can use backups to restore the operating system, application, and data files.

NOTE

When specifying the amount of storage you need, keep in mind that a well-built system should also have a reliable backup solution. (We discuss tape backup in the section "Tape Drives," later in this chapter.) The key point to remember is that if you are going to need 25 GB of hard drive storage, you will need an equivalent amount of storage space on something easily transportable—in this case, a hard drive, a thumb drive, or even a tape to which you can copy your data.

Here is a summary of the most common storage media.

Media	Description	Fixed or Removable	Data Capacity
Hard drive	Storage device that stores large amounts of data. Uses a series of magnetically coated disks to store ones and zeros.	Usually fixed, but some are removable	New drives are in the terabyte range.
Solid state drive (SSD)	Stores data in solid state memory instead of magnetically on platters, such as with SATA or SCSI drives.	Usually fixed, but some are removable	1 TB or larger
Compact disc (CD)	CDs are optical discs that store data by using lasers. Traditional CDs (CD-R) can be written to one time but read many times. Rewritable CDs (CD-RW) can be written to several times.	Removable	CDs hold up to 700 MB of data.
Digital video (or versatile) disc (DVD)	DVDs have been available for over 15 years. A single DVD has a storage capacity many times that of a CD.	Removable	A single-sided DVD can hold 4.7 GB of data. A double-sided version can hold more than 8.5 GB of data.
Blu-ray (BD)	Blu-rays are replacing DVDs. This technology is the new de facto standard for HDTV and laptops.	Removable	A single-sided Blu-ray disc can contain 25 GB and dual-layer discs can hold 50 GB and up to 128 GB for BD-XL.
Tape	Tape is a magnetic media that you commonly use for backup purposes. It is a slow media for seek times when accessing data, but its large capacity and low cost make it ideal for backup.	Removable	You can buy tapes that will store 500 GB or more.

Understanding Hard Drive Basics

hard drive
Stores data as a series of ones and zeros on a series of magnetically coated disks. A positive charge indicates a one, and the absence of a charge indicates a zero.

A *hard drive* is a series of magnetically coated disks that store data. Just above each disk in the drive sits a read/write head that adds a positive charge to indicate a one and removes the charge to indicate a zero.

The hard drive consists of these pieces:

◆ A series of disks, called platters, that are stacked together. Each platter has a hole in the middle, and a spindle is inserted through these holes. The platters rotate at high speeds measured in revolutions per minute (rpm).

◆ A read/write disk head sits on top of the disk surface and reads or writes to the disk as the disk rotates.

◆ An actuator arm, which is responsible for disk head movement, moves the read/write head across the platter to write or read data.

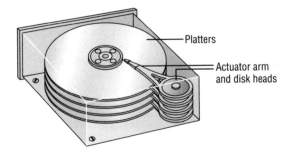

Platters

Actuator arm and disk heads

Selecting a Hard Drive

When choosing a hard drive, you should consider these factors:

◆ Is the drive type based on a common standard such as PATA, SATA, or SCSI?

◆ How much storage space do you need now and over the next year?

◆ What type of data will you be storing, and how will that affect performance?

◆ How critical is the data you are storing? In the event of a disk failure, how long can you afford for your system to be down before the problem is fixed?

◆ What is the speed of the drive?

◆ What is the cache of the drive?

◆ Does the drive need any additional hardware?

◆ How many drives can you chain together if you need more space in the future?

◆ How much will everything cost?

Two of the most common drive types are SATA (which is replacing PATA, the former Integrated Drive Electronics [IDE]) and SCSI. A new type of storage that is becoming very popular is the solid state drive (SSD). This is not a hard drive itself, but it is used in lieu of SATA or SCSI drives. You will learn about all of these in more detail in the following sections.

Because of the magnetic properties of disk drives, you should never place them near anything magnetic or near powerful electrical devices. The magnetic fields created by large power supplies can scramble data.

WARNING

Hard drives are one of the most essential forms of data storage. As with most PC components, the technology has changed significantly over the last 30 years. In the early 1980s, an average hard disk stored 10 MB of data, had an average disk access time of 87 milliseconds, and was substantially larger and heavier than disks used today. In addition, hard drives were extremely expensive. Now you can buy an internal hard drive that is 3 TB in size. Also, many SATA drives have an access time that is typically 8 milliseconds or less.

NOTE

Performance with Parallel ATA (PATA)

The *Parallel ATA (PATA)* specification was a continuation of the ATA standard, which evolved from the EIDE standard. PATA drives have largely been replaced by Serial ATA (SATA) drives, which will be discussed in the next section.

What makes PATA drives so popular is that the *disk controller* and drive were integrated into a single piece of hardware. This made PATA drives less expensive than SCSI drives (which you will learn about in a later section in this chapter titled "Performance with SCSI Drives"). PATA drives traditionally did not provide the same performance as SCSI drives —but even this changed over time. Several PATA standards, covered later in this section, increased drive performance to be comparable to SCSI. PATA hard drives have mostly been replaced by SATA drives in the past few years.

You can easily distinguish an PATA drive from a SCSI drive, because the PATA drive uses a 40-pin connector whereas traditional SCSI uses a 50-pin connector. If you are using other forms of SCSI, you may be familiar with wide SCSI, which uses a 68-pin connector, and SCA SCSI (sometimes referred to as Ultra wide SCSI), which uses an 80-pin connector.

Parallel ATA (PATA)
An IDE standard for connecting storage devices. PATA generally refers to the types of cables and connections that follow this standard. PATA is based on parallel signaling technology.

disk controller
Manages floppy and hard disks. It can be a separate piece of hardware, or it can be integrated with the hard drive.

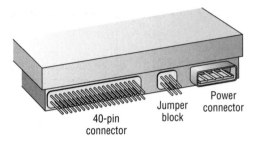

40-pin connector   Jumper block   Power connector

You can connect PATA drives to the computer in two ways:

◆ You can attach them directly to the motherboard if the IDE adapter is integrated as part of the motherboard.

◆ You can attach them to a paddleboard. The paddleboard is not a controller. It is a simple piece of hardware that facilitates the connection between the drive and the motherboard. This hardware is inexpensive, usually costing under $20.

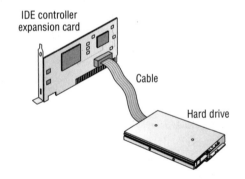

IDE controller expansion card

Cable

Hard drive

master
A device that is responsible for controlling one or more directly connected devices.

slave
A device that is controlled by another device called the master.

jumpers
Plastic-covered metal clips that are used to connect two pins on a motherboard. The connection creates a circuit that turns the setting to "on."

PATA technology enabled you to install two drives per slot on the motherboard through the use of a ribbon cable. You had to designate one drive on the ribbon cable as the *master* drive and the second drive as a *slave* drive (later changed to a Primary and Secondary drive, respectively). *Jumpers* on the hard drive usually determine the drive designation. You should refer to the drive's documentation to see how to configure your particular drive.

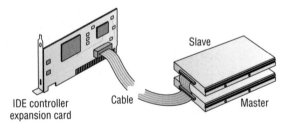

IDE controller expansion card   Cable   Slave   Master

You can start, or boot, your computer only from the master drive.

_____ *NOTE* _____

In some hardware books and manuals, you will see references to RLL, MFM, and ESDI on the subject of hard drives. These standards have been obsolete for some time.

_____ *NOTE* _____

When you refer to IDE drives that were popular, you were actually using *Enhanced IDE (EIDE)* drive. This specification was replaced by PATA (discussed earlier in this chapter). The original IDE specification supported drives that had a capacity up to 528 MB. The newer EIDE supported drives that were hundreds of GB in size.

Enhanced IDE (EIDE)
An extended version of the IDE standard. The benefits of EIDE include the support of hard drives over 528 MB, the capability to chain devices other than drives (for example, CD-ROM drives and tape drives), faster access time, and the capability to chain up to four devices.

IDE Interface Standards

IDE drives come in many formats, from 3.5-inch to 5.25-inch drives, with the former being the most popular today. But physical size doesn't matter much: what really counts is the speed and accuracy of the drive. Several standards have been developed to greatly improve IDE disk drive performance. These standards are actually protocols that the disk drive and the controller use to communicate with each other. Each protocol is made up of a set of rules that govern how communication will occur between the disk drive and the controller. Advancements in protocols can greatly improve hard disk performance. Faster communication between the hard disk and the rest of the computer means applications open more quickly and videos play more smoothly.

Several standards have been defined for IDE drives. As the standards have been released, they have typically doubled the amount of data that can be transferred. We explain each standard next.

Advanced Technology Attachment (ATA)

Advanced Technology Attachment (ATA) refers to a disk standard wherein the controller responsible for moving data on and off the disk is located in the drive. ATA was the original standard for IDE drives. ATA drives can have one or two drives connected to a single controller. As stated earlier, one of the attached drives is referred to as the master, and the second is the slave because of its dependency on the master. IDE drives slow the performance of the CPU because they must communicate directly with the CPU to access RAM. Some IDE/ATA drives have a transfer rate as high as 2 MBps.

ATA-2

Someone referring to a computer with an IDE drive is more than likely talking about an Enhanced IDE drive based on the ATA-2 standard. ATA-2, or EIDE, made two significant gains over the original ATA standard. The first major advance was that it was able to take advantage of the *direct memory access (DMA)* protocol. DMA improved CPU performance by accessing memory directly and avoiding the CPU whenever possible. The second enhancement was that its advanced BIOS could identify the type of hard drive from information on the drive itself, making installation much easier. ATA-2/EIDE has a maximum transfer rate of 16.7 MBps.

direct memory access (DMA)
DMA enables a device to transfer data directly to RAM without using the attention of the processor for the entire transfer period. The result is a faster and more direct method of data transfer.

Ultra-ATA

Ultra-ATA drives, like ATA-2/EIDE drives, also use the DMA protocol. Ultra-ATA uses a faster mode of the DMA protocol (mode 3, to be exact), which pushes transfer rates to 33 MBps. As with ATA-2/EIDE, your motherboard must support Ultra-ATA.

Ultra-ATA/66, ATA/100, and Ultra ATA/133

The ATA/66 and ATA/100 have been developed to complement today's larger applications and faster CPUs. With data transfer rates of 66 MBps and 100 Mbps, respectively, these two standards blur the lines between PATA and SCSI. Ultra ATA/133 has a maximum transfer rate of 133 MBps.

 NOTE

The Ultra-DMA/33 protocol was developed by Quantum Corporation to take advantage of faster Ultra-ATA disk drives. Ultra-DMA uses *burst mode* to temporarily take control of the bus to achieve data transfer rates of 33 MBps.

burst mode
The temporary increase in data transmission speeds beyond what is normal. The increase is not sustainable and usually prevents other devices from transmitting.

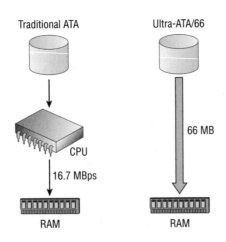

Performance with SATA Drives

Serial ATA (Serial Advanced Technology Attachment) is the successor to Parallel ATA (PATA). It is used to connect hard drives and optical drives. Several of SATA's improvements over PATA are the length of the connector cables, reduced voltage, and a vastly improved transfer rate.

Here are some benefits of SATA drives:

◆ Much faster transfer rate than PATA or IDE. Ultra-ATA/133 had a maximum transfer rate of only 133 MBps, while SATA 3.0 has a maximum transfer rate of 6 Gbps.

◆ Longer connecting cables. PATA was limited to only 18 inches, whereas SATA connector cables can have a maximum cable length of 3 feet.

◆ The PATA cable had a wide 40-pin connector. The SATA cable uses a 7-pin connector.

◆ Hot plug capability. This is available if both the motherboard and the connecting device meet the requirements for this capability.

SATA revision 1.0

Introduced in 2003, this was the original SATA standard (SATA 1.5 Gbps). The original release of SATA also included a chip to enable PATA devices with the SATA interface and adapters for the Molex power connector.

SATA revision 2.0

This is the second generation standard and still represents the majority of SATA devices sold, though SATA 3.0 is making quick inroads as users want faster throughput. SATA 2.0 has approximately twice the throughput of SATA 1.0 (157 MBps for SATA 1.0 vs. 300 MBps for SATA 2.0).

SATA revision 3.0

The SATA 3.0 (or as it is sometimes listed, SATA 6 Gbps) was formally adopted in May of 2009 and is backward compatible with SATA 2.0. Many of the new features were made to improve the performance of SATA drives for video streaming (home theater). The SATA 3.0 standard has a peak throughput of 600 MBps. Currently, the only drives that can realistically achieve these throughput results are solid state drives (SSD). In most cases, connecting cables and power connectors used with SATA 2.0 can also be used with SATA 3.0.

eSATA

The eSATA standard was designed for external connectivity and the consumer market. The standard was established in 2004 and competes with USB and FireWire. eSATA has a current maximum speed of 6 Gbps.

Performance with SDD Drives

A *solid state drive (SSD)* is a storage device that uses non-volatile memory chips to retain data. SSDs have none of the mechanical components that are present in traditional hard disk drives (i.e., platters that spin, actuator arms, and motors). As a result, SSDs use substantially less energy and generate almost no heat compared to conventional hard drives. Due to these two factors, SSDs are perfect for use in mobile devices; after all, mobile device users are always concerned with power consumption, heat, and weight.

As with conventional hard disk drives (HDD), SSD drives are generally available with a wide variety of commonly used connectors, including SATA, PATA, SCSI, Fibre Channel (SCSI and Fibre Channel are mainly used in enterprise environments), USB, and eSATA.

SSDs are more expensive than their SATA and even SCSI counterparts. One of the major differences in cost between HDDs and SDDs is that SSDs use integrated circuits (memory chips) instead of platters. Since they are using integrated circuit (IC) chips, the cost difference is almost zero seek latency. Another compelling reason to use SDDs is their MTBF (mean time between failure) of 1,000,000 hours (whereas a more expensive HDD might have a MTBF of "only" 750,000 hours).

These drives are designed to fit standard 1.8-inch laptops as well as 2.5-inch and 3.5-inch for desktops. SSDs are also used with PCI expansion cards for computers (mainly server applications due to their high cost).

Performance with SCSI Drives

Small Computer System Interface (SCSI)
An interface that connects SCSI devices to the computer. This interface uses high-speed parallel technology to connect devices that include hard disks, CD-ROM players, tape backup devices, and other hardware peripherals.

SCSI stands for *Small Computer System Interface* and is pronounced *scuzzy*. SCSI supports more than just drives; SCSI devices include hard disks, CD-ROM players, tape backup devices, and other hardware peripherals. Any SCSI device must communicate with the computer through a connection to a SCSI adapter. Because SCSI hard drives must be attached to an intelligent SCSI adapter, this disk storage solution is more expensive than IDE.

These are some benefits of SCSI:

♦ With a SCSI adapter, you can easily add or remove SCSI devices to/from your computer.

♦ SCSI is a high-performance storage solution with faster transfer rates and high-speed drive mechanisms.

♦ You can take advantage of new SCSI standards and adapters while maintaining compatibility with older SCSI devices.

◆ Multiple SCSI drives connected to a special adapter offer options that can greatly improve performance by enabling all the SCSI drives to work together as one; this approach is known as an *array*. Arrays are important technologies for digital video editing systems.

◆ SCSI is a widely available, widely used, mature technology.

◆ SCSI drives have a long and successful history as high-performance storage solutions for high-end workstations and servers.

array
A set of objects, all of which are the same size and type.

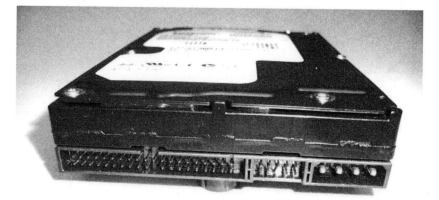

SCSI Standards

SCSI has been in development for nearly two decades. Since the first standard was released, SCSI has become the premier storage system for servers. Although other drive systems such as IDE and PATA drives have improved dramatically in performance, SATA is the preferred choice of network administrators despite its higher cost. Whether you decide to implement SCSI drives comes down to which SCSI standard your workstations and servers will support. The bus speed can significantly affect performance, so select wisely.

This table outlines the SCSI standards.

SCSI Standard	Bus Width	MBps Bus Speed	Maximum Number of Supported Devices
SCSI-1	8-bit	5	8
Fast SCSI (SCSI-2)	8-bit	8	8
Fast and Wide SCSI (SCSI-2)	16-bit	20	16
Ultra SCSI	8-bit	20	8–16
Ultra Wide SCSI (SCSI-3)	16-bit	40	8–16

SCSI Standard	Bus Width	MBps Bus Speed	Maximum Number of Supported Devices
Ultra2 SCSI	8-bit	40	8
Ultra2 Wide SCSI	16-bit	80	16
Ultra3 SCSI, or Ultra160	16-bit	160	16
Ultra320	16-bit	320	16

SCSI-1 and SCSI-2

The original SCSI-1 standard was introduced in 1986. SCSI-1 had an 8-bit bus with a 5 MBps transfer speed. It wasn't until 1994 that SCSI-2 was ratified. SCSI-2 is essentially SCSI-1 with some additional options. The most significant options were Fast SCSI and Wide SCSI. These two could be used with compatible devices to boost transfer speeds to 20 MBps. A SCSI device connected to a SCSI-2 adapter will still function, but at the lower speed of 8 MBps.

SCSI-3

SCSI-3 was developed to overcome several limitations of SCSI-2. SCSI-3 increased the total number of SCSI devices connected together from 8 in SCSI-2 to 16. The next problem was much more difficult to solve. SCSI-2 had a cable distance limitation of 3 meters. The limitation was a problem, especially as the data transfer speeds increased, because there was no way for SCSI devices to calculate transmission delays. Keeping the signals in order was difficult. SCSI-3 improved on this design by adding timing information to the data being sent. The additional timing information would keep the order of the data intact.

Ultra3 SCSI and Ultra320

The Ultra3 SCSI technology nearly doubles the transfer rate to 160 MBps. Like SCSI-3, Ultra3 SCSI uses timing information in the signal, but it adds a second piece of timing information to push twice the amount of data.

Ultra320 is a similar specification to Ultra3 SCSI, except it has a 16-bit-wide bus that can deliver a transfer rate of 320 MBps.

NOTE

Be sure to check which SCSI technology your computer will support. Some older implementations are not compatible with the newer Ultra Wide SCSI or Ultra3 SCSI. Also, keep in mind that if you use an older SCSI drive on a much faster Ultra3 SCSI bus, the SCSI bus will be only as fast as the older SCSI drive. So, if your drive is Ultra SCSI but your bus supports Ultra3, the SCSI bus will operate at a transfer rate of 20 MBps rather than the 160 MBps supported by Ultra3.

SCSI Termination

Traditionally, SCSI adapters enable you to *daisy chain* up to seven devices off each controller. The controller contains the *termination*. You must also terminate the last device in the SCSI chain. The termination at the beginning and the end forms the SCSI chain. Some devices use active termination, which means you don't have to do anything; other devices require you to manually remove the termination from devices in the middle of the chain and ensure that the last device is terminated.

The next graphic illustrates the daisy-chain technique used by SCSI and the locations of the termination. The ID numbers listed next to the drives are an important part of SCSI devices. Each SCSI device must have a unique address. The ID is used to address data to the correct device in the chain. Depending on the type of SCSI technology you are using, the ID can range from 0 to 15.

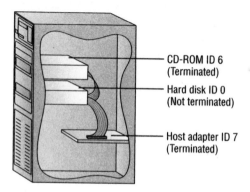

CD-ROM ID 6
(Terminated)

Hard disk ID 0
(Not terminated)

Host adapter ID 7
(Terminated)

On internal SCSI cables, the terminators are built into the ends of the cables.

daisy chain

To connect a series of devices, one after the other. When signals are transmitted on a daisy chain, they go to the first device, then to the second, and so on, until termination is reached.

termination

The use of a terminator at both ends of a SCSI daisy chain to keep data signals from bouncing back on the SCSI bus after they reach the end. The terminator is a small plastic connector that has a resistor (ceramic-based material that absorbs electricity) inside it.

NOTE

Organizing Disks

You can organize disk drives in several ways. The method you use is determined by how the disks are being used (just increasing space, providing for fault tolerance and redundancy). One way is to use multiple hard drives. Each partition or volume has an assigned drive identifier such as C, D, and so on. Usually, for this type of configuration, each *physical hard drive* represents just one storage location identified with a letter. This is sometimes referred to as JBOD (just a bunch of disks).

Another alternative is to organize the disk into a *volume* on the same physical disk. A volume is created from a partition in a Windows Server or Windows Desktop operating system into a dynamic disk. You can also create partitions. Each partition you create makes a physical change to the format of the disk.

physical hard drive

The physical (or real, as opposed to conceptual) drive; for example, drive 0 or drive 1 in a two-drive configuration.

volume

A part of a physical disk that is identified by a single drive label.

logical drive
Based on how you partition your physical drive, the area of the extended partition can be organized into multiple drives. Each drive is assigned a DOS identifier from D to Z.

The usable space defined through partitions is considered the *logical drive*. You can define disk space however you want, regardless of the physical size of the disk. Consider these examples:

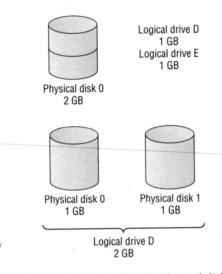

In the first example, you have a single 2 GB physical disk that is partitioned into two logical drives. Each logical drive is 1 GB.

In the second example, you have two physical disks that are each 1 GB. In this case, the two drives are configured as a single 2 GB logical drive by using software.

NOTE — To create partitions or logical drives in Windows 2000 or later, you can use Disk Management.

Understanding Partition Types

Before you create your partitions, you should first understand these disk concepts:

◆ Active and boot partitions

◆ Primary partition

◆ Extended partition

Active and Boot Partitions

active partition
The partition the computer identifies as the one that will boot it up and load the operating system.

When you start your computer, the start-up process looks for the partition that is marked as active. This is almost always the C: drive. The *active partition* should have the system files used by your computer to load the operating system. The partition that contains the operating system files is the *boot partition*. Normally, the active partition and the boot partition are the same. Only a primary partition can be designated as an active partition.

Primary Partition

Traditionally, the first partition you define is the *primary partition*. The primary partition is assigned all the disk space you allocate to it. For example, if you were to create the first partition as a primary partition and allocate 10 GB of space, the first drive by default (the primary drive) would be the C: drive and would consist of 10 GB of usable space.

With the Windows family of operating systems, you can have up to four partitions per physical disk. This means you can have four primary partitions, or three primary partitions and one *extended partition*. Each physical partition can have only one drive letter assigned to it.

Extended Partition

An extended partition is a physical partition that cannot be used as a boot partition. Within an extended partition, you can create up to 23 logical drives. For example, you could create a single extended partition that is 1 GB in size. Within the extended partition, you could then create four logical drives—D, E, F, and G—each 250 MB.

A Primer on Disk Drive Configurations

Several disk drive configurations are available. You can create the configurations listed next by using an operating system (software-based RAID, for example) or by using a hardware solution. Many of these types of configurations are called *Redundant Array of Inexpensive (or Independent) Disks (RAID)*. RAID storage systems require two or more disks, depending on the configuration. Each configuration has a specific level identifier that indicates the type of configuration. RAID systems are critical for servers because they provide improved performance, and in some cases *fault tolerance*.

> **Volume Set**   A volume set extends the size of a partition beyond a single physical drive. This is not a RAID configuration but is often the result of a RAID configuration. Disks that are used in a RAID configuration are physically separate from the RAID controller but appear as one large drive to software such as Windows Server 2003, Windows Vista, Windows 7, or Windows Server 2008.
>
> **Disk Stripe Set—RAID Level 0**   A disk stripe set combines several logical partitions of the same size into a single logical disk. Data is striped evenly

boot partition
Synonymous with the active partition on a disk. The boot partition contains the necessary files to start the operating system on the computer.

primary partition
The first and bootable partition you create on a hard drive.

extended partition
A non-bootable partition containing logical drives.

Redundant Array of Inexpensive (or Independent) Disks (RAID)
A method of using a series of hard disks as an array of drives. Some RAID implementations improve performance. Others improve performance and provide fault tolerance.

fault tolerance
The use of hardware and software to prevent the loss of data in the event of a system, hardware, or power disruption or failure.

over each partition. Performance is excellent in this RAID configuration, because of simultaneous reads and writes to all drives in the stripe; however, there is no way to recover data in the event of a hard disk failure.

RAID Level 0 is a good choice for digital-video editors and digital animators who need the storage capacity of many hard drives without sacrificing performance. Because of the improved performance inherent in RAID 0, you might consider it an option for disk-intensive applications such as databases. But keep in mind that RAID 0 provides no fault tolerance. If a disk fails, all data is lost on all drives!

NOTE On most computers that you purchase, the operating system and other software are already installed. The hard drive is usually represented by a single letter, which typically is C. Rarely, if ever, are other configurations present, regardless of the size of the drive. But there are other configurations to consider that can add better performance or higher insurance that the data will be protected.

Mirrored Set—RAID Level 1 A mirrored set contains a primary partition and a secondary partition. Any time data is written to the first partition, it is automatically written to the second partition. RAID Level 1 is often used to protect the drive where the operating system is located. The mirrored set provides the added fault tolerance needed for servers. It is not typically recommended that mirrored sets be created for all drives. Mirrored sets cost twice as much as non-RAID or RAID 0 to implement because for each disk you want to partition, you need a second disk of the exact same size.

parity
In the context of a stripe set, a series of mathematical calculations based on the data stored. If a disk fails, the stored parity information can be used to rebuild the data.

Stripe Set with Parity Drive—RAID Level 3 A stripe set with a *parity* drive is similar to a stripe set with a parity stripe. In a stripe set with a parity drive, the parity information is stored on a single drive as opposed to being striped across all drives.

Stripe Set with Parity Stripe—RAID Level 5 A stripe set with a parity stripe is similar to a stripe set, but it contains a parity stripe across all drives. This gives you the benefits of a stripe set while also offering fault tolerance. If one of the drives fails, the parity information from the other drives can be used to rebuild the data onto a new drive. RAID Level 5 is the most common configuration because of the low cost, ease of recovery of a failed disk, and performance. In cases where data availability is critical, such as databases, RAID Level 5 is the preferred choice. It adds a high level of reliability, provides good performance, and is relatively reasonable in cost.

Striping with double distributed parity—RAID Level 6 This stripe set allows for up to two drives to fail in an array and still provide fault tolerance. It does this by using block level striping with two parity blocks spread across the member disks.

Striped Mirrors—RAID Level 10   A stripe set that uses both a RAID 0 and a RAID 1 (or RAID 1+0 or just RAID 10). This uses separate mirror drives and stripes the data between them. To set this up, you need a minimum of four drives.

When deciding on a disk drive configuration, always consult the manufacturer of the computer first. Not only might you get some free instruction on the best type of configuration for your needs, you might even get some help implementing your new configuration.

TIP

Volume Set

A volume set extends the size of a single partition. For example, assume that you created a single partition on your 100 GB physical drive. You used the partition to store a database that is approaching 100 GB. You can add a second physical drive and with the free space create a volume set.

In volume sets, the data is written sequentially, so you can extend volume sets at any time without having to back up the data, create the volume set, and then restore the data. This makes volume sets an easy way to quickly and temporarily handle a shortage of disk space until you replace your disk drive with a larger drive.

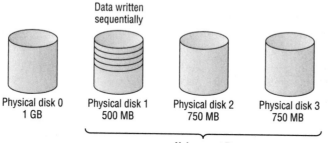

Data written sequentially

Physical disk 0
1 GB

Physical disk 1
500 MB

Physical disk 2
750 MB

Physical disk 3
750 MB

Volume set D

Consider these factors when you use volume sets:

Same-size partitions?   No. With volume sets, the partitions within the volume set do not have to be the same size.

Performance increase?   No. Volume sets write data sequentially, so there is no performance increase.

Fault tolerance?   No. Because volume sets contain no parity information, they are not fault tolerant. This means that if any physical drive within the volume set fails, the entire volume set is unusable.

———————————
NOTE   ———————————

With Windows Server 2003 and later, you can have up to 32 disks within a volume set or spanned volume.

Disk Stripe Set

In a disk stripe set, or RAID Level 0, you define logical partitions of the same size as a stripe set. There must be at least two partitions participating in a stripe set. After you create a stripe set, data is written across the set in stripes. The benefit of this disk configuration is that it enables you to take advantage of multiple disk *Input/Output (I/O) channels* for improved performance.

Input/Output (I/O) channel
A circuit that provides a path an input or output device can use to communicate with the processor.

Stripe set D

Consider these factors when you use stripe sets:

Same-size partitions?	Yes. Logical partitions have to be the same size in a stripe set.
Performance increase?	Yes. If the stripe set is located on multiple I/O channels, you will see a performance increase.
Fault tolerance?	No. Because stripe sets contain no parity information, if any drive within the stripe set fails, the entire stripe set will be lost. In this case, you would restore your data from your most recent backup.

———————————
TIP   ———————————

If you want fault tolerance, it is technically possible to mirror a stripe set; however, for this to be possible, the stripe set must be created using special RAID hardware. When Windows boots up, the stripe set appears as a single logical drive and not as multiple physical disks even though it is really made up of multiple disks. Using Disk Management, you create a software-based mirror set of two striped sets. The problem with software-based mirrored drives is that they are much slower than hardware-based drives. Also, software-based RAID configurations are prone to errors, which could cause data loss. It is not possible to mirror two stripe sets that were created with software.

Mirrored Set

A mirrored set, RAID Level 1, consists of a primary drive and a secondary drive. Any time data is written to the primary drive, it is copied (or mirrored) to the secondary drive. The benefit of a mirrored set is that if a disk fails, you do not lose any data.

There are two types of mirrored sets:

Disk mirroring   Uses one controller with two disks

Disk duplexing   Uses two controllers and two disks

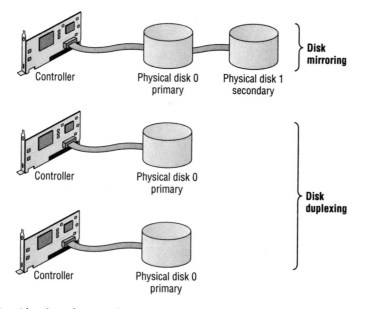

Consider these factors when you use mirrored sets:

Same-size partitions?	Yes. In a mirrored set, both logical partitions have to be the same size.
Performance increase?	Yes and no. With disk mirroring, performance decreases on writes, because one controller must write to both drives. With disk duplexing, you see a slight performance increase, because you are using two separate I/O channels.
Fault tolerance?	Yes. Mirrored sets are fault tolerant.

Stripe Set with Parity Drive

A stripe set with a parity drive, RAID Level 3, arranges logical drives of equal size into a stripe set. A separate drive stores parity information. In the event that a data drive fails, the parity information and the data on the functioning drives are used in a mathematical calculation that can reconstruct the lost data.

Stripe set with parity drive

Consider these factors when you use stripe sets with a parity drive:

Same-size partitions?	Yes. Within any stripe set, partitions must be equal in size.
Performance increase?	Yes. Each I/O channel that the stripe set uses increases the performance of the stripe set.
Fault tolerance?	Yes and no. As long as only one drive fails (assuming that the parity drive isn't the failed drive), the stripe set with the parity drive is fault tolerant. If two or more drives fail, you must re-create the stripe set with the parity drive and then restore the data from the most recent backup.

NOTE   Although most RAID configurations are implemented using special RAID hardware, RAID 3 is not typically available as a software-based option. Windows Server 2008, for example, only supports RAID 0, 1, and 5.

Stripe Set with Parity Stripe

A stripe set with a parity stripe, RAID 5, arranges logical drives of equal size into a stripe set. Each drive within the set has a parity stripe. As with stripe sets with a parity drive, discussed in the preceding section, the parity information and data from the functioning disks can be used to re-create a failed disk. Unlike the previous RAID examples, RAID 5 requires a minimum of three disks with a maximum limitation of 32 disks.

Stripe set with parity stripe 300

Consider these factors when you use stripe sets with a parity stripe:

Same-size partitions?	Yes. Within any stripe set, partitions must be equal in size.
Performance increase?	Yes. Each I/O channel that the stripe set uses increases the performance of the stripe set.
Fault tolerance?	Yes and no. As long as only one drive fails, the stripe set with the parity stripe is fault tolerant. If two or more drives fail, you must re-create the stripe set.

Windows 2000 Server introduced dynamic disks that do support software-based RAID 5. Dynamic disks minimize the need to restart Windows when a drive change such as creating a RAID 5 volume or mirror set has occurred. The RAID 5 drive configuration is supported by Windows Server 2003 and later and is considered a software implementation of RAID 5. With software implementations of RAID, you can use any disk drives that are of equal size.

NOTE

Types of Offline Data Storage

Hard drives are considered *online data storage*. This means that data is readily available at high speed. You do not need to do anything special to access online storage.

Another type of storage is called *offline storage*. Offline storage means that the data is not readily available without some type of user intervention. Offline storage is useful for transferring data between computers, storing large amounts of data, or providing a means of backup.

Offline storage is a major market for manufacturers as people take information and devices on the road. The mobile workforce demands that information be readily accessible on desktop computers, laptops, and handheld devices. Many products are available that offer incredible performance, reliability, and capacity. Some common forms of offline storage are *compact discs (CDs, DVDs, and Blu-rays)*, tapes, and external storage such as flash drives and external hard drives.

The storage capacity of flash drives and external hard drives has made them extremely convenient to use, but it has also made them a security threat

online data storage
Holds data that is immediately available and can be quickly accessed, as is the case with hard disks.

offline storage
Holds data that is currently unavailable. You use offline storage to store large amounts of infrequently accessed data or computer backups.

compact discs (CDs, DVDs, and Blu-rays)
Plastic or optical discs that can be read using lasers. Compact discs have a maximum storage capacity of 700 MB.

to organizations. External storage drives have nearly the same capacity and performance found with internal storage drives. External storage drives may be powered through the connecting port or through an external power adapter. Drives are usually connected with USB cables (both 2.0 and 3.0) though newer drives may also have Firewire or eSATA connectivity. Storage capacities of these drives are now 3 TB. Externally powered storage devices may have storage capacities of 16 TB.

digital video disc or digital versatile disc (DVD)
Based on the same technology as the CD-ROM, DVDs use a much smaller laser and are able to copy many times more data. DVDs can hold at least 4.7 GB of data and as much as 8.5 GB.

In addition to flash drives and external hard drives, *digital video disc* or *digital versatile disc (DVD)* technology has changed the way computer applications, audio, and high-quality digital video are stored and distributed.

In a networked environment, online data can also mean that the data is available through the network. Offline data can also refer to data that has been downloaded from the network for use on a local computer when it is not connected to the network.

NOTE

Near-line storage accessibility is somewhere between online and offline storage. For example, a magneto-optical drive that uses a jukebox to store data is not as readily available as a hard drive, but it can access data without user intervention.

Distribution Media for Applications

When PCs became mainstream in home and business environments, almost all applications were distributed on floppy disks. Now the most common distribution media are CDs, DVDs, or in some cases, a small install file that will be used to download the rest of the software package from a remote site on the Internet.

Removable Storage Devices

Removable disk drives were the storage choice of graphic designers. When a graphic designer was ready to send artwork to a printer, the artwork would be placed on a 20 MB or 40 MB removable disk and sent on its way. The mobility of the original removable drives, along with their storage capacity proved to be very valuable. A company could invest in an in-house graphic designer for all its original artwork needs.

Today, with the prominence of the USB port, the most common removable storage devices are flash drives and external hard drives.

Flash drives, also referred to as thumb drivers, are small and easily transportable, allowing you to take files with you on the go. Because of their size, they serve the same purpose as a CD. However, they are also usually more reliable.

Flash drive
A flash drive is a small, removable storage device typically used to take files on the go.

Flash drives use the USB mass storage standard, which is supported by Windows and most other operating systems. A flash drive consists of a circuit board and USB connector, which are enclosed in a plastic or rubber case. They draw power from the computer via external USB connection.

External hard drives are much larger in size, but also can carry very large amounts of data (up to 2 TBs or more). These are ideal for those who need extra storage space to hold things like music or photos, or need to backup their system. Like a flash drive, the external hard drive connects to the computer via a USB port.

External hard drive
An external hard drive is a larger removable storage device that connects to the computer via the USB port.

Compact Discs (CDs)

The compact disc (CD) has been a popular storage media for many years. CDs use an optical drive to read data. This is different from the magnetic media that standard hard disks use. This means that CDs are not susceptible to magnetism as hard drives and floppy disks are.

CDs offer several advantages:

◆ They can store up to 700 MB of data.

◆ They are inexpensive to reproduce.

- They are lightweight.
- If handled properly, they are durable and can archive data for 10 years or more.

CD-Recordable

Compact disc-recordable (CD-Rs) are excellent drives for archiving data. Many companies must keep data for three or more years. Maintaining data on the hard drive of a server is impractical, because it can lead to large stores of data that are rarely if ever used. Companies can write any set of data that they select to the CD-Rs and then archive that data for future use.

Writing to a CD requires the use of a strong laser. The laser in a CD-R heats the crystal material in a CD to a temperature between 900 and 1,300 degrees Fahrenheit. The heat causes the crystals to melt, creating a deformity that reflects less light. The less reflective area is called a pit and is interpreted by the computer as a one. A reflective area is called a land and is interpreted by the computer as a zero.

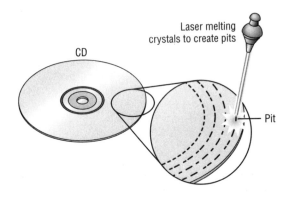

CD-Rewritable (CD-RW)

compact disc-rewritable (CD-RW)
A compact disc that can have data rewritten to it several times using lasers. Lasers record data to the disc like a CD-R, but slightly less powerful lasers are used to erase the data. Even weaker lasers are used to read the data.

Compact disc-rewritable (CD-RW) discs can be written to several times. CD-RW drives are excellent because they will work not only with CD-RW discs, but also with CD-R discs, which are less expensive. If you are considering CD-RW as an option, consider that CD-RW discs are not readable on conventional CD-ROM drives. If you need to use the CD on a CD-ROM drive, you will need to use a CD-R disc.

CD-RW works the same way as CD-R at writing data to disc. Rewrites require the CD-RW drive to use a second laser to change the nonreflective areas (the pits) so they become reflective. The laser heats the desired area to 400 degrees Fahrenheit. That is just enough heat to loosen the crystals in the disc. As the crystals cool, they assume their original structure, which reflects light.

Digital Video Discs (DVDs)

Digital video discs have long been sought after because of their high storage capacity and diverse usage. Now DVD technology is affordable for home entertainment systems, desktop computers, and laptops.

DVD's potential is in its data storage. DVDs can store a minimum of 4.7 GB to as much as 8.5 GB on a double-sided DVD. Coupled with its low cost per disc, DVD is an excellent choice for digital video and audio.

DVD has many variations. Like CD-ROM technology, DVD is versatile, meeting needs from video media to data archiving. The platforms are as follows:

> **DVD-ROM (Read-Only Media)**   Available as read-only. A typical DVD-ROM holds 4.7 GB of data—enough space for a full-length movie.

> **DVD-Video**   A standard designed for the video industry. DVD-Video is read-only, like DVD-ROM, but it requires a reader that is compatible with the Content Scrambling System (CSS). CSS is used to prevent people from illegally duplicating the video.

> **DVD-RAM**   A rewritable DVD format that will write as much as 2.6 GB of data per side.

Blu-ray is a sought-after replacement for DVD and CD technology, not only because of its storage capacity, but also because Blu-ray drives are backward compatible with DVDs and CDs. There is no loss in investment for users to migrate to Blu-ray.

NOTE

Blu-Ray Discs

Blu-ray discs and players were first introduced to the consumer market in 2006.

What makes Blu-ray more advantageous is its storage capacity. A single-layer Blu-ray can hold 25 GB worth of data and a dual-layer can hold 50 GB. A quadruple-layer (BD-XL) can hold up to 128 GB, though there is not much adoption of this format yet.

Tape Drives

Tape drives use a tape cartridge to store data. Tapes are a popular form of backup, because a single tape can hold huge amounts of data. Backups are critical for any computer, because you value your data. Any computer professional can tell you many horror stories of what happened when drives failed and they had outdated or no backups. The good news is there are people who usually can recover your data. The bad news is this method of data recovery is terribly expensive.

Although tape provides high-capacity storage, it is a slow medium to read from and write to. However, this is not typically a problem when backing up data, because backups are often scheduled during periods of inactivity. When choosing a tape backup device, consider these questions:

- How much storage space do you need?
- What *throughput* do you need for the backup?
- What are the costs of the tape device and the tapes themselves?
- What backup software is compatible with the drive you select?
- Does your computer operating system have a driver for the tape drive, and is the drive on the operating system's Hardware Compatibility List (a list that specifies what hardware can be used with the software)?

throughput
The amount of data that can be transferred in a set period of time.

Tape backups are only as good as the backup strategy in place. There are several methods of backing up data. The key to the strategies is that you are able to recover data quickly and without losing more than a day's data. An effective strategy requires the following components:

- Daily tape backups with a full backup at least once a week
- Regular use of a cleaning tape
- Monitoring of backup logs for failed backups
- Replacement of heavily used tapes after six months
- Offsite storage of tapes

In addition, a good backup strategy should cover at least a month's worth of data. This strategy requires at least 19 tapes. Four tapes are used for Monday through Thursday. Three tapes are used for the first, second, and third Fridays of the same month. The last tape is used on the fourth Friday of the month. This tape is archived for the year. At the end of a 12-month cycle, you should have a full backup on tape for each month. This ensures that you can restore the data from any month of the past year. In addition, the latest four weeks can be restored.

Terms to Know

active partition

array

backup

boot partition

burst mode

compact disc-recordable (CD-R)

compact disc-rewritable (CD-RW)

compact discs (CDs, DVDs, and Blu-rays)

daisy chain

direct memory access (DMA)

disk controller

digital video disc (DVD)

Enhanced IDE (EIDE)

extended partition

external hard drive

fault tolerance

flash drive

hard drive

input/output (I/O) channel

Integrated Drive Electronics (IDE)

jumpers

logical drive

master

offline storage

online data storage

Parallel ATA (PATA)

parity

physical hard drive

primary partition

Redundant Array of Inexpensive (or Independent) Disks (RAID)

slave

Small Computer System Interface (SCSI)

Solid State Drive (SSD)

termination

throughput

volume

Review Questions

1. The two most common types of hard drives are: _____ and _____.

2. True or false: SATA drives require a separate SATA adapter for installation.

3. You can easily identify a SATA hard drive because it uses a ____-pin adapter.

4. You can easily identify a typical (wide) SCSI hard drive because it uses a ____-pin adapter.

5. Which drive type typically offers better performance, SATA or SCSI?

6. What is the difference between a physical drive and a logical drive?

7. Define *volume set*.

8. List three disk drive configurations that are fault tolerant.

9. What is the difference between disk mirroring and disk duplexing?

10. True or false: If two drives in a stripe set with parity fail, you can still recover the stripe set if it consists of six or more drives.

11. True or false: In a drive configured as a stripe set with parity, all the partitions within the stripe set must be the same size.

12. What is the difference between online and offline storage?

13. How much data can be stored on a Blu-ray?

14. What is the advantage of using a thumb drive over a DVD?

15. Why might Blu-ray replace DVD technology?

16. True or false: You should keep all thumb drives away from any magnetic field.

Chapter 3

Data Movement:
Input/Output Devices

move•ment *n* : the act of moving something in a particular direction

Computers process, manipulate, and send data according to instructions from a user. Each computer has input and output interfaces to enable you to connect input or output devices. The input device enables information to enter the computer, and the output device enables information to exit the computer. Without providing the capability to enter or extract information, the computer is nothing more than a box with colored lights.

Understanding Ports

Ports are used to communicate between external devices and the computer or to communicate with other computers. Each port type has a specific shape, size, and pin count, and in some cases, the port may provide power for the device. Just as computer speed and capabilities have increased over the years, so has the speed at which devices can pass information.

Serial Ports

serial communication

The transmission of data one bit at a time.

clock signal

Controls the rate at which synchronous data is transmitted.

start bit

The bit that synchronizes the clock on the computer receiving the data. In asynchronous data transmission, the start bit is a space.

stop bit

The bit that identifies the end of the character being transmitted so that the character is clearly recognized.

A serial port is either an input or output port that supports *serial communication*. Data transmitted in a serial fashion can be sent using one of two methods: synchronous data transmission or asynchronous data transmission.

In synchronous data transmission, a *clock signal* regulates the flow of data over a cable or wire. This transmission method is used when large amounts of data must be transferred in a short period of time.

Asynchronous data transmission uses a single information bit, referred to as the *start bit*, to tell the computer when to start transmitting data and a *stop bit* to tell it when to stop. This method is used when you are transferring smaller amounts of data. Both the computer sending the data and the one receiving it must agree on the number of start and stop bits for communication to take place.

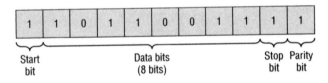

PCs used to be manufactured with two serial ports that were used to connect serial devices, such as a mouse, modem, or line printer, by way of a serial cable.

Serial port connectors (not USB) come in two types: 9-pin and 25-pin. A 9-pin connector is referred to as DB-9 and is a common serial connector for mice and handheld devices. DB-25 refers to 25-pin connectors and is frequently used by external modems.

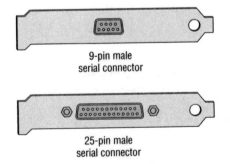

9-pin male
serial connector

25-pin male
serial connector

Parallel Ports

A parallel port is either an input or output port that supports *parallel communication*. Parallel communication occurs when data is transmitted and processed one *byte* at a time. Eight transmission lines carry the signal. Parallel communication is typically faster than serial communication.

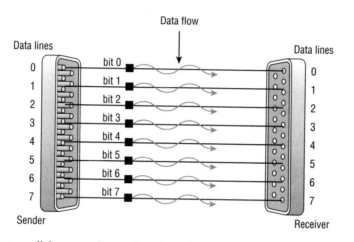

Most parallel ports today are based on the *Extended Capabilities Port (ECP)* or *Enhanced Parallel Port (EPP)* standards that support data transfer speeds of more than 2 *MBps*.

Historically, parallel communication has often been used to connect printers. Although parallel communication is not the fastest communication method, it is cost-effective. At one time, almost all computers were built with a parallel port or had an expansion card installed that provided a parallel port.

Besides printers, parallel ports have also been used to support external storage devices (discussed in Chapter 2, "Storing Your Files: Data Storage"). External devices that communicate using the parallel port connect via a 25-pin female connector.

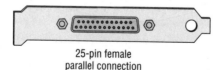

25-pin female
parallel connection

The original parallel port was designed to send information in one direction to a printer. Standards were later developed to improve the capabilities of the parallel port by allowing communication to occur in both directions and to support multiple devices on the same port.

parallel communication
The process of transmitting and processing data one byte (8 bits) at a time.

byte
A single binary character, or 8 bits.

Extended Capabilities Port (ECP)
The standard developed for parallel communication by Hewlett-Packard and Microsoft to allow for data-transfer rates of more than 2 MBps. In addition to the high data-transfer rates, it allows for bidirectional operation.

Enhanced Parallel Port (EPP)
The standard developed for parallel communication by Intel, Xircom, and Zenith Data Systems to allow for data-transfer rates of more than 2 Mbps. It supports bidirectional operation of attached devices and an addressing scheme.

megabits per second (Mbps)
A measurement of the amount of data, in the millions of bits per second, being transferred.

——— *NOTE* ———

USB Ports

Universal Serial Bus (USB) is an external bus technology for high-speed connection of peripheral devices. The USB specification was published in 1996 through the joint work of Compaq, Dell, IBM, Intel, Microsoft, NEC, and Nortel. USB has effectively replaced earlier, commonly used ports such as serial and parallel.

USB offers support for almost every kind of external computer device known. Monitors, mice and keyboards, joysticks, printers, scanners, cameras, storage devices, modems, and more can all be connected via USB. A single built-in USB controller can support up to 127 devices. The devices can be connected via additional *USB hub*s, daisy-chained from one device to another, or both.

USB 3.0 can transfer data at up to 5 Gbps (gigabits per second). That makes it an excellent choice for data-intensive applications such as video.

USB offers the following capabilities:

USB hub
A connectivity device that provides multiple USB connections so that several USB devices can communicate with the computer.

- It is capable of self-identifying devices that are attached.
- Hot-pluggable devices can be added or removed while the computer is running.
- Power can be supplied by the USB for devices that do not have a separate power supply.
- It can be used to charge devices as well as provide connectivity.
- It is easy to use; it would be very difficult to install a USB connecting cable incorrectly.
- USB 2.0 and earlier versions support cable lengths up to 5 meters (16.9 feet).
- USB 3.0 doesn't have a defined maximum length, but due to electrical signal current requirements, it is recommended that it not exceed 3 meters (10.1 feet).

Inside a computer that has USB ports, there is a USB controller. The controller is responsible for interfacing between software and hardware. Inside the controller, a host hub contains two USB connectors, or ports. The cables that attach to the USB ports have four wires: One wire supplies power and another is used as an electrical ground; the two remaining wires are used for signaling.

bandwidth
The capacity of a network line to carry information. Bandwidth is best thought of as a highway; four lanes support more traffic than two and have fewer slowdowns. One of the few basic rules of modern networking is that more bandwidth is always better.

When a USB device connects to the computer, it is automatically detected by the USB controller and is required to identify itself. After the device is recognized, the USB controller assigns it an ID. During this initial communication, the USB controller determines a device's *bandwidth* priority. Devices that require no interruption, such as video, have the highest priority. In contrast, printers, which send large amounts of data but don't care when it gets there, have the lowest priority.

The various versions of USB are described here and are summarized in the following table.

USB 1.0   USB 1.0 was officially released in January 1996. The original 1.0 specification had limitations with extension cables and pass-through monitors such that there were few USB 1.0 devices.

USB 1.1   The first widely adopted standard for USB was 1.1 in August of 1998. Maximum throughput was 12 Mbps.

USB 2.0   The standard for USB 2.0 was introduced in 2000 as a replacement for USB 1.1. USB 2.0 had a maximum throughput of 480 Mbps (compared with USB 1.1 of only 12 Mbps). Three new plug connectors were also introduced: Mini-A, Mini-B, and Micro-USB connectors (though these were not introduced until 2007).

USB 3.0   This is the latest USB standard introduced in 2008 and it offers a theoretical maximum throughput of 5 Gbps. A feature of USB is the Super Speed Bus, which provides for an expected throughput of 3.2 Gbps. The USB standard has been adopted by all computer manufacturers.

USB Version	Introduced	Throughput
1.0	1996	12 Mbps
1.1	1998	12 Mbps
2.0	2000	480 Mbps
3.0	2008	5 Gbps

Thunderbolt

The technology behind the new Thunderbolt data port was developed by Intel but was first used by Apple in the spring of 2011. This interface has a current maximum throughput of 10 Gbps (and that is not a theoretical throughput, but a usable value). The Thunderbolt port is basically a combination of PCI Express and DisplayPort. What this means to us is that external graphics cards for laptops are now feasible, as the throughput equals or exceeds that of PCIx16 cards. Now a true gaming laptop can be built.

Understanding Monitors

The monitor is the most common type of output device. It may look like a simple television or flat screen, but it is not. The monitor enables the human eye to interact with the computer. Without a monitor, the computer's output capabilities would be very limited. Imagine if the only output available were in printed or audible form. The monitor enables the computer to translate computer data into text and graphics and display them.

There are two main types of monitors (or displays): flat panels (LED, LCD, OLED) and cathode ray tube (CRT). The internals of the CRT monitor have remained virtually unchanged for 30+ years. They all contain an *electron gun* that shoots electrically charged particles called electrons toward the back of the monitor screen. The screen is coated with a phosphorous material that glows when an electron hits it. A beam is made up of these electrons that span across (horizontal) and down (vertical) the screen, forming an image by charging the rasters on the leaded glass screen. The image created is called a raster. In color CRTs there are red, green, and blue phosphers to produce a color image.

electron gun
The device that shoots electrically charged particles called electrons toward the back of the monitor screen.

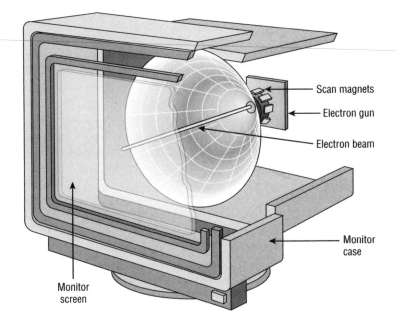

Scan magnets

Electron gun

Electron beam

Monitor case

Monitor screen

Two ways of measuring a monitor's quality are using the *refresh rate* and *dot pitch* characteristics. The refresh rate signifies the number of times the beam of electrons shot from the electron gun redraws the screen in one second. The dot pitch measures the distance between two dots of the same color on the monitor.

NOTE

refresh rate
A measurement of the number of times that an image is redrawn to the screen per second. Measured in Hertz; a higher number is better.

dot pitch
Measures the distance, in millimeters, between two dots of the same color on the monitor.

Video Display Adapter Standards

Video display adapters (the adapter inside your computer that connects to the monitor) have many standards. Each standard consists of specifications for the maximum supported resolution, colors supported for the maximum resolution, and connector type. Each video display adapter type has a different interface to allow for easier identification.

Resolution on the monitor is determined by the number of pixels. A *pixel* is the smallest addressable unit on a display screen. The higher the pixel resolution (the more rows and columns of pixels), the more information can be displayed.

Pixels are made up of one or more bits. The more bits you have, the greater the *bit depth*. Greater bit depth means that more shades and colors can be represented. A monochrome monitor uses one bit per pixel. On a color display, there can be 4 to 24 bits per pixel, which provides from 16 to over 16 million colors. What is common now is for systems to have an extra 8 bits for each 24-bit pixel (allowing for 32-bit pixels) color. These extra 8 bits are used when combining with another image (described as opacity).

This table defines the standards.

pixel
Short for picture element. A pixel is one dot in an image and is the smallest single component of a digital image.

bit depth
A value for the number of bits that are used to make up a pixel. The higher the number of bits, the more colors can be displayed.

Video Standard	Resolution (Pixels)
VGA	680×480
Super VGA (SVGA)	800×600
Extended Graphics Array (XGA)	1024×768
WXGA	1280×800
Super eXtended Graphics Array (SXGA)	1280×1024
Widescreen Super eXtended Graphics Array	1440×900
Widescreen Super eXtended Graphics Array Plus	1680×1050
Ultra eXtended Graphics Array (UXGA)	1600×1200
Full HDTV	1920×1080
Widescreen Ultra eXtended Graphics Array (WUXGA)	1920×1200

Taking advantage of the latest video technology is not exclusively a function of upgrading to Windows 7 or Windows Server 2008 R2. Software upgrades of the operating system only add support for new technologies. Your video display adapter and monitor—the hardware—must support the selected range of supported resolutions and maximum colors to function properly.

You can upgrade your video hardware to support higher resolutions and more colors. A video display adapter with additional memory will support higher-quality video. Many manufacturers include as much as 1 GB or more of RAM on the video card (in some cases you can use two video cards that are connected in tandem). If you intend to use advanced animation or video features, you can select video cards or 3D graphic accelerator cards that run faster (for smoother images and motion) and have more RAM. In addition to upgrading your video card, you will also need to select a monitor that will support more colors and higher resolutions.

Liquid Crystal Display (LCD)

Originally designed for watches, liquid crystal displays (LCDs) quickly grew to be a direct contender with traditional tube-based computer screens. The LCD's thin profile makes it suitable for portable devices from laptops to handheld devices. LCDs are popular for desktop use as well. Their sleek profile looks good and saves space.

LCD technology is available in two types: *passive matrix* and *active matrix*. The screen of passive matrix displays looks faded because the liquid crystal cells have fewer electrodes to maintain solid colors of light. The cells begin to fade before they can be recharged. Active matrix displays have transistors located throughout the display. Each transistor keeps the liquid display cell charged, providing a much brighter and sharper image.

passive matrix
A flat-panel LCD display technology that uses horizontal and vertical wires with LCD cells at each intersection to create a video image. Passive matrix is considered inferior to active matrix but is less expensive to produce.

active matrix
Sometimes referred to as Thin Film Transistor (TFT), active matrix LCD displays offer superior clarity and color. This is due mostly to faster refresh rates and more powerful LCD cells.

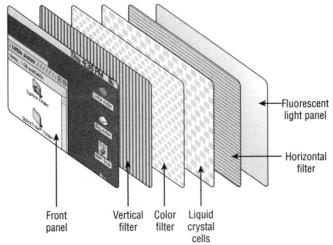

Front panel — Vertical filter — Color filter — Liquid crystal cells — Horizontal filter — Fluorescent light panel

Light Emitting Diode (LED)

An LED monitor is simply a new type of LCD monitor. The newer LCD monitors still use LCDs; it is how they use backlighting that differentiates them. There are three main types of LED monitors: Edge Backlight LEDs, RBG LEDs, and WLEDs.

LED monitors are gaining popularity because they use less energy than LCDs. LED monitors also offer more intense lighting and gradation, which explains their truer color quality. Another benefit of these displays is that they provide a significantly better dynamic contrast rate when compared with LCDs.

Organic Light Emitting Diode (OLED)

An OLED is a solid state device that uses thin films of organic molecules that create light when electricity is applied to them. What makes them unique is that they are bendable; in fact, you can roll up the screen of some devices. Also, OLEDs have a much brighter contrast than typical LCDs or LEDs and can be viewed from a broader angle. What might be the most compelling reason for using OLEDs is their response time (the number of times per second the display draws the data it has been given). A high-end LCD might have a refresh rate of 240 Hz or even higher whereas an OLED has a theoretical limit in excess of 100,000 Hz.

DisplayPort

DisplayPort is another display interface specification that was introduced by the Video Electronics Standards Association in 2006. It is designed to replace the DVI and VGA standards.

VGA

Video Graphics Array (VGA) was introduced in 1987 and, as of today, is still very popular. The VGA connector is found on almost all laptops, monitors, projectors, and on many desktop computers. VGA is also a video resolution most commonly used at 640x480 (later followed by Super-VGA at 800x600—which was a default standard for many projectors). The Video Graphics Array uses a 15-pin video connector.

DVI

Digital Video Interface (DVI) was introduced in 1999 as a replacement for analog VGA connectors. Most desktop computers and many laptop computers have a DVI port available as well as many newer projectors and HD televisions as the resolution and digital experience are superior to the output from analog devices.

Connecting a Keyboard and Mouse

The keyboard is the most common type of input device. The keyboard takes in information in the form of letters and numbers. The letters and numbers are translated into instructions that the computer must perform. The computer translates literally what is entered, so any typing mistakes will result in an error.

Certain aspects of keyboards are important to consider. For example, choose a keyboard that is comfortable for you. In most cases, it is beneficial to select an ergonomically designed product. These products are designed to blend smoothly with the contour of your body.

Keyboards can connect to computers in several ways. The most common type of connection is the Universal Serial Bus (USB) discussed earlier in this chapter. However, many computers still use the *DIN 6*, which is also referred to as a *PS/2* connector. This connector is small and looks identical to a PS/2-style mouse. In fact, it is easy to confuse these two when you are connecting them to

DIN
Deutsch Industrie Norm—a German standards organization.

PS/2
Also known as the mouse port and DIN 6, PS/2 was developed by IBM for connecting a mouse to the computer. PS/2 ports are supported for mice and keyboards alike.

the computer. Although the PS/2 connector isn't gone completely, and USB connections are pervasive, expect wireless keyboards to start challenging USB for keyboard and mouse connectivity.

Don't unplug the keyboard or mouse while the computer is on. You might damage your computer with a static charge. In some cases, older external USB hard drives may have required the computer to be rebooted to recognize the drive. However, today simply removing the device and reattaching will recognize the attached device.

DB-9   USB   DIN 8   DIN 6

The mouse is the second most common type of input device. You use the mouse for navigating, selecting, or drawing. The mouse movements are translated into computer instructions in the form of motion and button selection. The most common connector for mice is USB, though wireless mice (as with keyboards) are quickly dominating the market.

There are two main types of mice, Laser mice and the older (though still very common) roller ball mice. A laser (or optical) mouse uses a laser to track the movement of the mouse on virtually any surface.

In a roller ball mouse, the ball in the center touches the pad and rolls as you move the mouse. The ball moves two rollers that are connected to mechanical sensors. The movements of both rollers are interpreted into movements of the mouse pointer on the screen.

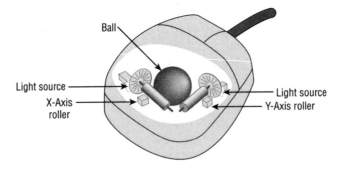

Many people use a mouse pad to provide a non-stick surface to roll the mouse on. The mouse pad serves two other important functions. First, it represents a finite physical space for moving the mouse. If you move off the pad, you sense the change and, given practice, move your mouse back onto the pad. Second, the pad offers a clean space that should be kept free of debris. Dust, hair, and food crumbs can degrade or damage the internal mechanical components found in roller ball mice. Laser mouse performance can be impacted if they are used on reflective surfaces such as glass or mirrored desks. In this case, the use of a mouse pad is advisable. Some higher end laser mice are not as susceptible when used on reflective surfaces.

Touch Screens

A touch screen can be thought of as having a built-in touch pad. The screen can detect where someone has touched the screen (with a stylus, finger, or other such device) and can respond to the action requested. This in effect removes the need for having an external keypad or keyboard.

Touch screens started to be developed in the late 1960s and saw their first commercial application in 1972. Since their first release, touch screens are found in banks, airports, lobby kiosks, and anyplace else where users can search for information. A touch screen blends the attributes of various input devices, such as a keyboard and mouse, with a computer screen. Most recently, touch screens have appeared in Smart Phones, iPads, and other such devices where having a separate keyboard would diminish the portability of these products.

Making Remote Connections

So far, this chapter has discussed input and output in relation to a single computer. Input and output also can occur between two remote computers or networks. The method chosen to remotely connect is determined by cost and what is available from telecom providers. What has traditionally been used (and is still in use in some rural areas) is the analog modem, which allows for slow (by today's standards of communication) connectivity over a Public Switch Telephone Network (PSTN). In most non-rural areas, you may have access to Asymmetric Digital Subscriber Line (ADSL), which runs over copper telephone lines or by using a cable modem which provides broadband access over cable Internet. Either of these methods will provide a substantially faster broadband connection—with downloads speeds up to 100 Mbps and upload speeds of 10+ Mbps.

Accessing the Internet through a traditional dial-up modem requires several steps. First, there must be a phone connection to the *central office (CO)* of the telephone company. The physical line between the CO and the commercial location is called the *local loop*. The local loop is terminated at both ends. At the commercial office end, the phone is plugged into a wall jack. At the telephone company, the cable terminates and is plugged into a telephone switch. Incoming calls to the switch are then forwarded to the appropriate location.

central office (CO)
A building in a given neighborhood where all local phone lines in that neighborhood terminate.

local loop
The two-wire copper telephone cable that runs from a home or office to the central office of the telephone company.

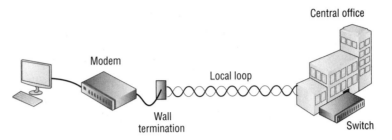

bits per second (bps)
The number of bits, or ones and zeros, transmitted each second.

When data is transmitted between two computers, the transmission speed is measured in terms of *bits per second (bps)* and not bytes per second. This table shows the difference between the two.

Bits	Transmission Speed
1 bit	1 bit per second (bps)
1,024 bits	1 kilobit per second (Kbps)
1,024,000 bits	1 megabit per second (Mbps)
1,024,000,000 bits	1 gigabit per second (Gbps)

There are several communication technologies that enable computers in different locations to share data. Each uses a different signaling format, medium, or both, which yields varying levels of performance. In the following pages, you will learn about these technologies.

Analog Modems

Modems function as input and output devices. They enable computers to communicate with one another over great distances. The word *modem* comes from the merging of the two words modulate and *demodulate*. Modems that send data convert digital signals from a computer into analog audible tone signals that can be transmitted over phone lines, and modems that receive data do the reverse.

modulate
To convert digital data into analog signals. Modulation enables digital computer data to be transferred over standard telephone lines.

demodulate
To convert an analog signal back to digital data. This is typically done on the receiving end of a computer transmission using standard phone service.

Digital signals are made up of discrete values. The values represent an on or off state, which are the ones and zeros of computer language. Discrete voltages represent the on or off conditions. An on condition is represented by +5 volts, and an off condition by −5 volts or a zero value. The values do not change over time; they change instantaneously from one state to another.

Analog signals are constantly changing values. The values represent fluctuations in voltage or sound. An analog signal can consist of an infinite number of possible values.

Modulation/Demodulation

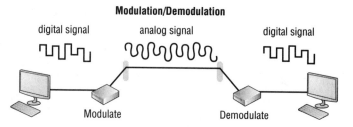

Modems can communicate at speeds from 300 bps to more than 56,000 bps (in the US, modems are regulated by the FCC to no more than 53,000 bps). Modems are backward compatible and slow their transmission speed to communicate with slower modems.

Modems come in two types: internal and external. External modems require a connection to an available serial port on the back of a computer using an *RS-232* cable. Internal modems plug into an expansion slot inside a computer. The use of dial-up modems is rapidly diminishing as more broadband providers are available that provide much faster technology. In some cases, users can *tether* their mobile phone to act as a modem and achieve speeds that are 10+ times faster than with their traditional dial-up.

A term often associated with modems is *baud*. Baud is the number of frequency changes made per second. This term is often used synonymously with bps. This is accurate at low speeds, such as 300 baud. At higher speeds, modems use a technique that enables multiple bits to be sent on each frequency change. So, for example, a modem operating at 9,600 bps may operate at only 2,400 baud.

RS-232
An interface standard for use between data communications equipment (DCE) and data terminal equipment (DTE).

tethering
Tethering is the process of connecting a mobile phone to allow connectivity to the internet.

NOTE
---

baud
A measurement of the number of signals that are transmitted each second.

Digital Subscriber Line (DSL)

Digital Subscriber Line (DSL) is still used and is a relatively inexpensive technology offered through the local telephone company. DSL has been successful in the residential/small office Internet access market because of its high bandwidth potential. Unlike modems, which must convert digital signals to analog to transmit over the public telephone network, DSL signals are digital from beginning to end.

The completely digital transmission vastly improves performance in several ways. First, DSL does not have the transmission limitation of 56 Kbps found with traditional modems. In fact, DSL is capable of transmitting 10+ Mbps (in most cases, the transmitting speed, or bandwidth as it is sometimes called, is limited by the carrier, not the DSL modem itself)—nearly as fast as a network connection. Second, the DSL modem does not have to convert a signal from analog to digital, and thus slow transmission, as modems do. A DSL modem is not a modem at all; it is actually a *bridge*. Since most people are comfortable

Digital Subscriber Line (DSL)
A digital signaling method used to transmit data over regular phone lines at speeds up to 6 Mbps. DSL uses Asynchronous Transfer Mode (ATM) to pass data in fixed-size cells.

bridge
A Layer 2 device that enables networks using different Layer 2 protocols to communicate with one another. A bridge can also minimize traffic between two networks by passing through only those packets that are addressed to the other network.

Asynchronous Transfer Mode (ATM)
A network technology that uses fixed-size cells to transfer data. The fixed-size cells enable it to provide better performance.

Internet service provider (ISP)
A company or organization that provides the user with access to the Internet, typically for a fee. Users may gain access by using any one of many remote connection technologies, including modems, DSL, ISDN, cable modems, and others.

with the term *modem*, it made more sense to use modem rather than introducing a new term.

DSL modems are able to achieve high transfer rates by using a technology called *Asynchronous Transfer Mode (ATM)*. ATM uses cells to transfer data. The DSL modem is a bridge that converts ATM cells coming from your *Internet service provider (ISP)* into *Ethernet* frames. Most computers with the right hardware can communicate via Ethernet network technology.

DSL is available in two flavors. Asymmetric DSL (ADSL) has a different download speed, usually faster, than the upload speed. This improves download times where file transfers are the largest. Symmetric DSL (SDSL) has equal download and upload speeds. If one of these versions of DSL seems more appealing than the other, you will need to find an ISP that supports your preferred technology. Most ISPs support only one of the technologies.

NOTE

DSL is not available everywhere. Two factors stand in the way of ubiquitous access. First, the current limitation for DSL connectivity is 18,000 feet (3.3 miles) from the CO. Longer distances are not able to support the minimum quality requirements for transmitting digital signals. Second, the telephone company in your area must invest a substantial amount of money toward upgrading their main facilities to support DSL. In metropolitan areas, this is not a problem, but in rural or semi-rural areas, justifying the cost is difficult.

Ethernet
A network communication technology developed by Xerox that encloses data with a destination and source address for delivery, which is called a frame. Additional information for Ethernet is also added to the frame.

When considering DSL make sure you can check-off each item in this list:

◆ Does your computer support Ethernet?

◆ Do you have a network card?

◆ Are you close enough to the CO in your area?

Cable Modems

Cable modems allow high-speed access to the Internet over cable TV (CATV) lines. The cable modem requires two connections: one to the cable outlet and the other to the computer. Cable modems are more economical than some other technologies. DSL is as cost-effective, but performance is more difficult to measure. One difficulty for DSL is that it has not had the rapid growth that cable technology has, and therefore DSL is not available in all locations everywhere. Compared to ISDN, described in the next section, cable modems offer much better performance at a fraction of the cost. There is no need to dial; the connection is always active.

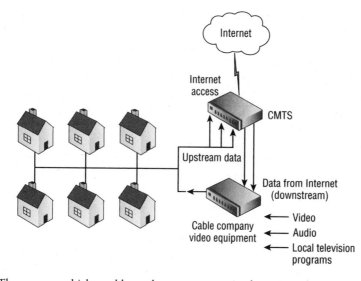

The range at which a cable modem operates varies from 500 Kbps to 25 Mbps. The typical range is more like from 2 Mbps to 10 Mbps. Data that is downloaded from the Internet is transmitted at a higher rate than data that is uploaded.

In your home, the cable company will attach a splitter to the incoming cable. One connection is used for your television and the other connects to the cable modem. Your computer connects to the cable modem via a *100BASE-T* Ethernet connection, which then connects to a switch or to a network card installed in your computer.

When you connect your computer to a cable network, you are actually part of a large Ethernet *wide area network (WAN)*. Each house plugs into the network via the cable in the home. The other end of that cable goes into a cable hub called a *Cable Modem Termination System (CMTS) device*. The CMTS will manage where data is being sent.

CMTS devices can be two-way, meaning that they support upstream (to the Internet) and downstream (to the user) data transmission. In some locations where CMTS devices are not installed or available, a telephone connection is used for upstream data.

ISDN

Integrated Services Digital Network (ISDN) is a digital dial service that transmits digital data at a higher transmission rate than a standard modem. This makes ISDN more expensive than using a modem. ISDN is still cost-effective, considering that the rate for one ISDN line is less than two business lines, and it can support data, voice, and faxing capabilities.

100BASE-T
An Ethernet standard that transmits at 100 Mbps.

wide area network (WAN)
A relatively low-speed data connection (typically 1.544 Mbps) that uses the telephone company to connect two locations separated by a large geographical area.

Cable Modem Termination System (CMTS) device
A device used to forward user data to the Internet. Downstream data from the Internet is forwarded to the cable television equipment in that neighborhood, where it is then forwarded to the home user.

Integrated Services Digital Network (ISDN)
A technology that combines digital and voice transmission onto a single wire.

telecommuter

Someone who remotely connects to his or her office to work from home or a remote location.

B channel

Stands for bearer channel and is a 64 Kbps circuit-switched channel. Used to carry voice and data.

D channel

Stands for delta channel and is a 16 Kbps circuit-switched channel. Used to manage control signals.

Basic Rate Interface (BRI)

The basic ISDN service offered by telecommunication companies. BRI consists of two B channels and a single D channel.

H0

Another ISDN channel that includes six B channels. Other H channel definitions include H-10 and H-11, which are just another way of identifying the 23 B channels of the Primary Rate Interface.

Primary Rate Interface (PRI)

The high-end ISDN service offered by telecommunication companies. PRI provides 23 B channels and one D channel. This is equivalent to the 24 channels of a T1 line.

You can connect ISDN adapters to the computer in two ways:

♦ Internal ISDN adapters plug into an available expansion slot inside a computer.

♦ External ISDN adapters connect to an available serial port on the back of a computer via a null-modem cable.

The most typical ISDN user is the *telecommuter*, who uses the high-speed service to connect with his or her main office from home.

ISDN adapters often link small branch offices that do not transmit large amounts of data to one another. A connection begins when data needs transmission.

ISDN is still used as a backup WAN link for some businesses, though it is being replaced as it is not a cost-effective measure and it is slow compared to newer technologies that can be implemented.

You can identify the speed of an ISDN adapter by the number of signal bearer channels, or *B channel*s. An ISDN adapter configured with a single B channel can support 64 Kbps, whereas a *D channel* supports only 16 Kbps.

Here is a summary of available ISDN services.

ISDN Service	Channel Type	Speed
Basic Rate Interface (BRI)	2 B + 1 D channel (2 × 64 K + 16 K)	128 Kbps
H0	6 B channels (6 × 64 K)	384 Kbps
Primary Rate Interface (PRI)	23 B + 1 D channel (23 × 64 K + 64 K)	1.472 Mbps

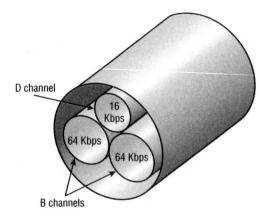

D channel

16 Kbps

64 Kbps

64 Kbps

B channels

Choosing a Printer

Printers are output devices that produce a hard-copy result in the form of printed text and graphics. Printers differ from other types of devices because they not only transfer an image to paper, but they also must move the paper through the process.

Several types of printers are available based on different technology standards. Most printer types operate in basically the same way. Paper is fed into the unit using a roller. The text and images are applied to the paper, and additional rollers push the paper out onto a tray.

Printers can vary in many ways, in addition to print method. For instance, print speed is a differentiating factor. This table defines printer types. *Method of Imprint* refers to the method of transferring information to paper.

Printers have two operating modes: text mode and graphics mode. In text mode, the computer's operating system and software look up *American Standard Code for Information Interchange (ASCII)* **characters, such as letters and numbers, from a character table and then produce the result in bit format to send to the printer. In graphics mode, the operating system and software work together to send instructions to the printer to control the print operation and produce a custom character or result.**

If you haven't already, at some point you may likely be faced with one seemingly simple question: inkjet or laser? Many people like inkjets because of their good quality, speed, and affordability—especially for color printing. Laser printers are high-speed networkable devices. Laser printers provide the same quality output as most inkjets but at a higher initial price for the device. The additional cost of laser printers usually means that one printer will be used to serve many. Inkjets are affordable so they can be ordered for each user. So why not just go with inkjets?

NOTE

American Standard Code for Information Interchange (ASCII)
A 7-bit coding scheme that translates symbolic characters into the ones and zeros that are stored as data on a computer. Extended ASCII uses an 8-bit coding scheme.

Printer Type	Method of Imprint
Impact	A wheel or ball that hits a ribbon and leaves a character on the paper printer ribbon.
Dot matrix	Tiny pins hit an ink-filled ribbon.
Inkjet/bubble jet	Ink squirts at the paper following a pattern to create an image.
Laser	A laser beam creates an image on a photo conductor drum that attracts ink from a special toner. The ink is then placed on paper, and heat bonds the ink to the paper to create a printed document.

Printer Type	Method of Imprint
Thermal dye transfer	Also known as dye sublimation, the process uses heat on ribbons containing dye to create photo-quality prints. The process is continuous so it creates a very high-quality output. It requires special paper.
Thermal wax transfer	Colored waxes are heated and placed on regular paper as dots. Quality is not quite photo-realistic but is less expensive and faster than thermal dye transfer.

In most offices, printers are heavily-used devices, so they need to be selected wisely. You should consider three factors before making your decision on an inkjet or laser printer. Mean Time Between Failure (MTBF) is a measurement of how long the printer will function before a component fails. Also, monthly print volume is a figure that can be used to determine whether the printer is designed to support the estimated usage of the printer. A final indicator is cost. Inkjet printers do cost less, but printing on inkjets is much more expensive with or without color. Depending on your printer, cartridges cost $30–$65 and may print only a few hundred pages. Laser cartridges typically cost $75 and support up to 15,000 pages or more. Laser printers are the best choice for heavy, long-term use by multiple users.

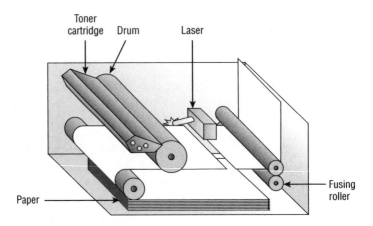

 NOTE

Printers are networked to provide many users with access to a single device, thus saving the money needed to purchase a print device for every user. Modern printers include an expansion slot to plug in a network printer card or they have one built in.

Choosing PC Cards

The PC Card (which was the Personal Computer Memory Card International Association—PCMCIA) is used as an interface for peripheral components. The original PCMCIA card was used as a memory expansion card. This quickly expanded to include such uses as modems, network interface cards as well as hard drives.

Several types of PC cards exist, such as those providing sound, network, video, and input/output capabilities. Regardless of the type of PC card, you attach them to the computer by plugging them into an available expansion bus slot on the motherboard. The expansion bus provides a pathway that links the device with the CPU and memory inside the computer.

There are several expansion bus design standards. It is important that you identify the slot type before you purchase a new PC card. Each bus design standard has a primary connector and might have one or more extension connectors to allow for additional capabilities. Other differences include the operating speed, interface, and method of configuration.

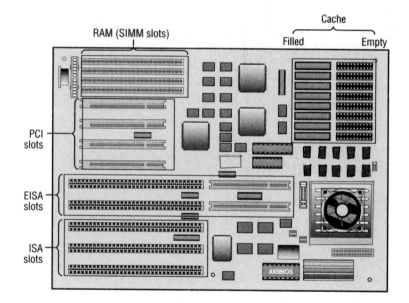

Bus Standards

When you are selecting a computer to purchase or build, you want to make sure that you are investing in the best technology to meet your needs. Most computers today will include support for the older ISA standard as well as support for the modern PCI standard. It is important that you select a computer that includes enough slots for your expansion cards. This table defines the key differences between the standards.

Bus Type	Interface	Speed	Configuration
ISA	8-bit or 16-bit	8–10 MHz	Hardware or software
Micro Channel	16-bit or 32-bit	10–20 MHz	Hardware or software
EISA	32-bit	8–10 MHz	Software
VL-Bus	32-bit	40 MHz	Hardware
PCI	32-bit or 64-bit	33 MHz	Plug and Play
PC Card (PCMCIA)	16-bit	33 MHz	Plug and Play
AGP	32-bit or 64-bit	66 MHz	Plug and Play
PCIe	32-bit or 64-bit	4 Gbps	Plug and Play
ExpressCard	PCI Express or USB 2.0 Serial Interface	2.5 GBps (PCI Express or 480 MBps (USB 2.0)	Plug and Play

Plug and Play

Microsoft Plug and Play technology was added to Windows 95 to greatly simplify the installation and configuration of new hardware. Plug and Play is currently supported with Windows XP and newer operating systems. Plug and Play just works—that is its intent. Some external hard drives and other hardware may require some additional work, but this percentage is very small. The technology works something like this: New hardware is installed into a Windows 7 computer. When the computer is first turned on, the BIOS checks to see what devices are attached to the motherboard or to any of the external ports. If it detects a new device, it notifies the operating system. After Windows 7 starts up, the Plug and Play wizard loads. If Windows 7 recognizes the new device, the software is automatically loaded from the hard drive. Also, the software is automatically configured by Windows 7. Only in rare cases does Windows 7 need assistance to configure a Plug and Play device. If the new device does not have software loaded into Windows 7, you will be presented with the option of inserting media that contains the necessary software.

Most adapter cards in the last couple of years have been designed to the Plug and Play specification. Older cards that are not Plug and Play–compatible require manual configuration through hardware, which consists of setting jumpers and *dual in-line package (DIP) switches*. This method of hardware configuration is nearly obsolete in most new hardware.

dual in-line package (DIP) switches
A set of tiny switches attached to a circuit board that are manually configured to alter the function of a chip for a specific computer or application.

NOTE

Plug and Play is part of Windows 2000 and later. But Plug and Play works only for devices that are included in Microsoft's Hardware Compatibility List (HCL). Devices on the HCL have been tested and verified to be compatible with Windows. If the device you are considering is not included on the HCL, you should seriously consider using another device that is. Besides the possibility of the device not working or causing Windows errors, Microsoft may not support your installation. You should also note that some motherboards require you to enable Plug and Play support through the computer's BIOS.

Unlike DIP switches, jumpers are still found on motherboards, hard drives, CD-ROMs, and some adapter cards. Jumpers are small connectors that are used to connect two pins to make a complete circuit. For example, most motherboards have a password reset jumper. You either enable or disable the jumper setting and restart the computer to reset the password. The password jumper can be used to erase a system password used when the computer first boots up. Most systems require that you remove the jumper for a set period of time to erase the password.

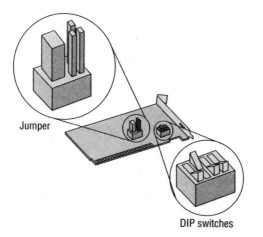

Jumper

DIP switches

Terms to Know

100BASE-T

active matrix

American Standard Code
for Information Interchange
(ASCII)

Asynchronous Transfer Mode
(ATM)

B channel

bandwidth

Basic Rate Interface (BRI)

baud

bit depth

bits per second (bps)

bridge

byte

Cable Modem Termination
System (CMTS) device

central office (CO)

clock signal

D channel

demodulate

Digital Subscriber Line (DSL)

DIN

dot pitch

dual in-line package (DIP)
switches

electron gun

Enhanced Parallel Port (EPP)

Ethernet

Extended Capabilities Port
(ECP)

H0

Integrated Services Digital
Network (ISDN)

Internet service provider (ISP)

local loop

megabits per second (Mbps)

modulate

parallel communication

passive matrix

pixel

Primary Rate Interface (PRI)

PS/2

refresh rate

RS-232

serial communication

start bit

stop bit

telecommuter

tether

USB hub

wide area network (WAN)

Review Questions

1. Define *serial communication*.

2. What is the difference between data that is transmitted serially and data that is transmitted in parallel?

3. True or false: The refresh rate determines how many dots of the same color are drawn on the screen.

4. Which display adapter type is the best choice for displaying the maximum resolution and most colors?

5. Name the five mouse interface types.

6. True or false: Digital signals represent constantly changing voltages.

7. What is the difference between a modem and a cable modem?

8. Why is performance on a DSL connection faster than with a modem?

9. True or false: ISDN transmits data at a higher rate than a standard modem.

10. True or false: Motherboards are manufactured to accommodate only one bus specification.

11. Why are printers often attached to a network?

Chapter 4

Hardware Configuration

con•fig•ure *v* : to assemble pieces so that they function as a single unit

Configuring your computer hardware can be an easy or difficult task to complete. Each hardware device must be configured with unique system resource settings. The resource settings enable the device to communicate with the computer's processor and memory without competing or conflicting with other devices. Most devices can accept various combinations of resource settings.

Installing Hardware

You install new hardware (for instance, a sound card or hard drive) through a multistep configuration process. The fundamental steps are to configure the device at a physical level and at one or more logical levels so that the system can communicate with the device. A device will not function properly unless it is correctly installed.

NOTE

Before you install any piece of hardware, take the precaution of wearing an anti-static wrist guard to protect the computer from any potential electrical shocks that might damage the circuitry.

When you install a piece of hardware, you should first properly configure it. You can determine configuration settings by reviewing the documentation that comes with the device. Traditionally, older hardware was configured through Dual in-line Package (DIP) switches and jumpers. Now this technology is fairly obsolete. Most hardware configuration is now done through software.

Each hardware device is unique and has its own settings that you need to configure. Installing new hardware these days does not involve the configuration steps it did in the past. In most cases, new hardware comes with an installation disk that you run after you have installed the hardware. The installation process will configure the hardware for use on your system. Previously you had to configure interrupt requests (IRQ), *interrupts*, *base memory*, *I/O memory*, and *direct memory access (DMA)*. These items are covered in more detail in the following subsections.

Completing the physical installation of the device requires plugging it into the motherboard via a slot, cables, or both. Be sure that you have all the necessary accessories, such as screws or cables, when you go to complete this step. If the device is a PC card, carefully plug it into an available bus slot of the same type, and secure it by screwing it into the case. It usually does not matter which slot you place the card into unless it is a Peripheral Component Interconnect (PCI), Extended Industry Standard Architecture (EISA), or Micro Channel Architecture (MCA) card; then it is identified by slot number.

After you have securely attached the device, you can begin the software configuration. In this step, you install the device drivers and set any configuration parameters that a particular operating system might need to communicate and interact with a device.

When installing new hardware in a Windows system, you want to ensure that the product has a "Certified for Windows" logo. This means the hardware or software device has gone through the Windows Hardware Quality Labs (WHQL) testing. Device drivers that have gone through this testing process have a digitally signed certificate created.

You can use the `sigverif` command to identify unsigned drivers on a system. You can create a Group Policy to prevent unsigned drivers from being installed.

interrupt

A type of signal that is used to get the attention of the central processing unit (CPU) when input/output (I/O) is required. An interrupt tells the CPU that the operating system is requesting a specific action. Interrupts are prioritized; higher-numbered interrupts are serviced first.

base memory

Memory addresses that are reserved and used to store low-level control software that is required by an add-on device.

I/O memory

Memory addresses that are reserved and assigned to add-on devices. Each assignment tells the CPU about the location of a specific device.

direct memory access (DMA)

DMA enables a device to transfer data directly to RAM without using the attention of the processor for the entire transfer period. The result is a faster and more direct method of data transfer.

One reason Plug and Play technology is so important is that it automatically configures hardware devices for you. Plug and Play has been supported since Windows 9.*x*.

NOTE

Installing Software Drivers

Software drivers are special programs that tell the computer how to communicate with and control a hardware device. Each device has a driver that enables it to communicate with the computer. The driver is written to operate only within a certain operating system as well as for 32-bit or 64-bit. Many device drivers are not backward compatible; that is, you cannot normally use a Windows 7 device driver on a Windows XP Professional computer.

Most software drivers are not usually generic in nature. Each piece of hardware contains unique components, and these components might not reside on a similar device, even if made by the same manufacturer. The software driver must communicate with that device to accurately interpret the instructions the operating system issued to the device.

Some devices, such as the mouse, are generic in that most do not contain special features or chips that need customized instruction code. Therefore, changing your mouse is much easier than swapping out your sound card or replacing your printer without changing the device drivers.

You might think of a software driver as the bridge between a piece of hardware and a specific operating system's software.

TIP

When you install a device, you should have the driver disk in hand and install it when the operating system prompts you. Operating systems such as Windows XP, Windows Vista, Windows 7, Windows Server 2003, and Windows Server 2008 R2 use Plug and Play to autodetect the presence of a new device and install the driver, provided they properly recognize the device. This is possible because these versions of Windows contain archives of the most common device drivers. You should install the latest device driver available for a particular operating system, because drivers are typically updated if incompatibility issues are reported.

Updating Software Drivers

Updating software drivers is an important part of a comprehensive system maintenance plan. You need to ensure that all devices have the most current and applicable software drivers. In some cases, the new drivers will remedy a problem with a piece of hardware; in others, they will provide new features or capabilities.

In order to update a driver, you need to go the manufacturer's site and download the latest one. Once you have downloaded the driver, you need to follow the instructions the manufacturer provides. In some cases this just means running a small executable file (assuming you have the requisite permissions). After you have installed the new driver, you may have to reboot the system for the changes to take effect.

Handling Interrupts

Each device interacts with the computer by interrupting the processor so that it can send or retrieve data or carry out a function. A device must have a method for telling the computer's processor that it needs attention. A hardware device tells the processor that it needs attention through an *interrupt request (IRQ)* line. By using this method of interruption, the processor can function without needing to ask a device every few seconds whether it needs service.

interrupt request (IRQ)
The method used by a device to inform the microprocessor (CPU) that the device needs attention. Through this method of interruption, the microprocessor can function without needing to poll each device to see whether it needs service.

When a device interrupts the system processor, the processor stops what it is doing and handles the interrupt request. Because each device is assigned a number when the device is configured, the system knows which device needs attention. After the processor has attended to the device, it returns to the function it was performing before the interruption.

Each device must have a unique IRQ so that the processor knows what to attend to when a service request is called. There are exceptions to this rule; for instance, serial ports (also referred to as communication, or COM, ports) can share the same IRQ, but they must be assigned another unique identifier (I/O address). In older systems, if any other devices shared the same interrupt request and needed attention from the processor, then the computer would hang or immediately reboot while it was trying to determine which device requested the service. Now that Plug and Play devices are on the scene, the computer just scans the system and determines what available interrupt request it can assign to a new device during installation. This prevents the potential problems that crop up with IRQ and DMA addressing schemes.

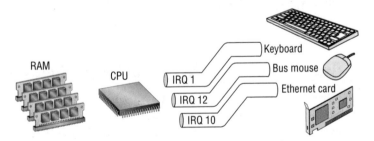

NOTE

The PCI bus standard enables devices connected to a PCI bus to communicate by using one common interrupt (IRQ 10).

The following table shows the standard interrupts that most systems use, including Windows 7 and Windows Server 2008 R2.

- *System Device* refers to the device that is configured to use the specified interrupt.

- *IRQ* refers to the interrupt request line that the hardware device uses to notify the processor that it needs attention.

- IRQ numbers that are listed as *available* can be allocated to new devices that are installed in the computer.

System Device	IRQ
System timer	0
Keyboard	1
Reserved	2
COMs 2, 4	3
COMs 1, 3	4
LPT2 (usually available for other devices)	5
Floppy disk controller	6
LPT1	7
Real-time clock	8
Redirected or cascaded to IRQ 2	9
Available (also used for PCI common interrupt)	10
Available	11
PS/2 or bus mouse port (available if not used)	12
Math coprocessor	13
Hard disk controller	14
Available (also used for PCI secondary IDE controller)	15

Using Base Memory and Identifying System Resources

Base memory refers to the reserved area in memory where devices can store data so that the processor can directly access that data. Some devices need this allocated memory range located in the system RAM. The area is typically located in the upper area of RAM memory called the *Upper Memory Area (UMA)*.

Upper Memory Area (UMA)
This was used by DOS memory management to address the area of memory between 640 KB and 1 MB in an IBM-compatible computer. The upper 384 KB of this UMA was originally used by IBM and IBM-compatible machines (8088 CPUs) for system and video use.

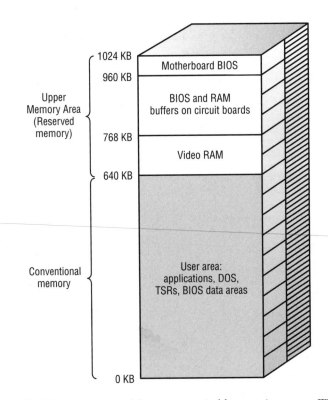

This table shows some typical base memory address assignments. When configuring address ranges, be sure that they do not overlap.

System Device	Memory Range
Video RAM	A0000–BFFFF
Available	C0000–CFFFF
Available	D0000–DFFFF
System ROM	E0000–EFFFF

If you run into a problem configuring the drives for your hardware or if you think there is a conflict, you may have to use the Device Manager in Windows XP and later versions to correct the problem. Device Manager gives you direct access to the specific settings for your hardware as well as other device resource information.

Besides being able to check what IRQ or I/O memory address is in use by a device, you can also check to see whether the driver is up to date. If it isn't, you can select the Update Driver option in the Properties window of the device. If there is a problem with a recently installed device driver, you can use the Device Driver Rollback feature to return to the previous, functional driver.

If you want to check which resources are already in use on your Windows 7 computer, you can try it out on your own.

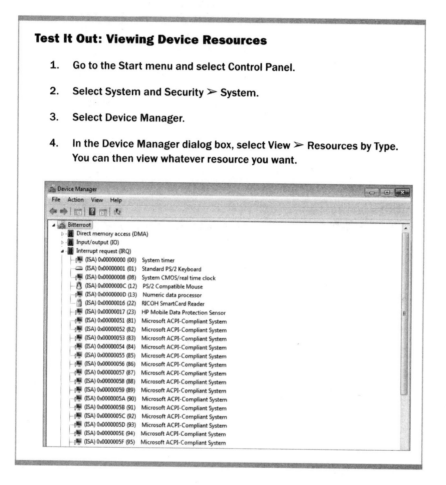

Test It Out: Viewing Device Resources

1. Go to the Start menu and select Control Panel.

2. Select System and Security ➢ System.

3. Select Device Manager.

4. In the Device Manager dialog box, select View ➢ Resources by Type. You can then view whatever resource you want.

Using I/O Memory

Each device has a memory address called an I/O address. The address acts like a mailbox that the processor uses to send instructions to the device. The I/O address is also commonly called the *port address*.

When the CPU sends instructions to this address, the device reads the instructions and carries them out. But the device does not talk to the processor through the same mechanism. It uses the interrupt assigned to it to request service or additional instructions from the processor.

port address
An address used by the computer to access devices such as expansion cards and printers.

Each device must have a unique I/O address so that the correct device receives the instructions from the processor. Some older devices are coded to use only one I/O address and cannot be changed.

Most PCs are designed to support more than one I/O address for a device. This feature helps prevent a conflict between two similar devices, such as the COM ports that share the same interrupt. The two ports would have separate I/O addresses, thus preventing a clash between them.

If your device does not support an I/O address that is available (not in use by another device), you may select an address used by another device, provided you can change the other device's address to an available I/O address.

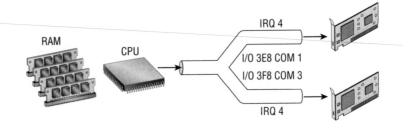

TIP Always note the addresses your system uses to make life easier when you're troubleshooting or adding a new device.

This table shows the typical I/O address assignments.

System Device	Memory Address
DMA controller	000–01F
Interrupt controller	020–03F
Timer	040–05F
Keyboard	060–06F
Real-time clock	070–07F
DMA page register	080–09F
Second interrupt controller	0A0–0BF
DMA controller 2	0C0–0DF
Math coprocessor	0F0–0FF
Primary hard disk controller	1F0–1F8
Joystick controller	200–20F
XT expansion unit	210–217
FM synthesis interface	220–22F
CD-ROM I/O port	230–233

System Device	Memory Address
Bus mouse	238–23B
Plug and Play I/O port	274–277
LPT2 (second parallel port)	278–27F
COM 4 (serial port 4)	2E8–2EF
COM 2 (serial port 2)	2F8–2FF
Available	280–31F
XT hard disk controller	320–32F
MIDI port	330–33F
Alternate floppy controller	370–377
LPT1 (primary printer port)	378–37F
LPT3 (third parallel port)	3BC–3BF
Color graphics adapter (CGA, EGA, VGA)	3D0–3DF
COM 3 (serial port 3)	3E8–3EF
Floppy disk controller	3F0–3F7
COM 1 (serial port 1)	3F8–3FF

Using DMA

As we stated earlier, DMA stands for direct memory access. DMA enables a device to transfer data directly to RAM without using the attention of the processor for the entire transfer period. The result is a faster and more direct method of data transfer. This method was especially useful in older PCs, enabling the DMA channel to transfer data in the background, thus freeing the processor to tend to other duties. DMA is typically used by devices such as floppy disks, hard disks, tape devices, and network cards.

This graphic shows the CPU intervening to transfer data.

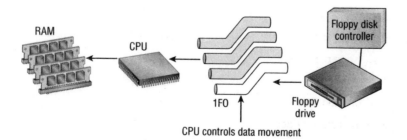

This graphic shows the use of DMA for direct transfer of data.

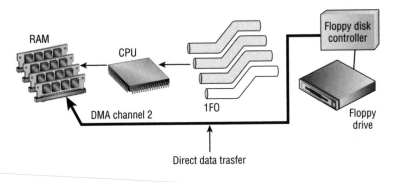

RAM

CPU

Floppy disk controller

1FO

DMA channel 2

Floppy drive

Direct data trasfer

The term *channel* is often used in describing DMA. In older PCs, a DMA controller chip handled DMA activities. The chip contained four DMA channels that were numbered 0 to 3. Technology enhancements now allow for up to eight channels. Each type of bus standard allows a different number of DMA channels.

The following table shows the standard DMA channels that most systems use. When two devices are configured to the same DMA channel, neither device can transfer the data to memory correctly. The only available DMA channel on older PCs is DMA channel 3.

System Device	DMA Channel
Available	0
Available	1
Floppy disk controller	2
Available	3
Not available (used for internal purposes or second DMA controller)	4
Available	5
Available	6
Available	7

TIP

If your device does not operate correctly using various combinations of DMA channel assignments, try the Disable DMA option.

If you install a piece of hardware and your computer does not work, remove the piece of hardware that you installed and restart your computer. Then, if the computer works, you know that the new piece of hardware conflicts with an existing piece of hardware.

TIP

Terms to Know

base memory   IRQ

direct memory access (DMA)   port address

interrupt   UMA

I/O memory

Review Questions

1. How do you accomplish the physical configuration of a hardware device?

2. What are the four hardware settings that you use to configure computer hardware?

3. How does an interrupt work?

4. Which interrupt does LPT2 typically use?

5. True or false: All devices need a reserved area of memory in which to operate (similar to video RAM).

6. What I/O address range is typically assigned to the primary hard disk controller?

7. How does DMA typically work?

8. Which DMA channel is typically assigned to the floppy disk controller?

9. What is a software driver?

10. True or false: A software driver will work with any operating system as long as it follows the Software Driver Association guidelines.

11. True or false: Two hardware devices can share the same IRQ.

12. What does DMA stand for?

13. What does I/O stand for?

14. What does IRQ stand for?

Chapter 5

Desktop Operating Systems: A Comparison

op•er•at•ing sys•tem *n*: Software that is used on an electronic device, usually a computer, to perform a set of tasks

Every computer consists of hardware and software. In the previous chapters, you learned about hardware. In this chapter, you will learn about local operating systems, which are the heart and brains of the computer's software. The local operating system manages system hardware and resources. In the past 30 years, operating systems have changed dramatically. This chapter provides an overview of common operating systems. Some of the information is provided as a historical summary to give you an idea of the evolution that has occurred in operating system development.

In The Beginning: Understanding DOS

If you used a computer between 1981 and the early 1990s, chances are the computer ran some version of DOS (Disk Operating System) as its operating system. Microsoft originally licensed DOS to IBM as an operating system to be used with IBM's personal computers. This version of DOS was called PC-DOS.

In what has become known as one of the smartest moves in the computer industry, Microsoft licensed DOS, as opposed to selling it, to IBM. Microsoft also retained the right to license other versions of DOS. The non-IBM version of DOS was called MS-DOS. It was used by hardware vendors who made PCs with the same Intel CPU that IBM used with its PCs. These computers were referred to as IBM clones and typically were more competitively priced than their IBM counterparts.

defragmentation
The reorganization of data on a hard disk to optimize performance.

compression
A method of reducing the size of data by using a mathematical calculation.

DOS 6.*x* provided the following:

◆ Disk utilities for tasks such as virus scanning and disk *defragmentation*, *compression* software, and backup software

◆ The EMM386.EXE utility, which enabled memory to be better managed

NOTE DOS 6.22 was the last version of DOS to be released. Currently, DOS is not a commonly used operating system, primarily because it lacks a truly graphical interface, but also due to its technical limitation of supporting 16-bit applications. However, many DOS commands continue to be supported under the Windows platform, and advanced users find knowing DOS commands very useful.

Understanding Windows

Although DOS provided many functions, users wanted these functions combined with a user-friendly interface. This led to Windows, a *graphical user interface (GUI)* operating system based on top of DOS (meaning that Windows is not an operating system by itself and requires DOS to be running). The Windows platform was based on technology that supported 16-bit processing.

graphical user interface (GUI)
An application that provides intuitive controls (such as icons, buttons, menus, and dialog boxes) for configuring, manipulating, and accessing applications and files.

The first version of Windows was version 1. This version broke new ground (in the PC market) by enabling more than one application to be open at the same time. It also had windows that you could tile (meaning that you could view many windows at the same time). In addition, Windows featured full mouse support, making this operating system easier to use than DOS, which primarily used a keyboard for user input. Version 1 of Windows supported the Intel 80286 processor.

Program Information Files (PIFs)
Files for a non-Windows application that include settings for running the application in Windows 3.x.

Windows 2, the second version of Windows, introduced icons to the Windows desktop. It also supported *Program Information Files (PIFs)*, which enabled users to better configure Windows. An enhanced version of Windows 2, called Windows/386, added support for the Intel 80386 processor.

The first widely accepted version of Windows was Windows 3, which introduced the File Manager and Program Manager utilities. It changed the way memory was managed and offered the option to run Windows in 386 Enhanced Mode. In 386 Enhanced Mode, Windows runs DOS applications in their own windows and uses part of the hard drive as *virtual RAM*. This feature offers better performance, and all modern operating systems include some variation of this concept.

The next versions of Windows to be released were Windows 3.1 and 3.11. Windows 3.1 added better graphical and multimedia support. This version of Windows had better error protection and supported *object linking and embedding (OLE)*. OLE is a technology that lets applications work together and share information. Windows 3.11, also known as Windows for Workgroups, added support for networking capabilities.

The Business Solution: Windows NT Workstation 4

Windows NT Workstation provided a higher level of performance and security compared to the Windows 95/98/Me desktop operating systems. It was relatively easy to use and had the same desktop interface as Windows 98. But don't make the mistake of equating Windows NT with Windows 98. The interface was the only thing that they shared. Windows NT's core technologies were completely different and were designed to support the needs of businesses. Windows 95 and 98 could not match its performance and security.

With NT Workstation, you got these features:

◆ A 32-bit multitasking operating system.

◆ The capability to support Intel, Alpha platforms, and PowerPC.

◆ Support for multiple processors and preemptive multitasking.

◆ Internet support as a client through Internet Explorer and support as a *server* through Peer Web Services, which enabled the workstation to act as a World Wide Web (WWW) and *File Transfer Protocol (FTP)* server. With the WWW service, users could access web documents from the web server. With the FTP service, users could transfer files to and from the web server.

◆ High security through mandatory logon and the NT File System (NTFS), which lets you apply security to users and groups and view resource access through auditing. NTFS is covered in more detail in Chapter 15, "File and Print Management."

◆ Support for applications written to work with DOS, 16-bit Windows, 32-bit Windows, *OS/2*, and *POSIX*.

◆ Full networking capabilities and integration with NT Server.

◆ Network services for sharing file and print resources, and support for up to 10 concurrent client connections.

virtual RAM
A function of the operating system that is used to simulate RAM by breaking computer programs into small units of data called pages and storing the pages in a page file on the hard disk.

object linking and embedding (OLE)
A technology that enables applications to share data. Each document is stored as an object, and one object can be embedded within another object. For example, an Excel spreadsheet can be embedded within a Word document. Because the objects are linked, changes through Excel or Word will be updated through the single linked object.

server
A computer that provides dedicated file, print, messaging, application, or other services to client computers.

File Transfer Protocol (FTP)
An application layer protocol for transferring files between two computers. FTP involves the use of FTP client software and an FTP server.

OS/2
A 32-bit operating system originally developed by Microsoft and IBM. OS/2 can support DOS, Windows, and OS/2 applications. Since Microsoft's abandonment of the program in the late 1980s, OS/2 has been produced and sold exclusively by IBM.

POSIX
A standard originally developed for Unix that defines the interface between applications and the operating system. It is now more widely used for the development of other operating systems, including Windows 2000.

- Support for up to 4 GB of RAM and 256 terabytes (TB) of disk space.

- One of the most reliable operating systems, because applications ran in separate memory spaces, preventing a failed application from affecting other applications on the operating system.

<hr>

NOTE   **The main disadvantages of NT Workstation over Windows 95 and 98 were that it had greater hardware requirements and was not as backward compatible. It also did not have Plug and Play capabilities.**

Windows 2000 Professional

On the heels of the new millennium came Microsoft's upgrade for Windows NT Workstation. Designed to replace Windows NT Workstation as the business desktop computer operating system, Windows 2000 Professional offered major improvements over NT. What did not change was the stability and performance that many had come to expect from NT.

Windows 2000 Professional offered these new and enhanced features:

- Windows file protection in the event that an application overwrote a system file.

Microsoft Management Console (MMC)
A Microsoft application framework for accessing administrative tools, called consoles.

- Access to system administration tools through the *Microsoft Management Console (MMC)*.

- An enhanced interface.

- Full 32-bit OS, which improved multitasking performance.

- Support for gigabit networking.

- Plug and Play support.

- The IntelliMirror function, which enabled users to work on files on a server and continue working even if they disconnected from the network. Files that had changed were updated with the latest content when the user connected again with the server.

- Power management for laptops.

IP Security (IPSec)
A protocol standard for encrypting Internet Protocol (IP) packets.

- Simplified installation, configuration, and removal of applications.

- Reduction in the number of reboots, especially when installing software.

virtual private networking (VPN)
Using encrypted envelopes to securely transmit sensitive data between two points over the unsecured Internet.

- *IP Security (IPSec)* support for *virtual private networking (VPN)*.

- Safe mode option available during startup that could be used to boot Windows 2000 with minimal settings.

Windows XP Home Edition and XP Professional

Windows XP was released in fall 2001. Windows XP Home Edition is Microsoft's upgrade to Windows 98/Me, while Windows XP Professional is Microsoft's upgrade to Windows 2000 Professional. Windows XP Home Edition is geared toward the home user, while Windows XP Professional adds extra features and is geared toward power users and businesses.

Mainstream support for Windows XP ended in 2009. However, extended support will be available until April 8, 2014, according to Microsoft.

NOTE

Windows XP Home Edition

Windows XP was built on the Windows 2000 operating system, which added features Microsoft had not traditionally included with its consumer operating systems. These included features related to power, security, reliability, and ease of use.

The following were major enhancements to this operating system:

♦ Windows File Protection, which protects the user from accidentally changing or overwriting core operating system files

♦ Protected Kernel Mode, which provides reliability by not allowing applications to access software kernel code

♦ System Monitor, which allows you to monitor processor, memory, disk, and network throughput metrics in real time or by creating logs for analysis

♦ Task Manager, which is used to manage applications and processes as well as view real-time computer performance

♦ Enhanced battery life by power options management through Lid Power and LCD dimming

♦ The Internet Connection Firewall, which safeguards your computer from unwanted attacks when it is connected to the Internet

♦ Credential Manager, a secure password storage mechanism

♦ Simplified setup through Easy Setup Wizards

♦ Dynamic updates for applications and device drivers

♦ A simplified user interface and Start menu, as well as simplified file management

- System Restore, which enables you to quickly restore your computer in the event of system failure
- The ability to run older versions of Windows applications with Compatibility mode
- Improved help support through the Help and Support Center
- Remote Assistance, which gives a remote administrator the ability to chat with you, view your screen, or remotely control your computer
- Windows Messenger, which lets you chat with other users in real time
- Internet Connection Sharing, which allows you to share a single Internet connection among several users
- Enhanced support for digital music, pictures, and home videos; also improved support for creating CD-Rs

Windows XP Professional

Windows XP Professional included features of Windows XP Home Edition and offered the following additional support for power and business users:

- Remote Desktop features, which can be used to access your desktop remotely
- Encrypting File System, which adds additional security by allowing you to selectively encrypt files or folders
- Better support for large networks by giving your computer the ability to be managed as a networked computer by a domain controller on a large network
- More robust features for system recovery in the event of system failure
- The ability to host personal websites through Internet Information Server (IIS)
- Support for multiple processors
- Support for multiple languages

Windows Vista

Windows Vista was officially released on January 30, 2007, five years after the release of Windows XP. Windows Vista was designed to correct many of the perceived vulnerabilities in Windows XP. Though Windows Vista was new in 2007, there were numerous complaints about high memory requirements and system resources, licensing, new digital rights management (DRM) features to reduce copying of digital media, and backward compatibility. New features that were touted included a new GUI named Aero and the ease with which you could create DVDs.

These are the major enhancements to this operating system:

◆ Windows Aero

◆ Instant Search

◆ Windows Sidebar, where you can place Desktop Gadgets

◆ Backup and Restore Center

◆ Windows Mail

◆ Windows Calendar

◆ Windows Media Center

◆ Shadow Copy

◆ Windows Ultimate Extras

The Latest Generation: Windows 7

Windows 7 was officially released on October 22, 2009, less than three years after the release of Windows Vista. Windows 7 is backward compatible with the hardware and applications supported on Windows Vista, and it is easier to use and has better functionality than Windows Vista.

The major enhancements to Windows 7 include the following:

◆ Windows Live Essentials (which includes Windows Calendar, Windows Mail, Windows Movie Maker, and Windows Photo Gallery)

◆ Support for Virtual Hard Disks

◆ Windows PowerShell

◆ Support for images in RAW image format

◆ Modified UAC (User Account Control), which is criticized by some for weakening security

◆ Windows Virtual PC

◆ Support for real-time multimedia in Remote Desktop Protocol

◆ Ability to pin applications to the taskbar

◆ Ability to snap documents to the screen

◆ Aero Peek

The following shows some of the feature sets in Windows 7.

Feature	Starter	Home Basic	Home Premium	Pro-fessional	Enterprise	Ultimate
Ram 32/64 Bit (GB)	2—32bit only	4/8	4/16	4/192	4/192	4/192
Versions	32 Bit only	32/64	32/64	32/64	32/64	32/64
Physical CPU	1	1	1	2	2	2
RDP Client	N	N	N	Y	Y	Y
Join a Domain	N	N	N	Y	Y	Y
Aero	N	Partial	Y	Y	Y	Y
XP Mode	N	N	N	Y	Y	Y
Dynamic Disks	N	N	N	Y	Y	Y
Encrypting File System	N	N	N	Y	Y	Y
Home Group	Join Only	Join Only	Y	Y	Y	Y
Bitlocker Drive Encryption	N	N	N	N	Y	Y
Direct Access	N	N	N	N	Y	Y

The following table shows the upgrade path from a current, upgradeable client version to a Windows 7 client version.

	Windows 7 Home Premium	Windows 7 Professional	Windows 7 Enterprise	Windows 7 Ultimate
Vista Home Premium	Upgrade	Fresh	Fresh	Upgrade
Vista Business	Fresh	Upgrade	Upgrade	Upgrade
Vista Ultimate	Fresh	Fresh	Fresh	Upgrade
XP	Fresh	Fresh	Fresh	Fresh
2000	Fresh	Fresh	Fresh	Fresh

System requirements for installing Windows 7 are:

◆ 1 Gigahertz or faster processor (32-bit x86 or 64-bit x64)

◆ 1 GB of RAM for 32-bit or 2 GB for 64-bit

◆ 16 GB hard drive space for 32-bit or 20 GB for 64-bit)

◆ sDirectX 9 or higher graphics device with WDDM 1.0 or higher driver

Understanding Unix and Linux

Unix is another popular operating system that is a 32-bit or 64-bit, multiuser, multitasking operating system. Linux is a derivative of the Unix operating system.

Unix

Unix was first developed in the late 1960s as an operating system for main-frame computers. The original development team consisted of Bell Telephone Laboratories, General Electric, and Massachusetts Institute of Technology (MIT). During the early development of Unix, many universities were able to obtain the Unix operating system by signing nondisclosure agreements that allowed them to use the software for educational purposes. Computer science students gained experience with Unix and contributed to its development.

Today two major versions of Unix exist:

◆ Unix System Laboratories (USL) System V UNIX

◆ Berkeley Software Distribution (BSD) Unix

There also are many other flavors of Unix, but most are derivatives of these versions.

Different versions of Unix have been produced as commercial software, *shareware*, and *freeware*. Each variation has its own features and offers differ-ent levels of hardware and software support. Different versions of Unix are also designed to support specific hardware platforms—for example, Intel, RISC, Alpha, and PowerPC.

Because the Unix operating system was designed for engineers by engineers, it has a stigma of being difficult to use and is not as user-friendly as other oper-ating systems. A standard for Unix called X Window System (X11) provides a graphical interface for Unix, making it easier to use.

freeware
Software that you can use without payment.

shareware
Software that is generally available for trial use. If you like the software, you should pay a small licensing fee.

You may notice that Unix is referred to as both *Unix* and *UNIX*. When *Unix* is used, it specifies Unix in general. When *UNIX* is used, it specifies the Unix used by USL and is a trademark name.

NOTE

Linux

Linux is an independent operating system that is similar in nature to Unix. The beauty of Linux is that it uses no proprietary code and is freely distributed. The code for Linux is developed and produced by the Free Software Foundation's Gnu's Not Unix (GNU) project. Linux is offered as freeware through the Web, and many applications have been written for Linux as shareware.

College student Linus Torvalds first introduced Linux to the world in 1991 as a hack operating system. By the end of the year, 100 people were using the operating system, sending feedback, and adding contributions to the code. In 1999, it was estimated that there were more than 20 million Linux users worldwide.

Linux is a popular version of Unix because it is *open source* software and can be distributed only for free or for a minimal cost. Many of the utilities included with the distribution of Linux are also freeware or shareware. This makes Linux an attractive offer for people who want a powerful desktop operating system at little or no cost.

Linux supports all the major software that is produced for the Unix operating system. It is mostly compatible with System V, BSD, and POSIX. It is primarily designed to run on an Intel platform but has been ported to other platforms.

There are numerous variants of Linux that you can choose from. Some are used for specific purposes, such as BackTrack, which is used in the security field. Some popular variants include Ubuntu, Red Hat, Mandriva, and even one called Puppy Linux.

The advantages of Linux include the following:

◆ It is a true 32-bit or 64-bit operating system.

◆ It supports preemptive multitasking.

◆ It offers the capability to support multiple users and includes networking capabilities.

◆ Security features are included, such as login/password and directory and file permissions.

◆ The distribution software includes development software.

The disadvantages of Linux include the following:

◆ The software that ships with Linux tends to be very basic.

◆ Text-based versions of Linux are difficult to learn. X Window Linux is easier to use.

◆ Linux accesses hardware directly, as opposed to going through a software interface, so hardware problems are more common under Linux than with Windows operating systems or other Unix operating systems.

open source
The free distribution of source code (software) for the purpose of improvement of the software by the programming community. Regardless of modifications or adaptations of open source software, the code is still protected by the Open Source Definition.

Apple Operating Systems

Apple makes a variety of types of computers: iPad2, PowerBook, MacBook Air, iMac, and Mac Pro. What makes Apple unique is that they build their own hardware as well as write their own operating systems (the latest OS is Lion). In addition, Apple adopted the use of Intel processors so that you could run Windows operating systems on a Macintosh computer. Apple released a program called Boot Camp that allows you to install these Windows programs.

The Macintosh was the first true use of a GUI on a computer. Historically, Macintoshes have not suffered the same degree of malware, viruses, and worms that have plagued other operating systems. Some of this is due to their inherently more secure environment and also because there are many fewer Apple systems than there are Windows systems.

The Apple OS is characterized by its ease of use and its simplicity of design. In many cases, you will find high school and elementary school computer labs filled with Macintoshes because they are easy to use and support.

Mac OS X Lion (10.7) is the latest release of the operating system, and it was initially only available through download from Apple. Some of the features of Lion include these:

◆ AirDrop—a Lion-to-Lion file share using Wi-Fi Direct.

◆ Apple Push Notification Service—sends alerts over the air for social network updates, news, etc.

◆ Multiuser screen sharing.

◆ Mail 5 and Address Book both use an interface similar to iPad.

Dual-Booting between OSs

With all the different operating systems out there, you may be wondering how you can test all that software without needing several computers. Fortunately, there is a way: You can run more than one operating system on one computer. The idea is especially useful in test environments where you have limited access to equipment. For example, say you have one computer at home and you want to learn Windows 7 and Windows Server 2008 R2. You cannot run both operating systems concurrently, but you can load both operating systems on the same computer and, depending on how you start your computer, access one operating system or the other.

It probably shouldn't have to be said, but different operating systems don't work well together. This doesn't mean you can't configure a *dual-boot* system; it just takes some advance planning. One feature of Windows 7 is that with it, you can create dual-boot systems without having to create different partitions.

You do this using the Boot From VHD feature. In effect, you use the DISKPART utility to create a virtual hard drive and then install the second operating system in this virtual machine.

If you want to create a dual-boot system in Windows versions prior to Windows 7, you have to create multiple partitions on your hard disk. If you have multiple hard disks, that will work as well. Using multiple partitions reduces the possibility of conflicts. In the case of dual-booting between Linux and Windows XP Professional, the operating systems must exist on different partitions or disks.

dual-booting
Having two or more operating systems on your computer. At system startup, you can select which operating system you will boot.

Terms to Know

compression

defragmentation

dual-booting

freeware

File Transfer Protocol (FTP)

graphical user interface (GUI)

IP Security (IPSec)

Microsoft Management Console (MMC)

object linking and embedding (OLE)

open source

OS/2

Program Information Files (PIFs)

POSIX

server

shareware

virtual RAM

Virtual Private Networking (VPN)

Review Questions

1. What does DOS stand for?

2. What does GUI stand for?

3. Which Microsoft operating system offers the highest performance and security options for desktop computers?

4. What was the last version of DOS to be released?

5. Which Microsoft desktop operating system first offered the Active Desktop as an integrated part of the operating system?

6. Which Unix service offers a graphical interface?

7. What are the two major versions of Unix?

8. What is the popular shareware/freeware version of Unix called?

9. True or false: You can dual-boot between Windows 2000 and Windows XP Professional.

10. What is the standard that defines the interface between Unix applications and Unix operating systems?

Chapter 6

Command Shell 101: Basics Every Administrator Should Know

com•mand *n*: a set of instructions given to perform a task

If you are new to the computer field, you may be asking yourself why you need to know the command shell. At times the command shell may be the fastest and easiest way to complete a specific task. You don't need to be an expert, but you should know the basics. This chapter covers the important commands and command shell concepts that every administrator should know.

Introducing the Command-Line Interface

command line

Refers to a command line or text based interface as opposed to the commonly seen graphical interfaces common today.

What do people mean when they mention the command line? The term *command line* can be used to refer to any one of multiple command-line tools, such as command.com, cmd.exe, and Windows PowerShell.

The command.com toolset was the original command-line shell included in the early Windows operating systems. It was very much like the original DOS interface and is rarely, if ever, used today. command.com is absent from the most recent operating systems like Windows 7 and Windows Server 2008 R2.

cmd.exe

Microsoft command-line interpreter that issues commands that are executed by the operating system.

cmd.exe is command.com's successor, and though it began as a 16-bit program, it was subsequently upgraded to a 32-bit program that was included in the Windows NT family of operating systems and has been part of all operating systems since. cmd.exe is still a widely utilized tool in administrative circles today.

Windows PowerShell is the latest incarnation of the command-line shell within the Windows operating systems. It contains significantly more muscle than its predecessors, as you will see in this chapter. Newer Windows operating systems contain both cmd.exe and Windows PowerShell.

In the very early days of system administration, the majority of administrative tasks were executed using a command-line interface. All system instructions were performed by typing lines and lines of text. As computing has evolved and favored the less technical user, the interface for the administrator has evolved as well.

Graphical tools and the ability to point and click have replaced the old-school task of issuing lines of text. For instance, you no longer need to navigate to a directory using the command line and then issue the md command to make a directory. Instead, simply navigate to the desired folder using the Windows Explorer interface and right-click within the screen to create a new folder. In much the same way, you can now easily perform many of the old advanced command-line tasks using the native Windows GUI point-and-click interface and a variety of administrative tools.

That being said, there is still a need for command-line interaction. Automation and remote administration are two of the primary reasons you need to look to command-line toolsets today, and more and more administrators are seeking to update their skill sets with the modern command-line interfaces.

The following sections will walk you through some of the more common actions you can complete using the current command-line tools; these range from creating and manipulating directories to automating tasks with Windows PowerShell.

Creating a Directory Structure

The directory structure is like a filing cabinet for your hard disk. It enables you to logically group files with similar functions. When creating your directory structure, a little planning can really pay off in terms of productivity. Think of a filing system. If you threw everything into one drawer, finding a specific document would be difficult. The same problem would occur on your computer if you put all your documents into one directory, or folder.

Consider the logic of the following sample directory structure. In this case, there are separate folders for applications and data. Each application and data folder is further divided into subdirectories to organize the contents at a finer level of detail.

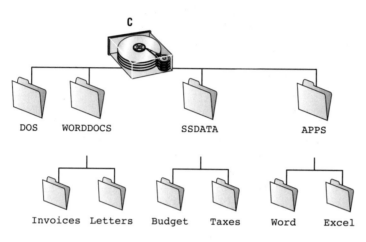

Manipulating the Directory Structure

You can use several commands to manipulate the directory structure. All of the commands mentioned in the following table function similarly in both Windows PowerShell and the cmd.exe interface.

This table summarizes the most useful commands for directory structure manipulation. The following subsections provide further details about these commands.

Command	Purpose	Syntax
DIR	DIRECTORY shows the directory listing, including files and subdirectories of the current directory.	**DIR**
MD	MAKE DIRECTORY creates a new directory or subdirectory.	**MD WORDDOCS**
RD	REMOVE DIRECTORY removes a directory or subdirectory.	**RD WORDDOCS**
CD	CHANGE DIRECTORY traverses the directory structure.	**CD WORDDOCS**

Listing Directories, Subdirectories, and Files

To show a list of all the files and directories on your logical drive, use the DIR command. This is perhaps the most commonly used directory command. After you type DIR, you see information about the files and directories that are relative to (in the same folder as) the directory path that you are in:

◆ Directory name or filename and extension

◆ Date and time you created the directory or file or the last time it was written to

◆ Size of the file in bytes

◆ Total number of files and the space used by the folder, as well as the remaining disk space in bytes (cmd.exe only)

```
C:\windows\system32\cmd.exe

C:\>dir
 Volume in drive C has no label.
 Volume Serial Number is 6A10-D588

 Directory of C:\

05/22/2011  09:26 PM    <DIR>          drivers
05/22/2011  09:11 PM    <DIR>          Intel
04/21/2011  11:12 AM                 0 msit-20110421-0812-amd64.txt
07/13/2009  11:20 PM    <DIR>          PerfLogs
07/03/2011  12:40 PM    <DIR>          Program Files
09/19/2011  12:02 AM    <DIR>          Program Files (x86)
09/19/2011  12:02 AM    <DIR>          ProgramData
04/21/2011  11:59 AM    <DIR>          Resources
09/09/2011  03:17 PM    <DIR>          Riot Games
05/22/2011  09:11 PM               211 setup.log
05/22/2011  09:29 PM    <DIR>          Users
09/18/2011  05:11 PM    <DIR>          Windows
               2 File(s)            211 bytes
              10 Dir(s)  86,431,793,152 bytes free

C:\>
```

You can use the following options from within cmd.exe with the DIR command for additional administrative flexibility:

DIR /P Pauses between screens—helpful when you have more than one screen of information

DIR /W Shows the list in a wide format

DIR /S Shows all the information within the subdirectories of the directory

NOTE Within the cmd.exe interface, you can combine the DIR command with one or more other switches. For example, the command DIR /W /P will show a wide list and will pause if there is more than one page of text to display.

Creating and Deleting Directories

To define your directory structure from within cmd.exe or Windows PowerShell, use commands to create and delete directories. To create a directory, use the MD command. To delete a directory, use the RD command.

Within cmd.exe, before you can remove a directory with the RD command, the directory must be empty of all files and subdirectories. To delete directories that contain files or subdirectories, you should use the RD /S command. Within Windows PowerShell, you can choose to remove a directory that contains files and subdirectories; PowerShell will prompt you to make sure that you want to execute this action.

TIP

Test It Out: Using the *MD* and *RD* Commands

Take these steps to practice creating and removing a directory from within cmd.exe:

1. From the C:\> prompt in a cmd.exe screen, type **MD WORDDOCS** and then press Enter.

2. From the C:\> prompt, type **MD SSDATA** and then press Enter. This creates the directory named SSDATA.

3. From the C:\> prompt, type **MD TEST** and then press Enter. This creates the directory named TEST.

4. From the C:\> prompt, type **DIR** and then press Enter. You should see a directory listing that includes the two directories you just created.

5. From the C:\> prompt, type **RD TEST** and then press Enter. This removes the directory named TEST.

6. From the C:\> prompt, type **DIR** and then press Enter. You should see a list that still includes the directory SSDATA but not the directory TEST.

At the cmd.exe prompt, you can type /? after any command for additional information and syntax options related to that command.

TIP

Changing Directories

From within cmd.exe, as well as within Windows PowerShell, you use the CD command to change directories. This command enables you to move fairly easily from one branch of the file system hierarchical structure to another.

As an example of how to use the CD command, again assume you have the directory structure shown in the graphic at the beginning of this section.

To move down a level—in this case from within cmd.exe, to the WORDDOCS directory—type this command at the C:\> prompt:

CD WORDDOCS

To move back up one level of the directory structure, use the CD.. command like this:

`C:\WORDDOCS>CD..`

If you are more than one level down the tree and want to return to the root drive (the C drive), you type **CD** like this:

`C:\WORDDOCS\LETTERS>CD\`

Test It Out: Using the *CD* Command

To test directory manipulation from within cmd.exe, you will complete the directory structure shown in the preceding section. If you completed "Test It Out: Using the *MD* and *RD* Commands," skip steps 1 and 2.

1. If you are not already at the `C:\>` prompt, type `C:` at the command prompt and press Enter.

2. From `C:\>` type **MD WORDDOCS** and press Enter. Type MD SSDATA and press Enter.

3. From `C:\>` type **MD DOCS** and press Enter. Type **MD APPS** and press Enter.

4. Change to the WORDDOCS directory by typing **CD WORDDOCS** and then press Enter.

5. From `C:\>WORDDOCS>` type **MD INVOICES** and press Enter. Type **MD LETTERS** and press Enter.

6. To return to the root level of `C:\`, from `C:\>WORDDOCS>` type **CD** and press Enter.

7. Take the steps needed to complete the directory structure shown in the previous section.

Copying and Moving Files

If you need to make copies of your files, adjust the location of your files, or if you want to rearrange your file structure you have multiple tools to choose from. From the cmd.exe interface you can use the COPY, XCOPY, ROBOCOPY, or MOVE commands to accomplish various administrative or maintenance tasks.

The COPY command copies the file(s) from the source directory to the destination directory. A copy of the file then exists in both the source and destination directories.

The syntax for performing a COPY is:

COPY `source path\filename destination path\filename`

For example:

COPY `C:\TEST\TEST.DOC C:\DOCS\TEST.DOC`

The XCOPY command stands for extended copy and is similar to the copy command. It allows you to copy all files and folders inside the target folder and not just the file(s) on the surface.

The syntax for performing an XCOPY is:

XCOPY `source path\filename(s) destination path\filename`

For example:

XCOPY `C:\TEST\*.* C:\DOCS\`

The ROBOCOPY command is the latest in the evolution of file copy commands and stands for robust file copy. It is similar to the COPY and XCOPY commands but has numerous amounts of additional features like being able to resume a copy operation if it gets interrupted.

The syntax for performing a ROBOCOPY is:

ROBOCOPY `source_directory destination_directory`

For example:

ROBOCOPY `C:\TEST\ C:\DOCS\`

The MOVE command functions in a different fashion, and instead of creating a copy of your files it only moves the file(s) from the source directory to the destination directory. The file then exists only in a single location, which would be within the destination directory.

The syntax for performing a MOVE is:

MOVE `source path\filename destination path\filename`

For example:

MOVE `C:\TEST\TEST.DOC C:\DOCS\TEST.DOC`

Test It Out: Using *COPY* and *MOVE* Commands

In this exercise, you will copy and move files from one directory to another.

1. At C:\TEST, create files TEST1.DOC, TEST2.DOC, TEST3.DOC, and MOVEME.DOC. Create the directory C:\DOCS.

2. From C:\TEST, type COPY TEST1.DOC C:\DOCS and press Enter.

3. Verify that the document was copied by using the DIR command at C:\
    TEST and C:\DOCS. **Does** TEST1.DOC **exist in both directories?**

4. Type MOVE MOVEME.DOC C:\DOCS and press Enter.

5. Verify that the document was moved by using the DIR command at
    C:\TEST and C:\DOCS. MOVEME.DOC should exist only in the C:\DOCS
    directory.

6. Type COPY T*.DOC C:\DOCS and press Enter.

    Using this command, all documents in the C:\TEST directory that
    begin with a "T" and end with the extension "DOC" will all be copied to
    the C:\DOCS directory. Use this method to quickly move many like files
    all at once.

NOTE   When you are working with a file that is located in the current directory, there is
no need to type the entire path for the file in the command.

Deleting and Renaming Files

After you no longer need a file, you can delete it from within cmd.exe or with
Windows PowerShell by using the DEL command. DEL is an easy command to
use. The syntax is

DEL *drive letter:directory\filename*

Or if you are already in the directory in which the file exists, the syntax is

DEL *filename*

```
Administrator: Command Prompt

C:\>del test.txt
C:\>
```

Third-party utilities—for example, Norton Utilities—can sometimes recover files that have been deleted.

NOTE

Do not delete files if you are unsure of what they are. They might be program, application, or configuration files you need.

WARNING

From within cmd.exe and Windows PowerShell you may use the REN command to rename files, using this syntax:

REN *oldname* newname

For example, assume that you have a file called ACCT.TXT that you want to rename ACCT03.TXT. You would use the command shown on the screen here:

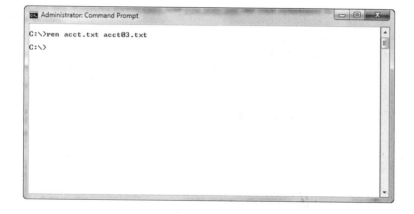

```
C:\>ren acct.txt acct03.txt
C:\>
```

Test It Out: Using the *REN* Command

In this exercise, you will use cmd.exe to create, rename, and then delete a file.

1. At the C:\ prompt, create a text file called OLD.TXT by using the EDIT or COPY CON command.

2. At the C:\> prompt, type REN OLD.TXT NEW.TXT and press Enter.

3. Use the DIR command to verify that your file has been renamed.

4. At the C:\> prompt, type DEL NEW.TXT and press Enter.

5. Use the DIR command to verify that your file has been deleted.

Using Command-Line Wildcards

The Windows file system uses wildcard characters to represent specific letters or numbers as variables. This is useful when you are using cmd.exe to look for a series of files or you want to perform an action on many files at the same time.

The asterisk (*) wildcard represents any number of characters that you are looking for.

The question mark (?) wildcard represents a single character or number. You can use multiple ? wildcards in a single query. This wildcard is not as commonly used as *.

Test It Out: Using cmd.exe Wildcards

1. Create the directory structure and files shown in the previous exercise. Refer to "Creating and Deleting Directories" for help on creating the directory structure and to "Editing Text Documents" for help on creating the text files.

2. Access the C:\TEST directory.

3. Type DIR *.TXT and press Enter.

   You should see FILE1.TXT, FILE2.TXT, FILE3.TXT, FILE4.TXT, PAPER1.TXT, and PAPER2.TXT.

4. Type DIR *.DOC and press Enter.

   You should see FILE5.DOC and FILE10.DOC.

5. Type DIR FILE?.* and press Enter.

   Notice that FILE10.DOC does not show up, because the ? wildcard indicates only a single placeholder.

6. Type DIR P*.TXT and press Enter.

   You should see PAPER1.TXT and PAPER2.TXT.

7. Type REN F*.DOC F*.TXT and press Enter.

   Type DIR *.DOC and press Enter to see whether any DOC files remain.

8. Type DEL P*.* and press Enter.

   Type DIR P*.* and press Enter to see whether any of the files beginning with P remain.

As an example of when to use these wildcards, assume you have this directory structure:

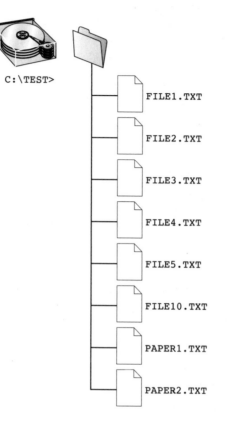

C:\TEST>

FILE1.TXT

FILE2.TXT

FILE3.TXT

FILE4.TXT

FILE5.TXT

FILE10.TXT

PAPER1.TXT

PAPER2.TXT

Working with Filenames

There are different types of file systems. Older systems may use the *File Allocation Table (FAT)* file system, which restricts the names of files and folders to only eight characters with a three-character extension. *FAT32* makes better use of disk space, supports large disk sizes greater than 2 GB, and improves disk performance.

Depending on the operating system version you are using, file or folder names longer than eight characters might be automatically assigned an abbreviated eight-character name. Sometimes the short names are not very intuitive. For this reason, it used to be a good idea to try to keep your filenames fairly short, but for the most part, this no longer applies. cmd.exe and Windows PowerShell, on the other hand, have a 255-character limit for filenames or directory paths.

You should also note that certain utilities may not understand spaces in filenames or long filenames. If you have a filename with spaces or a long filename, use quotation marks around the filename when using command line utilities.

File Allocation Table (FAT)
A table stored on the outer edge of the hard drive that indicates the location and order of files on the hard drive.

FAT32
A 32-bit version of the FAT file system that will recognize drives larger than 2 GB. FAT32 can adjust the size of the clusters (individual cells that are used to organize the data) on a hard drive to accommodate larger-sized drives.

As you can see, wildcards make directory management a lot easier and more efficient than managing files on an individual basis.

Understanding File Attributes

incremental backup
Uses the archive bit to determine which files have changed since the last incremental backup. After the incremental backup is complete, the archive bit is cleared. Incremental backups occur between normal or full backups.

differential backup
Uses the archive bit to determine which files have changed since the last normal backup. Files that have changed are backed up. The archive bit is not reset until the next normal backup. If you have to restore data, you need only your last full backup and your last differential tape.

hidden file
A file that is not viewable using the DIR command or visible in a folder. The hidden file attribute can be set to on or off using the ATTRIB command or by setting the file properties in Windows.

Each file has attributes that define the properties of the file. You can manipulate these attributes from cmd.exe and from within Windows PowerShell by using the ATTRIB command. The four attributes are described in this table.

Attribute	Purpose
read-only (R)	If you set the read-only attribute, you cannot modify or delete a file unless you remove it. This attribute safeguards a file from being accidentally modified or deleted.
archive (A)	You use the archive attribute with backups. When you use this attribute to mark a file, it indicates that the file is new or that it has been modified since the last backup. Use this attribute when you perform *incremental* or *differential backups*.
system (S)	The system attribute indicates that the file is a system or program file. To manipulate any of the other attributes, you must first remove the system attribute. This attribute implies that a file is read-only.
hidden (H)	The hidden attribute keeps a file from being listed through the DIR command or from being accidentally deleted.

The syntax for the ATTRIB command is

ATTRIB drive letter:\directory*file [+attribute|-attribute]*

- ◆ +*attribute* indicates that you are applying an attribute.
- ◆ −*attribute* indicates that you are removing an attribute.
- ◆ Note that you type only the letter abbreviation of the attribute, such as *H* for the hidden file attribute.

Assume that you have a directory, D:\TEST, and that the directory contains a file called TEST.DOCX.

To see the file attributes, type **ATTRIB TEST.DOCX** and press Enter.

```
Administrator: Command Prompt

C:\>attrib test.docx
A          C:\test.docx

C:\>
```

Note that the *A* in front of the filename indicates that the archive bit is set. This attribute is applied to all new files.

To apply the hidden file attribute to the TEST.DOC file, you would type **ATTRIB TEST.DOCX +H** and press Enter.

```
Administrator: Command Prompt

C:\>attrib test.docx +H
C:\>
```

To remove the hidden attribute from the TEST.DOC file, you would type **ATTRIB TEST.DOCX -H** and press Enter.

```
Administrator: Command Prompt

C:\>attrib test.docx -H
C:\>
```

Changing the Time and Date

You can see what time your computer is set to or change the time with the TIME command from the cmd.exe interface. From within the Windows PowerShell interface the DATE will display both the date and the time, while DATE from within cmd.exe will display only the date.

To see the time, type **TIME** at the cmd.exe interface. To change the time, type in the time after the command at the command prompt:

TIME time

To see the date from cmd.exe, type **DATE** at the command prompt. To change the date, type the date, using the syntax *mm-dd-yy*, after the command at the command prompt:

DATE *date*

```
Administrator: Command Prompt - date

C:\>date
The current date is: Mon 09/19/2011
Enter the new date: (mm-dd-yy)
```

Using Timesaving Keyboard Shortcuts

Some of the options that can help you save time are the F3 key, the TAB key, and the DOSKEY command.

The F3 key displays the last command that you typed. The F3 key can save you time when you are using the same lengthy command repeatedly and need only to change the variables slightly each time.

The TAB key cycles through potential matches for the command you are currently typing. In cmd.exe, the TAB key serves as a kind of auto complete.

It will try to complete your current command with possible legal matches. For example, typing **CD** and then the TAB key will cycle through the possible directories you can call. This functionality is similar in PowerShell though slightly more limited. In PowerShell, the TAB key lets you cycle through potential matches but only if you know the verb part of the cmdlet. To do this, you type the verb followed by the hyphen and then TAB will cycle through the potential matches.

The DOSKEY command keeps a history of the commands that you have typed. You access it by pressing the Up arrow (↑) and Down arrow (↓) keys on the keypad. When you use a set of commands repeatedly—for example, when you create and move files—DOSKEY can save you a significant amount of time that you would have otherwise spent typing.

Another useful command-line command is CLS. When you type CLS at the command prompt, it clears the current screen and leaves you with a DOS prompt.

Test It Out: Using the F3 Key, *DOSKEY*, *TIME*, and *DATE* Commands

In this exercise, you learn how to apply new timesaving commands in addition to resetting the time and date of your system. You will need to use some of the commands that you have learned in previous sections. Refer back to those sections if you forget a command.

1. From a command-line prompt, type **DOSKEY** and press Enter. You will see the message DOSKEY installed displayed. Newer operating systems have DOSKEY functionality already built in and will not display the DOSKEY installed message, but will still work appropriately.

2. Type several of the commands that you have learned about in this chapter.

3. Press the F3 key to display the last command that you typed.

4. Use the Up arrow (↑) and Down arrow (↓) keys on the keypad to view the history of the commands you have issued since you invoked DOSKEY.

5. From a cmd.exe prompt, type **TIME**. If the time is correct, press Enter. If not, type the correct time and press Enter.

6. From a cmd.exe prompt, type **DATE**. If the date is correct, press Enter. If not, type the correct date and press Enter.

Introducing PowerShell

PowerShell

A robust command-line shell built on the .NET Framework that includes an associated scripting language. PowerShell generally utilizes cmdlets to interact with the operating system.

PowerShell script

A file that contains a set of cmdlets to be executed by PowerShell. All PowerShell scripts end in `.ps1`.

batch file

A file that contains a set of commands to be executed by the operating system. All batch files end in `.BAT`.

Every version of Windows has included some sort of command-line interface. Unfortunately, as time went on, it became apparent that the power in these tools was lacking. When compared to what was needed, the command-line interface had a limited number of commands and from it, you couldn't perform the same functions as you could in the Windows graphical user interface (GUI).

In 2002, Microsoft started to address this need by developing a unique command-line shell, code-named Monad. This was eventually renamed Windows PowerShell and the first version was released in 2006. As of this writing, the latest version is 2.0, which was released in October 2009.

The first question many users might want to know is "What is PowerShell?" *PowerShell* is a powerful command-based shell and scripting language built on the .NET Framework. It is a command-line interface just like cmd.exe, but it has a lot more muscle. It accepts DOS- and Unix-style commands. In addition, it supports scripts and *batch files*, and since it was built on the .NET Framework, it also boasts full scripting capability.

Installing PowerShell

Before you can do anything with PowerShell, you must make sure you have it installed. If you are running Windows 7 or Windows Server 2008 R2, then you don't really need to do anything, since PowerShell is installed by default.

If you are not sure if you have it installed there is an easy way to check. Open a Run window by clicking on Start and then selecting Run, type in **PowerShell,** and hit Enter. If it is present, a command-line interface window for PowerShell will open. If you don't have PowerShell installed and want to follow along with the examples in the book, then you will need to download it.

As of this writing, the latest version of PowerShell is version 2.0. Since the PowerShell scripting language is built on the .NET Framework, it requires the .NET Framework with Service Pack 1 (SP1) to be installed. In addition to Windows 7 and Windows Server 2008 R2, PowerShell 2.0 will run on any of the following platforms.

Windows Server 2003 SP2
Windows Server 2008 SP2
Windows XP SP3
Windows Vista SP1 or later

You can download and install the latest version of PowerShell 2.0 from http://support.microsoft.com/kb/968929/en-us. Once you have done this, you are ready to move on to the PowerShell command syntax. Keep in mind that if you already have an older version of PowerShell installed, you should uninstall it before installing the newer version.

PowerShell Command Syntax

PowerShell commands are called *cmdlet*s, pronounced commandlets. All cmdlets are similar in syntax in that they are a verb-noun combo. For example, a verb-noun combo that would represent you reading this book would be "Read-Book." "Read" explains the action that you would like to take, while "Book" represents the object the action should be taken on. This format stands true for all PowerShell cmdlets.

Discoverability

The two most important cmdlets in PowerShell are Get-Help and Get-Command. These cmdlets allow you to discover additional information from within PowerShell about the various cmdlets and their syntax.

PowerShell has been designed to be user friendly and allow users to easily discover new features and get help. This is what is referred to as *discoverability* and it is considered an innovative feature of PowerShell when compared to previous Windows command-line iterations.

Adding Arguments

If we continue with our Read-Book example earlier, we need to give the system additional information so that it understands which book we are referring to. For this reason, most verb-noun combinations are usually followed by an argument. The argument specified in a cmdlet represents additional information that is required to successfully perform the action. In this case, we would follow the Read-Book cmdlet with an argument that identifies the title of the book, for instance, "JumpStart." These components come together, resulting in the following cmdlet string: Read-Book Jumpstart.

Let's apply this concept to some actual cmdlets, Get-Help and Get-Command. First, open a PowerShell window from the Run window by typing **PowerShell** and hitting Enter. Let's first try the Get-Help cmdlet, where you will specify the argument of help.

The result of this cmdlet is a screen similar to the following one. Your cmdlet has requested that PowerShell display the help content that is available on using help. The Get-Help cmdlet can be used in combination with any cmdlet in PowerShell to get more information about that cmdlet as well as its syntax. Get-Help functions as PowerShell's version of a built-in user manual, and it is definitely a feature that you should use as frequently as you need to.

cmdlet
A command executed within Windows PowerShell that performs an action and can be used to create powerful scripts for local or remote administration. The command is issued in a verb-noun format.

```
Windows PowerShell                                                          _ □ X
PS C:\> Get-Help help

NAME
    Get-Help

SYNOPSIS
    Displays information about Windows PowerShell commands and concepts.

SYNTAX
    Get-Help [-Full] [[-Name] <string>] [-Category <string[]>] [-Component <string[]>] [-Functionality <string[]>] [-On
    line] [-Path <string>] [-Role <string[]>] [<CommonParameters>]

    Get-Help [-Detailed] [[-Name] <string>] [-Category <string[]>] [-Component <string[]>] [-Functionality <string[]>]
    [-Online] [-Path <string>] [-Role <string[]>] [<CommonParameters>]

    Get-Help [-Examples] [[-Name] <string>] [-Category <string[]>] [-Component <string[]>] [-Functionality <string[]>]
    [-Online] [-Path <string>] [-Role <string[]>] [<CommonParameters>]

    Get-Help [-Parameter <string>] [[-Name] <string>] [-Category <string[]>] [-Component <string[]>] [-Functionality <s
    tring[]>] [-Online] [-Path <string>] [-Role <string[]>] [<CommonParameters>]

DESCRIPTION
    The Get-Help cmdlet displays information about Windows PowerShell concepts and commands, including cmdlets, provide
    rs, functions and scripts. To get a list of all cmdlet help topic titles, type "get-help *".

    If you type "Get-Help" followed by the exact name of a help topic, or by a word unique to a help topic, Get-Help di
    splays the topic contents. If you enter a word or word pattern that appears in several help topic titles, Get-Help
    displays a list of the matching titles. If you enter a word that does not appear in any help topic titles, Get-Help
    displays a list of topics that include that word in their contents.

    In addition to "get-help", you can also type "help" or "man", which displays one screen of text at a time, or "<cmd
    let-name> -?", which is identical to Get-Help but works only for cmdlets.

    You can display the entire help file or selected parts of the file, such as the syntax, parameters, or examples. Yo
    u can also use the Online parameter to display an online version of a help file in your Internet browser. These par
    ameters have no effect on conceptual help topics.

    Conceptual help topics in Windows PowerShell begin with "about_", such as "about_Comparison_Operators". To see all
    "about_" topics, type "get-help about_*". To see a particular topic, type "get-help about_<topic-name>", such as "g
    et-help about_Comparison_Operators".

RELATED LINKS
    Online version: http://go.microsoft.com/fwlink/?LinkID=113316

    about_Comment_Based_Help
    Get-Command
    Get-PSDrive
```

As you start to get into the routine of running Get-Help, you might notice that sometimes it will give you too much information at once and your screen will scroll so that the information displayed isn't absorbable. In these cases, abbreviate the Get-Help cmdlet by using only help (e.g., help disk).

```
Windows PowerShell                                                          _ □ X
PS C:\> help disk

Name                       Category  Synopsis
----                       --------  --------
Get-WinEvent               Cmdlet    Gets events from event logs and event tracing log files on local and rem...
Get-Counter                Cmdlet    Gets performance counter data from local and remote computers.
Import-Counter             Cmdlet    Imports performance counter log files (.blg, .csv, .tsv) and creates the...
Export-Counter             Cmdlet    The Export-Counter cmdlet takes PerformanceCounterSampleSet objects and ...
Get-WSManInstance          Cmdlet    Displays management information for a resource instance specified by a R...
Invoke-Command             Cmdlet    Runs commands on local and remote computers.
New-Module                 Cmdlet    Creates a new dynamic module that exists only in memory.
New-Event                  Cmdlet    Creates a new event.
ConvertFrom-StringData     Cmdlet    Converts a string containing one or more key/value pairs to a hash table.
Import-PSSession           Cmdlet    Imports commands from another session into the current session.
Set-PSBreakpoint           Cmdlet    Sets a breakpoint on a line, command, or variable.
Get-WmiObject              Cmdlet    Gets instances of Windows Management Instrumentation (WMI) classes or in...
New-PSDrive                Cmdlet    Creates a Windows PowerShell drive in the current session.
Get-PSDrive                Cmdlet    Gets the Windows PowerShell drives in the current session.
Get-Process                Cmdlet    Gets the processes that are running on the local computer or a remote co...
Get-Credential             Cmdlet    Gets a credential object based on a user name and password.
-- More --
```

This saves time on input and also enacts a pausing feature that shows only one screen of information at a time. Administrators who have a Unix background should be aware of the man command, which allows listing of help content. This command is also supported within PowerShell and works just like the help command.

Another option is to use the pipeline operator (|) and pipeline the result of the get-help cmdlet to more which will pause each page for you.

TIP

A pipeline is a series of commands in PowerShell connected by the pipeline operator. Each pipeline operator sends the results of the preceding command to the next command creating a chain.

Make sure you are also familiar with the Get-Command cmdlet. At the most basic level, the Get-Command cmdlet will get a list of all the PowerShell cmdlets. If you enter the Get-Command cmdlet alone, all the cmdlets shown in the following screen appear. The Get-Command cmdlet has more uses than that, however. You can use it to target a specific cmdlet, for instance. Assume you want to look up a cmdlet that you remember ended with session. Just type **Get-Command *session** and get all the cmdlets that fit that pattern.

```
Windows PowerShell

PS C:\> Get-Command *session

CommandType     Name                          Definition
-----------     ----                          ----------
Cmdlet          Enter-PSSession               Enter-PSSession [-ComputerName] <String> [-Crede...
Cmdlet          Exit-PSSession                Exit-PSSession [-Verbose] [-Debug] [-ErrorAction...
Cmdlet          Export-PSSession              Export-PSSession [-Session] <PSSession> [-Output...
Cmdlet          Get-PSSession                 Get-PSSession [[-ComputerName] <String[]>] [-Ver...
Cmdlet          Import-PSSession              Import-PSSession [-Session] <PSSession> [[-Comma...
Cmdlet          New-PSSession                 New-PSSession [[-ComputerName] <String[]>] [-Cre...
Cmdlet          Remove-PSSession              Remove-PSSession [-Id] <Int32[]> [-Verbose] [-De...

PS C:\>
```

To further familiarize yourself with PowerShell, use the Get-Help about command to list available subjects. Select a subject that interests you and specify it following the Get-Help command to view additional information. They are there for the express purpose of being informative.

PowerShell Execution Policy

Powershell, like many Windows programs, will try to protect you from yourself. This means that it will not let you execute many of the examples in this book by default; it uses an execution policy to limit what you can do.

You can view the execution policy with the Get-ExecutionPolicy cmdlet. By default, it will be set to Restricted, which means it will not allow any scripts to be run and will generally limit your interaction with the system. In order to execute a wider range of activities, you will need to change the policy to one of the following three configurations:

AllSigned   Allows only scripts that are signed by a trusted publisher to be run.

RemoteSigned   Scripts can be run, and downloaded scripts must be signed by a trusted publisher.

Unrestricted   All scripts can be run, regardless of signed state.

You can use the Set-ExecutionPolicy cmdlet to set the policy. To ensure that you like the change to the process, PowerShell prompts you to confirm the change. Once you confirm the change, it goes into effect immediately. Remember that you can always use the same Set-ExecutionPolicy cmdlet to revert the setting back to the default setting at any time. To work through the examples that follow, change the setting to RemoteSigned.

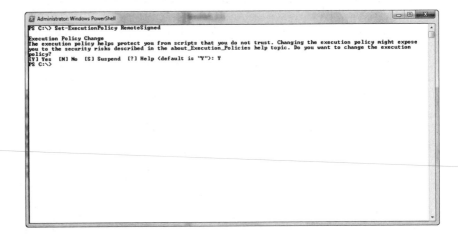

Using PowerShell Wildcards

Another feature of PowerShell is its user-friendly support for wildcards. A *wildcard* is a special character that serves as a placeholder for an unknown character or group of characters. By using wildcards you can find commands or help without having all the information about a specific cmdlet. The wildcard characters for PowerShell include * and ? and work the same way as they did in the section "Command-Line Wildcards" earlier in this chapter.

The square brackets [and] are another set of wildcard characters used in PowerShell. The brackets are used to match a specific range. The way to use them is to either specify all the matches you are interested in or actually to specify a range. For example, [bdeg]ark would match bark and dark, but not lark, since the l is not specified in the brackets. [a-k]art is a range example and would return any match with the characters in the range inclusively, like cart or dart.

When working with PowerShell wildcards, keep in mind that wildcards are not case sensitive; they do not care if the match is uppercase or lowercase, only that it matches. Once you are familiar with wildcards you will have a much easier time using cmdlets in PowerShell to accomplish what you want.

Understanding PowerShell Modules and Snap-Ins

PowerShell modules and snap-ins are feature sets that contribute to PowerShell being considered, by some, to be a fully fledged programming language instead of just a command-line tool like cmd.exe. By importing the modules or adding snap-ins, the user is able to expand PowerShell's already-existing functionality even further. It is also this feature that makes PowerShell a fully extensible scripting language.

Snap-ins and modules are, in essence, collections of code that are separate from PowerShell but when imported, provide additional functionality via extra cmdlets and other code in the same way code libraries are imported in other programming languages. What this means to you as an administrator is twofold: first, you can import additional functionality to better fit your needs, and second, if you are a skilled programmer, you can write your own modules as well.

Although modules and snap-ins might be similar in what they accomplish, they also have some very important differences. Snap-ins have been around since PowerShell version 1.0, and they are limited to cmdlets and providers. You can see a list of all the snap-ins you currently have active by using the Get-PSSnapin cmdlet as shown here.

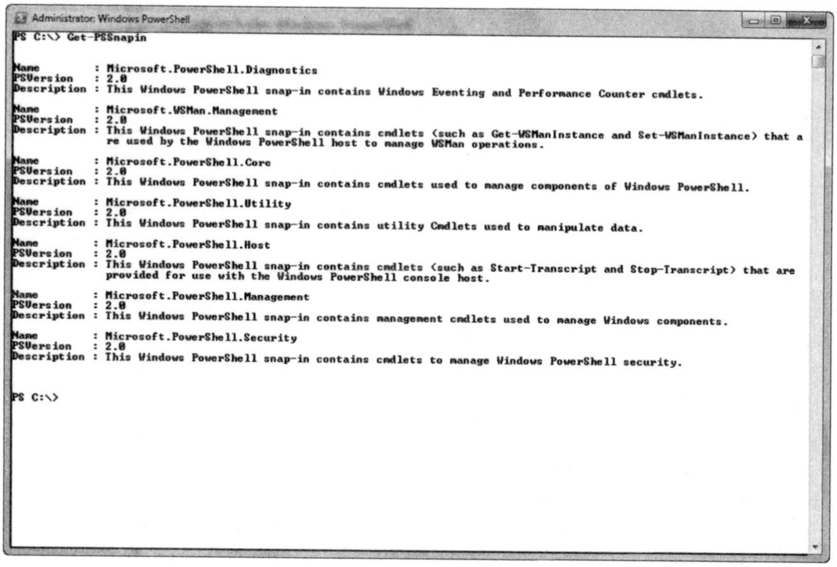

You already know what a cmdlet is, but what is a provider? A provider is a data store that is available for you to use in PowerShell, and it behaves very much like a hard drive partition, allowing you to view and manage it. To see what providers you have available, use the Get-PSProvider cmdlet as show here. Snap-ins are available as soon as you add them but usually only affect the current session.

Modules are new to PowerShell version 2.0. They also allow you to extend the functionality of PowerShell much like a snap-in. Modules can contain cmdlets and providers just like snap-ins, but they are not limited to only these functionalities. For example, modules can include images, help files, and many other items. PowerShell also lets you use modules to organize your cmdlets and other files so that you can share them with other users. You can use the `Get-Module` cmdlet to see what modules you have imported.

Using snap-ins and modules is very beneficial and in most administrative situations, becomes a necessity. For example, if you want to use the Active Directory cmdlets in Windows Server 2008 R2, you first need to import the Active Directory module.

The following image demonstrates how you can easily import a PowerShell module and view the modules that have been imported.

PowerShell Functions and Scripts

When some system administrators hear "scripting," they immediately assume the worst. They think that scripting is more for their programmer friends. Well, there is some good news in PowerShell; PowerShell is geared toward system administrators and it makes scripting extremely easy and unintimidating.

PowerShell makes no distinction between cmdlets executed from a script and cmdlets you enter manually at a command-line prompt. This means that if you can issue cmdlets or *function* calls to PowerShell one at a time, you can write a script. When you start writing scripts, you will find that you need to use functions as well as cmdlets. Although writing a function by yourself is beyond the scope of this book, it is helpful to know something about them.

Functions are blocks of code that perform an action. Most of them take a parameter or additional instruction from inside curly brackets to help them execute the desired action. For instance, let's assume a function existed that made a gold bar appear under your pillow in the morning. Let us call this fictional function DreamGold. To call this function in PowerShell, we would have to type **Function DreamGold** {} and place the ounces that we wanted inside the curly brackets. So, if we wanted to wake up to a 20-ounce bar of gold, we would type **Function DreamGold** {20} at the PowerShell prompt, go to bed, and never worry about working again.

Some functions require a parameter inside the curly brackets in order to work properly, while for others, the parameter may be preset, and therefore the input is optional. For example, let's assume that if you did not place a value inside the DreamGold function it would always work as if you had requested an 8-ounce bar.

For your first function call you will change your prompt using the prompt {} function. This function takes a parameter that you give it inside {} and changes the prompt to this parameter. To begin, launch PowerShell and then type in **Function prompt** { 'Your Will? >' }, and then hit Enter.

Your prompt now changes to display what you typed inside the brackets. Feel free to try it again with anything you might want it to say. Make sure you enclose your desired text inside the curly brackets and the single quotes. Be aware that this will change your prompt for this session only. If you exit the PowerShell session and open a new session window, you will see that the old prompt is back. This is one reason many people write scripts. Once you write a script and save it, you can call that script as desired without ever having to re-enter the desired commands.

One of the many advantages of using a script is that that they are reusable. Once you become able to write a sophisticated series of cmdlet sequences to accomplish a task, you will be able to write them once and then save them as a script so that you can execute them anytime thereafter.

function
A block of code that performs an action or operation. A function may or may not require parameters.

Terms to Know

batch file	function
cmdlet	hidden file
cmd.exe	incremental backup
differential backup	PowerShell
File Allocation Table (FAT)	PowerShell script
File Allocation Table 32 bit (FAT32)	wildcard

Review Questions

1. If you were at C:\TEST\DOCS and you wanted to go to the root of C:\, which command would you use?

2. Which command would you use from the C:\ prompt to delete the TEST.DOCX file that is located in C:\TEST?

3. You use the _____ command to rename a file.

4. What is the difference between the * and ? wildcards?

5. What is the difference between the MAKE DIRECTORY and REMOVE DIRECTORY commands?

6. What are the command and syntax to specify that TEST.DOCX should have a hidden file attribute?

7. What is a PowerShell module and why is it used?

8. What cmdlet is used to look for help on a subject?

9. What cmdlet lets you check which modules are installed?

10. What cmdlet allows you to check the configured execution policy?

Chapter 7

Graphical Interface: Windows 7 Basics

in•ter•face *n* : a point of interaction between two systems

One of the most basic tasks in Windows management is being able to navigate the graphical interface. In this chapter, you will learn the fundamental components of the graphical interface in Windows 7.

A Quick Introduction

Windows 7 offers many ways to configure the desktop to make it easy to use and to accommodate personal preference. The Windows 7 operating system was designed around many of the original goals of Windows Vista. The design makes this operating system user friendly while offering the highest level of features. The design goals for Windows 7 included:

- It had to be easy for people to use.
- The platform needed to be stable so that users would feel comfortable storing data on the computer.
- The interface needed to be visually pleasing and intuitive so that users would have an experience that was comfortable and productive.
- It had to provide superior integration of the latest Internet technologies, including Internet-based email, web browsing, and Internet access configuration. These features needed to have wide-reaching support for different technologies and be easy to set up.
- It needed to have support for the latest hardware.
- Performance and stability needed to improve compared to earlier versions of Windows.

Windows 7, like its predecessors, has a graphical user interface (GUI), which makes it much more intuitive and straightforward to use than the old DOS *command-line* environment. Windows 7 is designed to be a *discoverable* operating system, which means that users can intuitively complete necessary tasks.

command line
The prompt in a DOS screen from which a command is executed by typing letters and characters.

In Windows 7, using the left mouse button, sometimes called the primary mouse button, enables you to complete basic tasks, such as launching a program or opening a folder. The right, or secondary, mouse button enables you to perform more advanced tasks, such as changing a file's properties.

—————— TIP ——————

To introduce new users to a GUI and the mouse, let them play the game Solitaire. Depending on the version of Windows 7, Solitaire might need to be enabled via the Turn Windows Features On or Off functionality. Playing helps them practice using the mouse. The only drawback is that most users become addicted to this game!

As a brand-new user of Windows you should first learn these tasks:

- To use the mouse. You do this through practice.
- To open windows so that you can easily complete common tasks. To open windows, you simply point to and click on what you want to open. You can also select items with a single click. When a window is open, you will see a screen similar to this one.

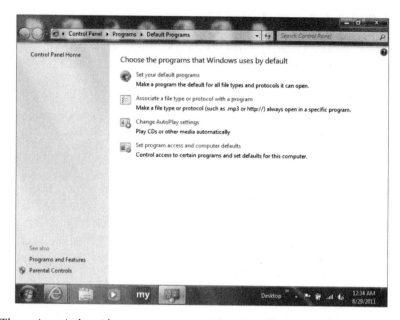

The active window (the one you are using) has three buttons in the upper-right corner:

- The ▭ button minimizes the window, making it disappear and leaving only a button in the Taskbar to make the window reappear. The application is still running while minimized, and you can easily re-access it by clicking the item on the Taskbar.

- The ▭ button maximizes the window so that it takes up the entire screen.

- The ▭x▭ button closes the application.

You can see which applications are running by looking at the Taskbar. The Taskbar is the bar that runs along the bottom of the Windows Desktop by default. By clicking an application button in the Taskbar, you specify the application that will be the active window. The Taskbar also allows additional operations such as the new Peek function, which will be discussed later in this chapter.

Introduction to the Windows 7 Desktop

The Windows 7 Desktop comes with many new features aimed at enhancing the user experience. The new Desktop features try to make it easier for the user to move and manage open windows. An integral part of these new features is what the operating system calls the *Aero Desktop experience*. The Aero Desktop experience is the integration of light translucent windows that don't obscure the current active window. This allows you to preview other windows without interfering with your current activity.

The following table shows the Desktop features that will be covered in this chapter along with a brief description.

Feature	Description
Snap	Lets the user dynamically arrange and resize windows on the desktop.
Shake	Allows the user to quickly minimize all open windows.
Peek	Lets the user preview open windows and the desktop.
Gadgets	Replaces the Windows sidebar in Windows 7.
Desktop Customization	Allows the user to change the arrangement of the desktop icons and the Taskbar to suit specific tastes or needs.

Snap

Snap is a new Windows 7 Desktop feature aimed at making things easier for the user. It allows them to arrange and resize Windows with simple mouse movements. You can now quickly maximize a window, expand it vertically keeping it the same width, or expand it to fit half the screen. You accomplish all these movements by "snapping" the window onto a screen edge.

To maximize a window using the mouse, drag the title bar of the window you would like to maximize to the top of the desktop. This causes the window to automatically maximize.

To expand a window vertically while keeping its current width, first hover over the top edge of the window until the mouse pointer changes into a double headed arrow. Next, while the double headed arrow is being displayed, click and hold the top edge of the window and drag straight up to the top of the screen. This causes the windows to expand vertically and fill the screen from top to bottom while maintaining the previous width. This is useful if you have a long document, a large monitor, and would like to view a larger portion of the document at once.

To expand a window to fill half the screen to either the left or the right, you simply drag the title bar of the window flush with the side of the desktop that you wish it to snap onto. This expands the window to fill only the half of the screen that corresponds to the side that it was dragged against. This is useful when you want to compare two documents or view two different windows in a side-by-side fashion. You simply snap one window on each side of the desktop and each will automatically take up only half of the screen's real estate.

Shake

The Shake feature introduces a quick and simple way to minimize all open windows except for the one you are currently working on. You accomplish this by "shaking" the active window—quickly dragging it in a side-to-side motion on the screen. To do so, click the title bar of the window that you want to keep open and then shake it back and forth; all other windows will minimize, leaving the shaken window as the only visible window on the desktop. If you would like to maximize all of the windows that were minimized by the shake, simply shake the current window again. Only windows that are minimized during a shake will be restored.

Peek

The Peek feature is very powerful and handy and is new to the Windows 7 Desktop. It takes advantage of the Aero Desktop functionality to allow you to preview windows as well as preview the desktop without interrupting your current activity.

You can take advantage of the Peek functionality in two main ways. To use Peek to preview the desktop, simply hold the mouse pointer over the Show Desktop button on the bottom-right side of the Taskbar without clicking it. This button allows you to peek at your current desktop. To restore the current active window, move the cursor off the Show Desktop button. If you want to actually show the desktop instead of just taking a peek, then click the Show Desktop button. This minimizes all your windows and shows the desktop.

The Peek functionality also lets you preview other open windows without minimizing or closing the current window. To use this feature, move the mouse pointer over the Taskbar and hover over any open item without clicking it. This immediately shows a pop-up that displays a smaller version of the open items in the Taskbar group. If you move the mouse pointer over a single file in the group, a preview of that item will appear on the screen. To make it disappear, just move the mouse away from it and your current window appears again. Clicking the window or file you are previewing will immediately maximize it and make it your active window. This allows you to move swiftly and easily between multiple open windows without having to guess which window is the one you are trying to find.

Gadgets

The new Desktop gadgets replace the old Windows Sidebar function from Windows Vista. Gadgets are mini-programs that you can place anywhere on the user's desktop. They provide snippets of information depending on their function. A handful of built-in gadgets are available within Windows 7, including these:

- Bing Search
- Calendar
- Clock
- CPU Meter
- Currency
- Feed Headlines
- Picture Puzzle
- Slide Show
- Weather
- Windows Media Center

Since gadgets can be placed anywhere on the desktop, a user can take advantage of the Peek functionality to look at them without interrupting productivity. To view the list of available gadgets, right-click the desktop and select gadgets from the shortcut menu. This opens a window with all the gadgets available on the system. You can now place them anywhere on the desktop and Peek at them whenever you like, even while working actively in other windows. You can download additional gadgets by using the Get More Gadgets Online link from within the Gadgets window.

Desktop Background and Appearance

The Windows 7 Desktop appears after a user logs onto a Windows 7 computer. The user can then configure their desktop to suit their personal preferences or to work more efficiently.

The Windows 7 Desktop offers similar yet enhanced customization features to those that existed in previous versions of the Windows operating system. One of the easiest and most uniform ways to customize the desktop is by applying a Windows Desktop theme. Themes typically include ways to customize the desktop background, sounds, screen saver, and window color.

You can customize the Windows 7 Desktop by applying the Windows 7 default theme or any customized theme you wish. As an administrator, you may need to troubleshoot an improperly configured desktop. To look at the desktop at any time, click the Show Desktop button on the bottom right-hand side of the Windows Taskbar.

If you have installed Windows 7 from a clean install, you will notice that the desktop is clean and that all of the options for managing the computer are under the Start option.

If your computer came with Windows 7 already installed, your desktop might look different because of customization from the hardware manufacturer. As you use Windows 7, you can customize the desktop to reflect your preferences. In addition, some companies configure their desktops in a specific way to reflect the corporate culture.

NOTE

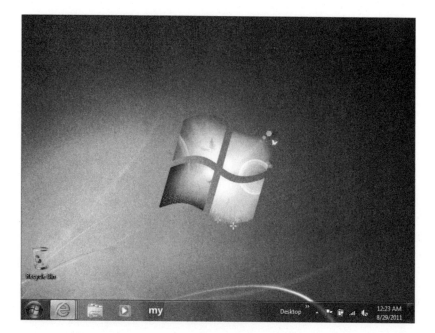

The following table provides an overview of some of the built-in components included with Windows 7. The main topics will be covered in more detail throughout this chapter.

Option	Description
Internet Explorer	The built-in web browser. Along with an Internet connection, *Internet Explorer* provides an interface through which to access the Internet or a local intranet.
Windows Media Player	Used to play multimedia files.
Windows Media Center	Used to view TV.
Windows Easy Transfer	Used to transfer files and settings from an old computer (using a previous version of Windows) to a new computer that has Windows 7 installed.
Discover Windows	Provides an online tutorial for Windows 7.
Documents	By default, stores the documents that are created. Each user has a unique Documents folder, even if a computer is shared.
Recent Items	Lists the most recently accessed documents. Might need to be enabled for some users.
Pictures	Used to display and edit any pictures that are in the Pictures folder.
Music	Used to store and manage any music files that are in the Music folder.
Libraries	Used to show content-specific collections instead of location-specific collections.
Control Panel	Used to configure and manage the computer.
Devices and Printers	Used to connect to, create, or manage print and device resources.
Help and Support	Used to access Windows 7 Help and Support resources.
Search Programs and Files	Searches for pictures, music, videos, documents, files and folders, computers, or people.
Run	Used to run a program or application.
The Start button	From the Start button, you can run applications, access documents, configure your computer, and shut down your computer.

Option	Description
The Taskbar	The Taskbar runs across the bottom of the screen. It shows which applications are running and enables you to switch between them.
Notification Area	The right-most portion of the Taskbar that can be customized to display icons and notifications.
Recycle Bin	The Recycle Bin enables you to store files that you have deleted so that you can undelete them if necessary.
Desktop Background	The desktop background in Windows 7 is more powerful than before. It is no longer limited to a single picture. You can set a full slide show as the background for the desktop. This personalization can be accomplished by right-clicking the desktop and selecting Personalize from the menu.

Using the Start Button

You can do almost anything from the Windows 7 Start button. When you click the Start button, you see a menu with the following options:

- ◆ All Programs
- ◆ Search Programs and Files
- ◆ Documents
- ◆ Pictures
- ◆ Music
- ◆ Computer
- ◆ Control Panel
- ◆ Devices and Printers
- ◆ Default Programs
- ◆ Help and Support
- ◆ Run
- ◆ Shut Down

These are the basic options you will use most often in Windows 7.

Internet Explorer

If your computer has access to the Internet, Internet Explorer is the main utility for accessing Internet resources.

All Programs

When you click on or hold the mouse pointer over All Programs within the Start menu, you see all the programs that have been installed on your computer. The way the programs display is completely customizable; just right-click and select Properties on the Start menu.

Within the Programs menu, you will see folder icons and specific program icons. You can further expand the folder icons to show their contents by clicking them. The programs and folders that appear can, in turn, be further expanded. The specific program icons that are not folders represent applications or programs that can be opened directly by the icons. This screen shows an example of the Programs menu.

Search Programs and Files

The Start menu's Search option enables you to search files and folders based on name, location, or the time that the file was created or modified. You can also search for pictures, music, video, computers, or people. Advanced searches allow you to search for files based on file type, text within the file, and the size of the file. As you type in characters inside the search field, Windows will start to search for you and start to show you potential matches, as seen in the following screenshot.

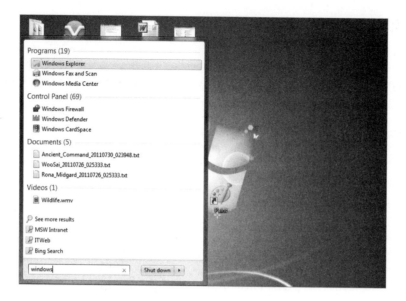

Help and Support

Help and Support provides online help for Windows 7. This component is arranged so that you can read it like a list with related links, or you can use the Search Help field at the top to search for information on a specific topic. Features that used to be found in Help and Support—for example, Windows Updates—have been moved to the Control Panel.

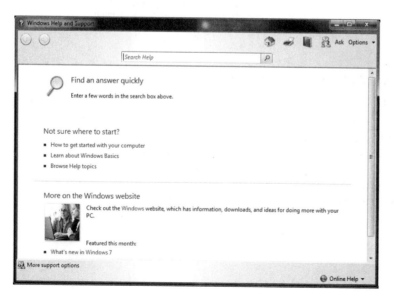

Test It Out: Accessing the Windows 7 Help

If you are not familiar with Windows 7, the search feature within the Help and Support utility can be very useful. Follow these steps to access the tutorial:

1. Select Start ➢ Help and Support.

2. Select Learn About Windows Basics.

3. After the list loads, just click the links that interest you.

Run

The Run option enables you to run command-line utilities or to launch applications. Within Run, you can browse for files by using the Browse button. Using Run can be a faster way of launching programs or a way to launch programs that are not defined as part of the Start menu.

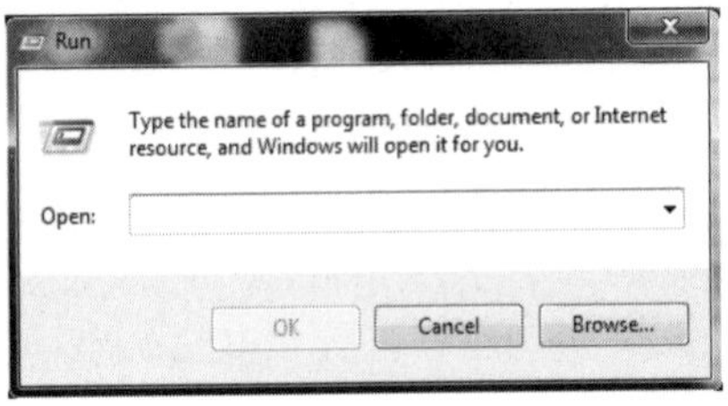

Shut Down

The Shut Down menu offers seven choices, as defined in the following table. The menu is customizable, allowing you to choose to display whichever function you prefer on the main button by right-clicking the button and selecting Properties. This brings up the Taskbar and Start Menu Properties screen. From this screen, select the Start Menu tab and use the Power Button Action drop-down menu to select the option you want displayed on the button.

Shut Down Option	Purpose
Switch User	Switches the active user without logging the current user off from the computer.
Log Off	Logs off the current user.

Shut Down Option	Purpose
Lock	Locks the computer so that only an administrator or the currently logged on user can unlock it.
Restart	Saves any changes that you have made and restarts your computer. Many changes to your computer require you to restart the computer for the changes to take effect.
Sleep	If your computer hardware supports the Sleep option, this enables you to suspend operation or put your computer in sleep mode, which conserves power. When you return your computer to a running state, you should be able to continue your work from where you left off. During sleep mode, low power is used to maintain the current state of the computer.
Hibernate	Saves the current status of your computer on the hard disk and then turns off the computer. Hibernation consumes no power but requires hard disk space to save the current state.
Shut Down	Saves any changes that you have made and prepares the computer to be turned off.

Depending on the permissions of the logged on user or the way the system has been configured, you might have fewer options than this. In addition, some of these options might not be available on all computers.

Managing the Computer's Settings: Appearance and Personalization

The main utility for managing your computer's settings is the Control Panel. Windows 7 improves ease of use for this utility by grouping common tasks logically into eight categories. While the Control Panel is in Category view, as shown in the following image, each category of tasks is displayed with some of the related common operations listed directly underneath the category heading. Clicking a category will change the view so that all of the categories are listed on the left, and all of the corresponding tasks related to the selected category display in a list format on the right. The main categories found in the Control Panel are defined in the following table. We will cover the common options for configuring your computer's appearance and themes in greater detail later in this chapter.

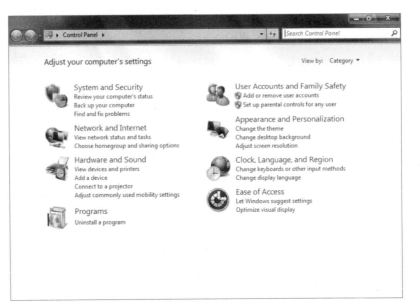

Control Panel Category	Description
System and Security	Allows you to see basic information about your computer, adjust visual effects, free up space on your hard disk, back up data, and rearrange items on your hard disk to make programs run faster. Used to manage the security aspects of the computer, including the Windows Firewall settings and the Windows Update settings.
User Accounts and Family Safety	Used to create and manage local users and group accounts and parental controls.

Control Panel Category	Description
Network and Internet	Used to configure local network or Internet options ranging from the home page to the type of connection.
Appearance and Personalization	Used to manage all personalization aspects of your computer. Used to change the computer's theme, the desktop background, colors, sound effects, and the screen saver; to manage the display; to manage the Start menu and Taskbar options; and to modify folder options and computer fonts as well as some of the ease of access options, like an onscreen keyboard. Everything used to customize Windows 7 is found here.
Hardware and Sound	Used to manage printers and faxes, game controllers, the mouse, the keyboard, phone and modem options, scanners and cameras, and wireless links. Used to display and manage audio devices as well.
Clock, Language, And Region	Used to configure the date and time and to set up support for multiple languages.
Programs	Used to view currently installed applications or to add or remove programs. Also allows the user to specify the default program settings as well as the gadgets for the desktop.
Ease of Access	Used to configure accessibility options for users with impaired vision, hearing, or mobility. Also used to configure speech recognition.

The main utility for configuring your computer's desktop is Appearance and Personalization. Having the capability to customize your desktop means that you can personalize it to suit your needs and personality. This section shows you how to change the appearance of items on your desktop. You can do any of the following:

- Change the computer's theme.
- Change the Desktop background.
- Choose whether to use a screen saver.
- Change the screen resolution.
- View and manage folder options.
- View and manage Taskbar and Start Menu options.
- Customize fonts.
- Manage Desktop gadgets.
- Configure accessibility options.

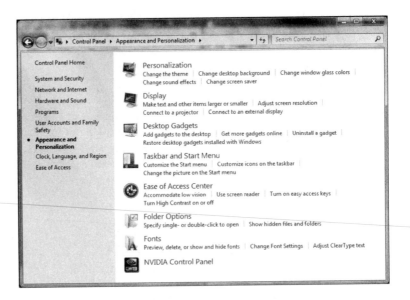

Changing Your Computer's Theme

Under Appearance and Personalization, you can click Personalization to specify the specific theme, background, sounds, icons, and other elements that allow you to customize your computer. Windows 7 comes with built-in themes to choose from; these include a collection of Aero Themes and Basic and High Contrast Themes.

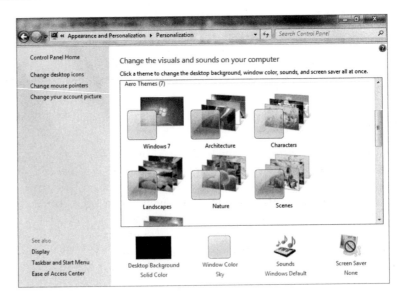

Changing Your Desktop's Background

Under Appearance and Personalization, look under Personalization and click Change Desktop Background. The drop-down list lets you specify what you want to set the desktop background to. This is what the computer displays when the user logs on. A *desktop background* is a predefined set of colors, patterns, and sometimes images that you apply to change the look of your desktop. Windows 7 has many choices available. From the drop-down list, you can specify a solid color, a picture, or more than one picture as your background. If you select more than one picture, your desktop background will be a slide show of the selected pictures. You are free to use your own pictures as well as create your own colors if the ones on the list are not to your liking.

Using a Screen Saver

The Change Screen Saver option under Personalization in Appearance and Personalization opens the Screen Saver Settings screen. This screen enables you to specify whether your computer will use a screen saver if there is no activity for a certain amount of time. The screen saver applies your choice of image or text to the screen in a continually changing, random order. (Beware, they can be addictive to watch!) Screen savers were created to prevent a chemical inside the computer screen from leaving a permanent ghost image on the display. Even though for many modern-day computer monitors this is no longer an issue, screen savers can instead be employed as effective security mechanisms. For example, screen savers can be configured to require a password to stop them before the user can access the system. The following options are configurable for screen savers:

- Which screen saver to use
- Whether you need a password to disable the screen saver
- The amount of time without any activity before the screen saver starts

Click the Change Power Settings link at the bottom of this tab to view the power plans, which are most commonly used with laptop computers. These power plans allow you to configure how the computer will react to periods of inactivity.

Changing the Screen Resolution

When you select Appearance and Personalization in the Control Panel, Display is one of the subcategories listed. By clicking the Adjust Screen Resolution option under Display, you can open the screen resolution window that allows you to configure the appearance of your various displays.

By accessing this screen, you can change the screen resolution for each recognized display, as well as manage the screen orientation and text size. You should not modify the settings without understanding what you are doing, however. Make sure you take a moment to view the new settings before you apply them. But don't worry, if you configure settings incorrectly, you are able to revert to the previous configuration. To do so, either select Revert on the Display Settings pop-up screen, or if the display is no longer being properly displayed and you cannot see the pop-up, either press Enter on the keyboard (this works because Revert is the default option), or simply wait 15 seconds and the screen will automatically revert on its own to the previous settings.

Viewing and Managing Folder Options

Choose Folder Options in the Appearance and Personalization window to open the dialog box shown here. You can specify how folder browsing behaves, how folders are displayed when they are opened, and whether you use a single click or a double click to complete specific tasks.

Viewing and Managing Taskbar and Start Menu Options

You can configure all of the Taskbar and Start Menu options by choosing Taskbar and Start Menu in the Appearance and Personalization screen. In the resulting dialog box, you use the Taskbar tab to configure options related to the Taskbar, such as whether the Taskbar is displayed and what icons appear in the Notification area (the bottom right of the Taskbar).

Use the Start Menu tab to specify which programs are displayed on the Start menu, how these programs look and behave, and how the Power Button Action is configured, as discussed previously. The final tab labeled Toolbars allows the user to select which of the available toolbars are displayed on the Taskbar. Built-in toolbars include the Address bar, the Links bar, and the Desktop bar.

Accessing the Computer Window

On the Start menu you will find a menu option called Computer. This replaces the My Computer menu option from previous Windows versions. The Computer option contains information about your computer's installed drives. From the main Computer window, you will typically see icons that represent some or all of the following:

- ◆ Diskette drives
- ◆ Logical drives (the logical disk partitions you have created, such as C:)
- ◆ CD-ROM drives
- ◆ External hard drives
- ◆ Other external devices, such as USB drives, cellphones, MP3 players, or any other devices with removable storage.

The contents of the Computer window depend on your computer's configuration. Here is a sample screen:

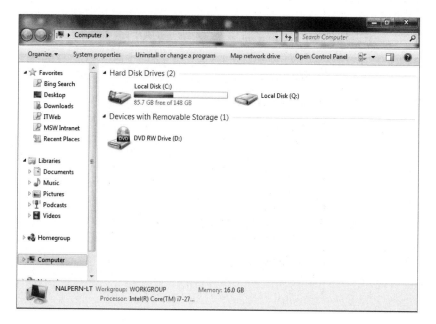

NOTE **Notice the Open Control Panel button in the top area of the window, along with other options like Uninstall or Change a Program. These options also exist in other locations as discussed in the Control Panel section of this chapter. By providing several ways to access these items, Windows 7 makes finding them easier for the user.**

By double-clicking an item within the Computer window, you can obtain more information about that item. For example, if you click a diskette drive, a logical drive, or a CD-ROM drive, you see the contents of those drives, such as folders and files. Here you can see the contents of a sample C: drive:

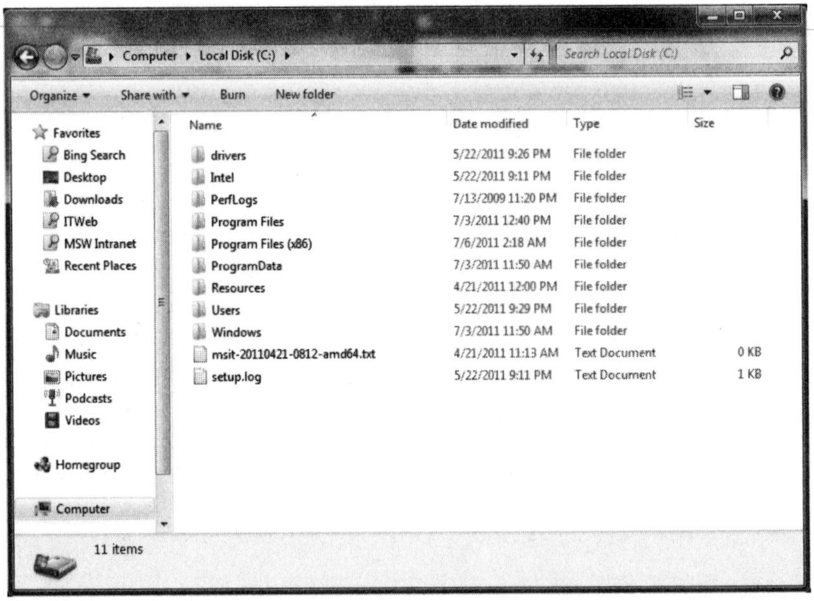

By right-clicking an item within the Computer window, you access a menu that enables you to open the item, scan it for viruses (assuming antivirus software is installed), format the drive, create a shortcut for the item, and use the Properties option to view the object's specifics.

If you choose to see Properties, you can get detailed information about capacity and also access tools such as error checking, backup, and defragmentation. The following screen shows general information about the C: drive.

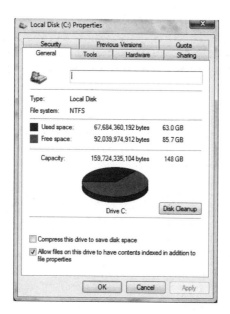

Accessing Network Resources

You access network resources through the Network and Sharing Center. You can access this utility from the Control Panel or through several different alternate methods, including through the Computer window. Once the Computer window is open, simply click Network on the left-hand side of the screen, and the Network and Sharing Center will appear at the top of the window.

Using the Network and Sharing Center, you can complete the following tasks:

◆ View your active networks and connect to or disconnect from them.

◆ Set up a new connection or network.

◆ Configure sharing of printers and files.

◆ Troubleshoot and fix network problems.

◆ Manage wireless networks.

◆ Change adapter settings.

◆ Change advanced sharing settings.

Depending on the network circumstances, each of these options allows for variations in configuration. For most users it is best for them to check with their network administrator before they make significant changes to their network properties.

Using the Recycle Bin

If you've ever thrown anything away and then pulled it out of the trash, you already know how the Recycle Bin works. When you delete files, they are placed in the Recycle Bin. You recover the files by restoring them from the Recycle Bin, typically back to their original source of deletion.

When you open the Recycle Bin, this is what you see:

◆ The names of the files that you deleted

◆ The original path where the files existed

◆ The date and time you deleted the files

◆ The type of files

◆ The size of the files

WARNING   **When you delete files from another networked computer, the files will not go to your Recycle Bin. You are actually deleting the files from the networked computer outright. You will be prompted to confirm that you want to permanently delete the files.**

Within the Recycle Bin, you can organize files, restore files, empty the Recycle Bin (at which point, you cannot recover those files), delete specific files, and see file properties.

Creating Shortcuts

Shortcuts are icons that point to any Windows 7 object—applications, files, folders, disk drives, Control Panel items, and more. You can place shortcuts on the Windows Desktop or within any folder. The main advantage of shortcuts is that they enable you to quickly access resources. You can recognize a shortcut by the small arrow in the lower-left corner of the icon.

To create a shortcut, you select an object and then choose Create Shortcut from the File menu. You can also create shortcuts by right-clicking an object and choosing Create Shortcut. After you create a shortcut, you can drag and drop it anywhere you like, for example, to the desktop.

You can also create a shortcut by right-clicking the desktop and choosing New ➤ Shortcut. This brings up the Create Shortcut wizard.

Test It Out: Creating a Shortcut

1. From an empty place on the desktop, right-click and choose New ➤ Shortcut in order to launch the Create Shortcut wizard.

2. In the Create Shortcut screen, use the Browse button to select the target object and then click Next.

3. In the Type a Name for the Shortcut dialog box, type in a customized name or accept the default name that has been selected and then click the Finish button.

4. The shortcut will appear on your desktop.

Using Wizards

*Wizard*s are built into Windows 7 to help you perform specific tasks more easily. To install a printer, for example, you simply open Devices and Printers and click Add a Printer. This starts the Add Printer wizard, which walks you through the installation by asking a series of questions.

wizard
A configuration assistant that walks the user through a short series of guided steps to complete a task.

In addition to the Printer wizard, Windows 7 has wizards for almost any common maintenance task.

Using Windows Explorer

Windows Explorer is an easy-to-use application that simplifies the task of accessing and managing folders, files, applications, and resources. Windows Explorer can be used to manage local, network, or Internet resources. From Windows Explorer, you can manage the following:

- ◆ Libraries
- ◆ Favorites including:
    - ◆ Desktop
    - ◆ Downloads
    - ◆ Recent Places
- ◆ HomeGroup
- ◆ Computer including:
    - ◆ Diskette drives
    - ◆ Logical drives
    - ◆ CD-ROM drives
- ◆ Network

You can access Windows Explorer from the Taskbar, from the Search window by entering Run, or by clicking the Start menu and then choosing All Programs and accessing the Accessories folder.

Within Windows Explorer, the left side of the dialog box shows you a hierarchical structure of all objects. The right side of the dialog box shows you details of the object that you have highlighted on the left.

Through Windows Explorer, you can manage objects by adding, deleting, or manipulating properties. You can also use drag-and-drop to copy or move objects within Windows Explorer.

If your computer is connected to a network, you can also map *network drives*, which enables you to access network resources in the same way that you access a local resource on your C: drive. You can also disconnect network drives.

Clicking on the Windows Explorer button on the Taskbar or running it from the Start menu will bring up a window like the one shown here. Clicking an item you wish to examine further will allow you to navigate around your computer.

network drive
A mapping to a network path that appears to the user as a drive letter. You access it the same way that you access a local drive.

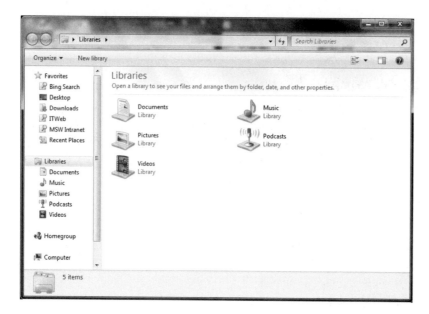

Traditionally in Windows operating systems, a handful of folders were pre-created with the intention of encouraging users to utilize them to organize content. The folder names are self-explanatory and ideally a user would store their files types in the folder with the corresponding name. So for instance, picture files in the Pictures folder, and documents and files in the Documents folder and so on. These folders were indexed by the system to allow for faster searching. However, one short fall of these folders was their static nature.

Each folder was only ever capable of displaying a static view of its contents and subfolders. Since users frequently store content in additional places on their machine—the Desktop for instance—this limited usability. The chances of the Pictures folder truly containing all the picture files on the machine were remote. The reality was that unless a user was diligent about the usage of the various built-in folders ensuring to place all folders of that type in the folder at best the folder would render a partial view of the document type.

To address this, Windows 7 introduces a feature called Libraries. Libraries are intended to give users additional organizational control of their information while making it easier than ever to find data files and content. They take the concept of well-known built-in folders such as Documents and Pictures and enhance their functionality by making them dynamic. Instead of the folders containing a static set of contents, the default Libraries instead render a view.

There are four default Libraries:

- Documents
- Music
- Pictures
- Videos

When accessed by a user, each Library will show the combined contents of two locations by default. The two locations are corresponding folders within the user's profile as well as folders within the public profile path. So for instance, when viewing the Music library the view rendered will include all files from the My Music folder in a user's profile path as well as all files from the Public Music folder in the Public profile path.

Libraries are very customizable and have multiple options available for configuration. One such option is the ability to choose a default save location. When a Library is chosen as the target save path for a file, the default save location provides the system information about where to save the data on the hard drive. Since Libraries are simply views and typically consist of multiple file paths the system must understand which folder within the Library to use to place the on file on the hard disk.

Additional folders can be included within existing Libraries at any time so that the data within the additional folder is then included in the view. Libraries can be optimized for particular file types, such as pictures, videos, or documents. This optimization serves to control the options for arranging the files within the Library.

Terms to Know

command-line   network drive

Internet Explorer   wizard

Review Questions

1. Which item on the Windows Desktop enables you to recover files that you have deleted?

2. Which item in Windows 7 allows you to connect to Internet resources?

3. Which item on the Start menu enables you to access disk resources?

4. Which item on the Windows Desktop enables you to see which applications are running?

5. Which item on the Windows Desktop provides a starting point for accessing almost anything in Windows 7?

6. You go to Start ➤ _____ to see the printers installed on the machine.

7. How can you configure Start and Taskbar properties from the Start menu?

8. Through Start ➤ _____, you can access Help information.

9. What are three of the Shut Down Menu options?

10. True or false: You can access the Control Panel program from Computer, Windows Explorer, and Start ➤ Settings.

11. What is the advantage of using shortcuts?

12. What is a wizard?

Chapter 8

A Communications Framework

In This Chapter

- The need for a standard communications model
- The flow of data in the model
- The seven layers of the OSI model

com•mu•ni•ca•tion *n* : the transfer of information between two or more people or devices over a medium

Communication occurs all around us in many forms. Usually, when communication happens, it is between two things that can easily understand each other. For example, two people in the same country who speak the same language can communicate with little or no problem. The same can be said for species of birds. They understand each other. But not everyone speaks the same language, and there are thousands of types of birds. Needless to say, life and work can get difficult when communication breaks down.

Communication between computers can be challenging. Many types of computers can communicate in any number of forms. Making them able to talk to one another and understand the information being passed is a whole other challenge. The Open Systems Interconnection (OSI) model sets a standard that, when followed, helps make communication between devices work.

Understanding OSI Model Basics

network
Two or more computers connected for the purpose of sharing resources such as files or printers.

protocol
A set of rules for communication between two devices.

standard
An agreed-upon set of rules, procedures, and functions that are widely accepted.

International Standards Organization (ISO)
An organization dedicated to defining global communication and informational exchange standards. The American National Standards Institute (ANSI) is the American representative to the ISO.

The *International Standards Organization (ISO)* began developing the OSI model in 1974 and finally adopted the model in 1977. The OSI model is the basis for nearly all networking devices today. It is a theoretical multilayer model that defines how *networks* are built and how they function from the ground up. When you understand the OSI model, you can develop a better understanding of networking *protocols* and *standards*. Even though networks may be implemented differently, they are all based on the same or a similar reference model. The OSI model defines seven layers and includes a description of the function and the data flow within each layer.

Data moves both up and down through the seven layers of the OSI model, and the layers are always passed through in the same order. For instance, the smallest unit of data may begin at the Application layer, which is the highest layer in the model. As data moves down the OSI model, more information is added at each layer to enable network communication to take place. At the receiving computer, the data enters the system at the bottom-most layer and then makes its way up the layers; during this process components are stripped off at corresponding layers, called peer layers. The process is then reversed for the reply.

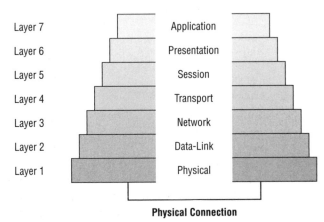

Layer 7	Application
Layer 6	Presentation
Layer 5	Session
Layer 4	Transport
Layer 3	Network
Layer 2	Data-Link
Layer 1	Physical

Physical Connection

Using this type of model has three main advantages:

♦ It breaks down a large concept such as a network into smaller parts (in this case, layers), which makes it easier to understand.

♦ It compartmentalizes network functions, which enables you to easily replace specific technologies without having to replace the entire network.

♦ Devices that are built around a common model should work together, or interoperate, regardless of the manufacturer that built the device.

The seven layers of the OSI model and their functions are displayed in the following table:

OSI Layer	Function	Example of Layer Function
Layer 7: Application	Supports the communication of applications with the network.	Examples of Application layer services include sending and receiving messages and transferring files.
Layer 6: Presentation	Formats and translates data.	An example of a Presentation layer service is the compression or *encryption* of data.
Layer 5: Session	Manages communication sessions between service requesters and service providers. This layer manages communications by establishing, synchronizing, and maintaining the connection between sender and receiver.	At the Session layer, a web server may close the session with a user after a specified period of time has elapsed without activity.
Layer 4: Transport	Is usually associated with reliable end-to-end communication. It is the layer responsible for managing connections, *error control*, and *flow control* between sender and receiver.	When part of a web page does not download due to heavy traffic, the Transport layer will resend the missing data.
Layer 3: Network	Moves *packets* over an *internetwork* so that they can be routed to the correct network.	The IP address of a device is used on the Internet to determine the route that information travels to get to the correct sender and receiver.
Layer 2: Data-Link	Includes information about the source and destination hardware addresses of the communicating devices. It also specifies lower-layer flow control and error control.	Devices that use Data-Link layer protocols are network cards and *bridges*.
Layer 1: Physical	Transmits data over a physical medium.	Cables and physical connection specifications are defined at the Physical layer.

encryption
The process of encoding data to prevent unauthorized access.

error control
A mechanism for assuring that data received is in the same condition and format in which it was sent.

flow control
A feature of the Transport layer that manages the amount of data being transmitted between sender and receiver. If the receiving computer is unable to accept more data, it tells the sending computer to pause transmission.

packet
Data that has been encapsulated with information from the Transport and Network layers of the OSI model.

internetwork
Two or more networks that are connected by using a router.

bridge
A Data-Link layer device that enables networks using different Layer 2 protocols to communicate with one another. A bridge can also minimize traffic between two networks by passing through only those packets that are addressed to the other network.

frame
Data that has been encapsulated by the Data-Link layer protocol before being transmitted on the wire.

Data Transfer in the OSI Model

When communication occurs between two computers on different networks, data is transferred across the networks through *routers*.

Assume you have a file that you want to send from computer A to computer B. Many steps must occur:

routers

Devices that connect two or more networks. Routers work at the Network layer of the OSI model, receiving packets and forwarding them to their correct destination.

1. The user on computer A creates an email message using his or her favorite email program. The email program supports specific network services that pertain to sending and receiving email. The services that enable the email program to communicate with email servers are all part of the Application layer.

2. The next step is to translate the message into a language that is common to both computers. As humans, we see "hello," but each computer wants to see the message in a format that it can interpret. The Presentation layer translates "hello" into ASCII code, which is internationally recognized as 96 numbers and letters and 32 nonprinting characters. The computer can then convert the ASCII code into ones and zeros, which is understood by both computers.

3. At the next layer of communication, the Session layer, a connection, or session, is established and maintained. This connection determines when requests are made so that appropriate responses can be returned. Just like human conversations, computer communications are usually a series of requests and responses that must be answered sequentially.

connection-oriented

A method of communication that is considered reliable because the sender is notified when data is not received or is unrecognizable.

4. If you want to make sure that the connection is reliable (similar to when you send a letter with a return receipt to confirm that it was received as opposed to a letter you send via regular mail), you might use *connection-oriented* services that guarantee reliable delivery. These services exist at the Transport layer.

5. In this example, computer A and computer B are on different networks. The Network layer routes the packets to the correct network by identifying network addresses and calculating the best route the packet should take.

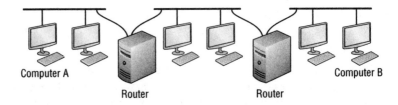

Computer A   Computer B

Router   Router

6. After the data gets to the correct network, it must be delivered to the correct computer (sometimes called a *node*) on the network. On an Ethernet network, the packet is sent out on the network. Each computer receives the packet and reads the physical address—called the *Media Access Control (MAC) address*—to determine who the packet is intended for. The computer with the matching physical address accepts the packet and all other computers disregard the packet. Physical layer addressing occurs at the Data-Link layer of the OSI model.

7. The only physical connection that exists between the two computers is defined at the Physical layer of the OSI model. Network cables, connectors, and the hardware portion of the NIC (rather than the software) are all part of the Physical layer specification.

node
A connection point on a network. Nodes include computers, servers, and printers.

Media Access Control (MAC) address
A hexadecimal number that is allocated by an international organization and is burned into the network interface card (NIC) by the NIC manufacturer. MAC is a sublayer of the Data-Link layer.

Here are two mnemonic devices to help you remember the seven layers:

Layer	Memory Trick (Top to Bottom)	Memory Trick (Bottom to Top)
Application	All	Away
Presentation	People	Pizza
Session	Seem	Sausage
Transport	To	Throw
Network	Need	Not
Data-Link	Data	Do
Physical	Processing	Please

Layer 1: The Physical Layer

When you get down to the nitty-gritty details of putting the ones and zeros onto a cable, you are dealing with the Physical layer.

The Physical layer of the OSI model determines

♦ The physical network structure you will use.

♦ The mechanical and electrical specifications of the transmission media that will be used.

♦ How data will be encoded and transmitted. There are all kinds of schemes used for encoding data that specify how the ones and zeros will be transmitted. For example, Ethernet networks use a scheme called *Manchester encoding*.

The following graphic illustrates devices in the Physical layer (including an RJ-45, which is used in most environments for connecting computers to the network).

Manchester encoding
A method of identifying the beginning and end of a bit signal (one or zero) when it is transmitted on the network.

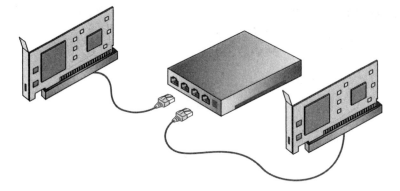

NOTE   Topologies, Ethernet, and Token Ring are covered in greater detail in Chapter 10, "Data-Link and Network Layer Protocols."

Physical Layer Technologies

The category of technologies that the Physical layer defines includes the following:

Connection type   Connections can be point-to-point or multipoint. Point-to-point assumes that only two devices are connected. Multipoint means that three or more devices are connected.

Physical topology   Topologies define the physical layout of the network. Common topologies include star, bus, ring, and mesh.

Type of signal   Signals can be analog or digital. Local computer networks use digital signals, and the public telephone system uses analog signals.

Type of bit synchronization   You can send data by asynchronous or synchronous means. *Asynchronous communication* requires less expensive equipment but is less efficient when transferring large blocks of data. The data is sent without timing being considered between the sender and the receiver. The data can flow intermittently between the two parties over a set period of time. When a file is being downloaded, asynchronous transfer can occur without a negative impact on the transmission potentially resulting in data loss. *Synchronous communication* requires more expensive equipment but provides better efficiency. Before data is transmitted, the two parties involved will synchronize on timing and the data is transmitted in a steady stream instead of intermittently as with asynchronous transfers. Technologies that are time sensitive, such as video streaming, are best served with synchronous communications.

Transmission signaling technology   You can use *baseband* technology, which is the signaling type used on Ethernet networks, or *broadband* signaling, which is used in cable and DSL networks.

asynchronous communication
Begins transmission of each character with a start bit and ends transmission of each character with a stop bit. This method is not as efficient as synchronous communication but is less expensive.

synchronous communication
Transmits data by synchronizing the data signal between the sender and receiver and sending data as a continuous stream. This is the most efficient way to send large amounts of data but requires expensive equipment.

baseband
A technology that permits a single transmission of data at a fixed frequency on a wire at any given moment.

broadband
A type of transmission that can use a single wire to transmit multiple streams of data simultaneously using different frequencies. This method is similar to the method used by radio stations all sharing the airwaves to send their signals.

Physical Layer Hardware

Here are examples of Physical layer hardware:

- Network interface cards
- Network cables
- *Hubs* (also referred to as concentrators)
- *Repeaters*
- Modems
- ISDN adapters

At the Physical layer, data is referred to as bits.

Layer 2: The Data-Link Layer

The Data-Link layer of the OSI model has three primary responsibilities:

- Establishing and maintaining the communication channel
- Identifying computers on the network by physical address
- Organizing the data into a logical group called a *frame*

Establishing and maintaining the communication channel is low-level work. At the Data-Link layer, it just means confirming that a data channel exists and that it is open. At the Session layer, there is higher-level communication management.

Each computer on the network is identified with a unique physical address, the MAC address. On Ethernet and *Token Ring* cards, this is a 6-byte *hexadecimal* address that is burned into an EPROM chip on the network card. This address uniquely identifies computers when you send data from a source to a destination. Both the source MAC address and the destination MAC address are added to data as it passes through this layer of the OSI model.

Data is logically grouped into a frame at the Data-Link layer. A frame logically organizes the bits from the Physical layer. Here is an example of a frame:

Start	Destination address	Source address	LLC header	Data	CRC	End

Frame Description

In the preceding frame

- The Start field identifies the beginning of the frame. This might be 10101010.
- The destination address is the MAC address of the computer to which the frame is being sent.

hub
A Physical layer device that connects computers and other devices to make a network. A hub regenerates an incoming signal from one device and broadcasts the signal out all other ports.

repeater
A network device, similar to a hub but with only two or three ports, that can be used to extend the transmission distance of a network signal or to join two networks.

— *NOTE* —

Token Ring
A Data-Link layer protocol developed by IBM that uses a token-passing method for transmitting data. Each device on the ring takes turns using the token. The token can be used by only one device at a time.

hexadecimal
A numbering system that uses 16 instead of 10 as its base; it uses the digits 0–9 and the letters A–F to represent the decimal numbers 0–15.

- The source address is the MAC address of the computer from which the frame is being sent.
- The *Logical Link Control (LLC)* header manages the LLC connection.
- The Data field contains the data from the upper-layer protocols.
- The *cyclic redundancy check (CRC)* is used for low-level error control. For instance, it may be used to ensure that the connection is valid.
- The End field indicates that this is the last field of the current frame.

Logical Link Control (LLC)
A Data-Link sublayer that establishes whether communication with another device is going to be connectionless or connection oriented.

cyclic redundancy check (CRC)
A form of error detection that performs a mathematical calculation on data at both the sender's end and the receiver's end to ensure that the data is received reliably.

Sublayers of Data-Link

The Data-Link layer has two sublayers:

- The LLC sublayer
- The MAC sublayer

The LLC sublayer provides the upper layers with access to the physical hardware at the lower layers, and the MAC sublayer is used for physical addressing as described earlier.

NOTE   **Data is referred to as a frame at the Data-Link layer.**

Data-Link Layer Devices

Here are examples of Data-Link layer devices:

- Bridges
- *Managed hubs*
- *Switches*
- Network interface cards

managed hubs
Similar to hubs except the device can be managed using software to monitor and control network communication.

switch
The modern name used for a multiport bridge. Like a regular bridge, each port on a switch represents a separate network. Traffic on each port is kept isolated except when the packet is destined for another device on a different port or if the packet is a broadcast. Broadcasts must be sent out all ports.

Layer 3: The Network Layer

The primary responsibility of the Network layer is to move data over an internetwork. This is called routing.

At the Data-Link layer, addressing is physical. At the Network layer, addressing is logical. The Internet Protocol (IP) resides at this layer and is used to perform the logical addressing. Each network must have a unique network address. This address routes packets to the correct network.

The main functions of the Network layer are to

◆ Logically define networks based on unique network addresses.

◆ Determine how packets should be delivered based on current routing information. A route, or path, to a destination network can be created in several ways. The path can be manually entered by the network administrator; the path can be learned from other routers; or the path can be a default route, which means that the router relies on the next router to determine the best path.

◆ Provide network-level connection services.

Sending data through the Network layer is considered to be a connectionless service. This is like sending a letter through the regular mail. You drop the mail in a postal box and assume that it will reach its destination. The Network layer is similar in that you send a packet and assume that it will reach its destination. This layer depends on other layers in the OSI model, such as the Transport layer, to provide connection-oriented services.

Network Layer Example

Refer to the example network shown momentarily; assume that you want to send a packet from computer A to computer B. These steps will occur:

1. Each router contains *routing tables* that define the best path to all known networks. The first packet leaves computer A and is destined for computer B.

2. The packet first reaches the New York router. That router compares the destination IP address of the packet to its routing table.

3. The New York router determines that it must send the packet to the L.A. router to reach computer B. Each pass through an external router, not the New York router, is considered a *hop*.

4. The L.A. router determines the shortest path to computer B is through the Seattle router. The packet is sent on its way.

5. Seattle performs the same process as the preceding routers and sends the packet onto computer B's network, where computer B receives it.

Data is referred to as datagrams or packets at the Network layer.

routing table

A table created by a router that contains information on how to reach networks that are directly attached to the router and networks that are distant.

hop

A foreign gateway (router other than your own) that a packet must pass through between the source and destination computers.

NOTE

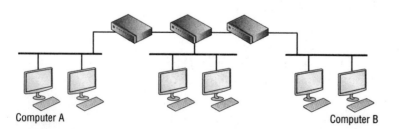

Computer A   Computer B

Layer 4: The Transport Layer

There are two mechanisms for sending data through the Transport layer: connection-oriented transmission and connectionless transmission.

Connection-oriented transmission

- Is reliable
- Involves more overhead, so is slower and less efficient
- Can provide guaranteed file transfer

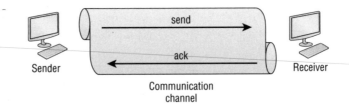

Connectionless transmission

- Is less reliable
- Involves less overhead, so is faster and more efficient
- Does not resend packets

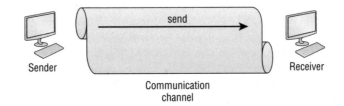

The Transport layer of the OSI model is most commonly associated with reliable, or connection-oriented delivery. With reliable delivery, the sender and receiver establish a connection, and the receiver acknowledges receipt of the data by sending an acknowledgment (ACK) packet to the sender. The protocol that exists at the Transport layer that is responsible for this behavior is called the Transmission Control Protocol (TCP).

Reliable delivery is a concept that can be applied to the telephone system. You place a call to a friend hoping that they answer. When they answer, you begin a conversation. If everything is going well, you will each take turns talking. But if the connection is bad, you may not hear a question that was asked. In that case, your friend, having not received an answer, would ask you again.

Connectionless transmissions are also possible, though they are less common in software today compared to TCP's connection-oriented transmissions. The Transport layer protocol, User Datagram Protocol (UDP), is responsible for connectionless transmissions.

Other Transport Layer Functions

Data moves down the layers of the OSI model in large chunks. After data reaches the Transport layer, it is segmented into smaller units that do not exceed the maximum packet length specified by the network in use. The Transport layer is responsible for dividing and then reassembling the data back into the original order at the receiver's end.

The Transport layer is capable of performing some error control. If a particular unit of data does not arrive at the receiver's end, the Transport layer can request that the missing data be retransmitted.

This layer of the OSI model also performs some flow control. The sender and receiver determine how much data can be sent before an acknowledgment is required.

Data at the Transport layer is referred to as a datagram, segment, or packet.

NOTE

Network and Transport Layer Technologies

The Network and Transport layers of the OSI model work closely together. Many protocol suites function across these layers. Here are two:

TCP/IP The leading industry protocol for the Internet. TCP/IP consists of a suite of protocols that function together. The two primary protocols are the Transmission Control Protocol (TCP), which functions at the Transport layer, and the Internet Protocol (IP), which functions at the Network layer. Additional protocols include the User Datagram Protocol (UDP), the Address Resolution Protocol (ARP), and the Internet Control Message Protocol (ICMP).

IPX/SPX A proprietary protocol developed by Novell for their NetWare software. With Internetwork Packet Exchange/Sequenced Packet Exchange (IPX/SPX), IPX functions primarily at the Network layer, and SPX functions at the Transport layer. This protocol is rarely used in network environments today.

Layer 5: The Session Layer

The Session layer of the OSI model is responsible for managing communications between a sender and a receiver. Here are some of the communication tasks performed at this layer:

- ◆ Establishing connections
- ◆ Maintaining connections

- ◆ Synchronizing communication
- ◆ Controlling dialog
- ◆ Terminating connections

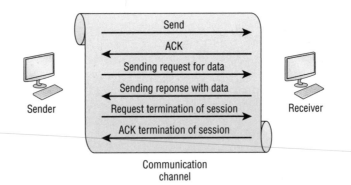

Communication
channel

Creating a Connection

Creating a connection requires

- ◆ Authenticating through a username and password that are valid on the receiving computer
- ◆ Determining which computer will be the sender, which will be the receiver, and which will send first
- ◆ Figuring out which type of communication will take place
- ◆ Specifying which lower-layer protocols will be used for transmission

Transferring Data and Using Dialog Control

dialog control

Manages the dialog between the sender and receiver. This consists of managing the transfer of data, determining whether an acknowledgment is required, and determining the appropriate responses to the sender.

Data transfer and *dialog control* consist of

- ◆ The actual transfer of data
- ◆ Any acknowledgments that are needed
- ◆ Responses to requests that the sender or the receiver makes

There are three types of dialog control at the Session layer:

Simplex communication Specifies that communication is one-way only. Simplex is more common in less complex systems for which two-way communication is not necessary.

Half-duplex communication Specifies that communication can be two-way but only one channel can communicate at a time. Most computer networks can communicate in half-duplex mode.

Full-duplex communication   Specifies that communication can be two-way simultaneously. This is a valuable function found in many network devices. Full-duplex is typically implemented with computers for improved performance.

Terminating a Connection

After the session is complete, the connection is terminated. This enables other devices to open new sessions. Sometimes termination of the connection will come from the receiver. Other times the sender will terminate the session if it does not hear back from the receiver within a specified time.

Layer 6: The Presentation Layer

The Presentation layer of the OSI model is responsible for

◆ Character code translation

◆ Data encryption

◆ Data compression and expansion

Character Code Translation

People understand symbolic characters; for example, "hello." Computers do not understand human vocabulary and instead understand data as a series of ones and zeros (binary code). In order to communicate, there must be some translation. This process occurs at the Presentation layer of the OSI model through character code translation. Examples of character codes include

◆ American Standard Code for Information Interchange (ASCII)

◆ *Extended Binary Coded Decimal Interchange Code (EBCDIC)*

Extended Binary Coded Decimal Interchange Code (EBCDIC)
The 8-bit character set used by IBM mainframes.

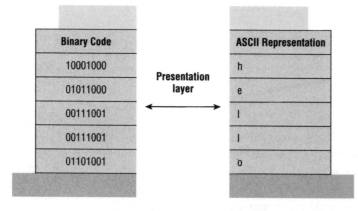

After data moves from the Application to the Presentation layer, it must be converted from its original form to a format that will be understood by the receiving device. As noted earlier, this format may be in ASCII or it may be in EBCDIC. The data may also need to be encrypted or compressed before it is passed on to the Session layer.

Data Encryption

Data encryption is the process of encoding data so that it is protected from unauthorized access. Some of the methods used to encrypt data include these:

◆ Transposing information within the data.

◆ Substituting one character for another. (Think of this as the secret code you used when you were a kid.)

◆ Scrambling the data with mathematical calculations that the sender and the receiver determine. This is the most secure encryption method and is the most complex. Almost all Internet sites that have security use this method.

Data Compression and Expansion

Data compression occurs at the sender's end and compacts the data so that it can be sent more efficiently.

Data expansion, or decompression, occurs at the receiver's end when the data is returned to its original format.

NOTE

There are many encryption methods that can be implemented at the Presentation layer. Some encryption methods are easily broken using available software.

Layer 7: The Application Layer

The Application layer of the OSI model is the highest layer and it supports primarily user facing services including these:

File services   Store, move, control access to, and retrieve files

Print services   Send data to local or networked printers

Message services   Transfer text, graphics, audio, and video over a network

Application services   Process applications locally or through *distributed processing*

Database services   Use the local computer to access a network server for database storage and retrieval functions.

distributed processing
Sharing the task of processing instructions between a server and a client CPU.

NOTE

Applications such as Microsoft Word and Excel do not directly interface with the Application layer of the OSI model. However, the Application layer provides those applications with underlying services, such as file and print services.

In addition, the Application layer of the OSI model advertises any services that are being offered and determines whether requests made by the client should be serviced locally or remotely.

Service Advertisement

Service advertisement means that the computer is making its resources available over the network. For example, any Microsoft Windows Workstation or Server computer running the server service can be configured to automatically advertise any file or print resources that it is sharing.

Service Processing

Service processing determines whether a request should be processed locally or remotely.

Assume, as an example, that you have two computers: computer A and computer B. If computer A makes a request to its local hard drive, the I/O manager (which handles all input and output) will direct the request to be handled locally. If the computer makes a network request—in this case, computer A is using the drive letter F to represent a shared folder on computer B—the I/O manager will process the request and redirect it to the network.

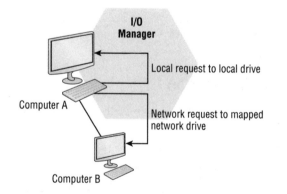

At the Application layer of the OSI model, data is referred to as a message or simply data.

NOTE

Terms to Know

asynchronous communication	ISO
baseband	LLC
bridge	MAC address
broadband	managed hubs
connection-oriented	Manchester encoding
CRC	network
dialog control	node
distributed processing	packet
EBCDIC	protocol
encryption	repeater
error control	routers
flow control	routing table
frame	standard
hexadecimal	switch
hop	synchronous communication
hub	Token Ring
internetwork	

Review Questions

1. List the two main advantages of the OSI model.

2. Which layer of the OSI model is responsible for establishing, maintaining, and synchronizing the data connection?

3. Which layer of the OSI model is responsible for identifying the source and destination hardware addresses and organizing bits into frames?

4. Which layer of the OSI model is responsible for file and print services and determines whether a service request should be processed locally or routed to the network?

5. Which layer of the OSI model is responsible for moving data over an internetwork?

6. Which layer of the OSI model is responsible for moving bits over physical media?

7. Which layer of the OSI model is responsible for formatting and translating data?

8. Which layer of the OSI model is responsible for reliable delivery of data, management of connections, error control, and flow control?

9. What are the two sublayers of the Data-Link layer?

10. Which device routes packets between two networks at the Network layer of the OSI model?

11. What is the difference between connection-oriented services and connectionless services? Which is more reliable? Which is more efficient?

12. What is the difference between a physical address and a network address?

13. List the seven layers of the OSI model from bottom to top.

Chapter 9

Network Models

In This Chapter
◆ Peer-to-peer
◆ Client-server, including the directory services model

mod•el *n* : a description or representation of a system

An architect who designs a building has to consider the kind of structure that is needed. The design of a skyscraper, for example, reflects a very different model than a warehouse. There are different tools, systems, and uses for each design. Computer networks also have various models that are used to suit specific scenarios.

When designing a network, you can choose from several network models. Some things you should consider when choosing a network model include the size of the network, the number of users you will support, and the network operating system you will use. This chapter provides an overview of two common network models.

Considering Peer-to-Peer Networks

You might be familiar with the following scenario. A small office has a couple of computers that are not connected to one another. Everyone is used to using USB drives to transfer files, and each person has to use his or her own printer or email the file to another person so he or she can print it. Now, the small company isn't so small anymore; it has 10 employees who each have a computer. The cost of supplying everyone with a printer would be expensive, and physically moving the files between machines using USB drives or sending them via email to print is slowing productivity. The company is ready for a better solution.

As you might have guessed, a *peer-to-peer network* is one solution. As a network model, peer-to-peer is an excellent choice for this budding company because it enables users to share resources from their computers. Resources can include files, printers, and Internet connections. More than anything else, peer-to-peer networks offer a cost-effective solution that does not require significant expertise, management, or support.

peer-to-peer network
This type of network does not use dedicated network servers for logging in users or providing secure access to network resources. Instead, clients simply share resources, and other clients have access to whatever has been shared.

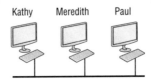

As you can see in this graphic, a peer-to-peer network does not require a dedicated computer called a server. Instead, each user can share resources on his or her computer. From a management standpoint, each user carries some of the responsibility for networking. If Paul needs access to a file on Meredith's computer, Meredith must share the folder that contains the file. Also, Meredith's computer will have the added responsibility of performing tasks that Paul's computer requests, such as transferring files. This transfer could happen at the same time that Meredith is using her computer to print a document. In other words, a user sitting at a computer, called a network *client*, can share network resources while also accessing local resources, such as the hard drive for running local applications.

client
A computer on the network that requests network services.

Even though setup and usage is simple, the tradeoff in this configuration is a sacrifice in security. Since each computer is responsible for regulating the security of its own resources, security is distributed and more loosely controlled. Resource access is completely unregulated; anyone on the network may have full access. Even though each user may need to use a username and password to access a specific resource, these usernames are often shared and the passwords are infrequently changed. Keep in mind that in a peer-to-peer configuration, all the users on the network are peers and ideally each should have equal privileges and equal power. They are meant to work this way without any sort of centralized control or regulation.

When Appropriate

Typically, you use the peer-to-peer network model in small workgroups of 10 or fewer people. Larger peer-to-peer networks become difficult to manage and support. In addition, all versions of Windows 7 are limited to 20 or fewer users accessing one computer from the network at the same time. The peer-to-peer model is well suited to organizations that need a cost-effective solution for fulfilling basic networking needs, such as file and print sharing.

Here are some advantages to choosing a peer-to-peer network:

♦ It is easy to set up because it is designed for a small network.

♦ Administration is maintained by each user (so that a dedicated administrator is not required).

♦ It does not require dedicated server hardware and software.

♦ Peer-to-peer networking software is built into all popular operating system software.

♦ If one computer goes down, this doesn't affect the files on a different computer.

There are also some disadvantages:

♦ This model does not work well with a large number of users.

♦ Security is poor because each individual is responsible for assigning and maintaining the shared resources. These responsibilities range from assigning passwords to actually properly sharing the files.

♦ Because network resources are dispersed, backup of critical data is irregular.

Common OS Examples

Most commonly used operating systems today support peer-to-peer networking. Examples of operating systems that are commonly used with peer-to-peer networks include these:

♦ Windows XP, Windows Vista, Windows 7

♦ Apple Macintosh OS

Viewing Network Configurations for Windows 7 Computers

Windows 7 is primarily designed to act as a client desktop operating system. These types of operating systems are covered in Chapter 5, "Desktop Operating Systems: A Comparison."

However, in addition to providing client support, Windows 7, as well as previous versions of Windows, includes extensive network support. If the network consists exclusively of desktop operating systems such as Windows XP, Windows Vista, and Windows 7 computers, the network is typically a peer-to-peer type. If a machine is functioning as a dedicated server, each of the other Windows computers functions as a *workstation* within the client-server network. Or more typically, in a corporate environment, they are a part of a directory services model. In any configuration, network support enables the Windows computers to use network resources or provide network resources through file and print sharing.

The way a Windows 7 machine is configured to participate in a network will depend on the makeup of the rest of the computers that are going to belong to the network. If all the computers on the network are running Windows 7, then a homegroup is a convenient and simple-to-configure choice. If the network contains computers running multiple versions of Windows, then it is best to use a workgroup. It is important to make sure that all computers are using the same workgroup name as this is an easy-to-miss mistake.

This section details how to view and configure a Windows 7 computer for networking. It serves as an example of an operating system configured for a peer-to-peer network.

When you set up a Windows 7 computer, you can specify whether to install the networking components. You configure a Windows 7 computer for networking through Control Panel ➤ Network and Internet.

When you access Network and Internet, you can manage your connections through the following components:

workstation
Another name for a computer that is used by users. This term is sometimes used to describe powerful computers that are used for completing complex mathematical, engineering, and animation tasks.

Network and Sharing Center   View your network status, connect to a network, view network computers and devices, or add a wireless network.

HomeGroup   Connect to a homegroup or create a homegroup. It is from here that you can manage your homegroup and change its settings. Using homegroups is a quick and easy way to create a peer-to-peer network if all the computers are running Windows 7. Depending on the edition of Windows 7 being run, there are limitations on the available actions. Windows 7 Basic and Windows 7 Starter can only join a homegroup but not create one.

Internet Options   Manage your Internet browsing options by changing your homepage, managing browser add-ons, deleting cookies or history, as well as using many other Internet-specific settings.

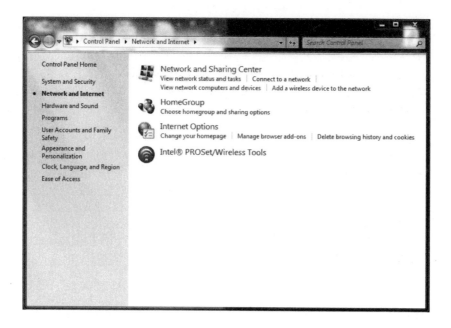

Configuring Local Area Connection Properties

To configure network components, select Start ➤ Control Panel ➤ Network
and Internet, then choose the Network and Sharing Center, and then from the
left pane, choose Change Adapter Settings. This option allows you to view and
select your Local Area Connection in order to manipulate its properties.

The resulting dialog box contains two tabs: Networking and Sharing. The Sharing tab is utilized to enable and manage Internet Connection Sharing. This topic is beyond the scope of this book. On the Networking tab, click the Configure button to view the current configuration of your network adapter, its status, and whether it is working properly.

Also on the Networking tab, under This Connection Uses the Following Items, you can see the network components that are installed by default when you install a computer for networking: the Client for Microsoft Networks (which allows your computer to access network services), the Quality of Service (QoS) Packet Scheduler, and File and Printer Sharing for Microsoft Networks, which provides network services by allowing your computer's files and printers to be shared. In addition this list includes The Internet Protocol Version 6 (TCP/IPv6) component, which is installed by default when you install Windows 7. The Internet Protocol Version 4 (TCP/IPv4) component is also installed by default and is the option you are most likely to configure. All computers on a network must be configured with compatible TCP/IP configurations.

Identifying the Computer

Another important part of a computer's network configuration is identifying the computer. If the computer is configured through one of the network setup wizards, this identification step is a part of the wizard. If you use manual configuration, you can specify identification by clicking Start, right-clicking on the Computer and selecting Properties; then scroll down to the Computer Name, Domain, and Workgroup Settings and click the Change Settings options to view the Computer Name tab of System Properties.

On this tab, you can specify a computer description, which is for informational purposes and can contain any text you want. This tab also displays the name of the computer and the domain or workgroup it is a part of. The computer name must be unique to all other computer names on the network. By clicking the Change button, you can change your computer's name and specify what workgroup or domain the computer should be a part of.

Considering Client-Server Networks

As the number of users grows, the peer-to-peer network model loses its value and eventually becomes unfeasible. Also, large or growing companies might have different needs than a small company has. They might need to support hundreds of users or create a centralized order processing system that can be accessed by retail stores and on the Internet. Such needs require a powerful and flexible model.

The *client-server network* was designed specifically to meet the complex and challenging needs of larger organizations. The name *client-server* originates from a design that requires some tasks to be completed by the user's workstation and other tasks to be processed centrally on a server. As an example of a client-server model, consider a user accessing a site on the Internet.

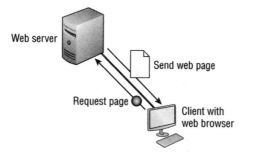

Web server

Send web page

Request page

Client with web browser

client-server network
Uses a dedicated server to centralize user and group account management. Users at a client, or workstation, log on to a server where they have user accounts and access resources on the server to which their user account has permission.

In this graphic, a user at a workstation opens a web browser. The web browser is the client application. The user enters the URL of a website into the browser, which then makes a request to the web server for that site. The server sends the page with all its *Hypertext Markup Language (HTML)* code. Now that the server has completed its job, the client application is responsible for converting the HTML into a web page.

When Appropriate

Deciding between a peer-to-peer model and a client-server model is not as difficult as it may seem. First, the client-server model can be recommended to companies of all sizes and should be the first choice when there are 15 or more

Hypertext Markup Language (HTML)
A text-based scripting language that is used in the creation of web pages to control the presentation of text and graphics. It can also be used to add functionality to the web page for navigation or for interfacing with other technologies like databases and multimedia.

users. Second, you should consider potential growth. You might be a company of 10 people now, but plans might include increasing personnel to 20 or more in a short time. Planning for that growth can have a significant effect on cost savings and user productivity. Finally, certain application needs, especially those involving the Internet, require a client-server model. Common applications for centralizing resources include messaging (for example, email), file and print sharing, databases, and voice services.

The client-server network offers several key advantages:

◆ Administration is centralized.

◆ This model provides centralization of resources for easier backups.

◆ Multiple levels of network security exist through management of usernames and passwords and through controlled access to network resources.

◆ The network offers performance and reliability that can grow as demand grows.

However, the client-server model has some drawbacks:

◆ A dedicated server or multiple servers are normally required.

◆ It requires a more experienced administrator to install and manage the network than the peer-to-peer network model does.

Common OS Examples

Here are common examples of software that supports the client-server model:

◆ Novell Open Enterprise Server (OES) 2

◆ Unix

◆ Linux

◆ Windows Server 2008 and Windows Server 2008 R2

◆ Apple OS X Lion Server

The Directory Services Model

directory services model
Uses a hierarchical database to logically organize the network resources. This model scales well to small, medium, or large enterprise networks.

The concept of the *directory services model* grew out of a need to better manage the large, complex networks found in today's organizations. The complexity was due in large part to two factors: First, applications used over the network were becoming more popular and created a greater demand; second, it was becoming increasingly common to have software and hardware from different vendors operating on the same network. Directory services provides a centralized system for managing applications, files, printers, people, and other resources in large groups or individually.

In a directory services model, a hierarchical database contains all the network resources. Conceptually, the database looks like an upside-down tree structure. The root of the tree is at the top and is used to represent the organization. Users logging on to the network are actually logging on to and being processed by the directory services database. The user can access any objects within the database that they have been given access to. Objects can be users, groups, servers, printers, and so on as shown in the picture below.

The directory services database consists of a hierarchical structure of objects. You can think of objects as towns located along a river. Each town has characteristics that make it unique. Like the town, each object in directory services has properties that can be managed. If we continue with the analogy, the towns are linked together by water whether they are on the river or a tributary that connects to the river. Similar to the river that links the towns, the link between the objects is called the directory tree. The directory tree is what helps organize the management of directory services. This structure enables the administrator to logically group directory service objects.

The directory services database file is hosted on servers that are referred to as *domain controllers (DCs)*. Once a DC is installed and configured, it will retain a local copy of the database file and is responsible for processing any changes to the directory. Administrators may delete objects from the directory, modify objects, or add new objects. All of these changes are processed on a DC.

In order to ensure that the directory is always available, multiple DCs are typically installed in an environment. The servers will replicate any changes to the directory between themselves to ensure that they all have the most recent copy of the database.

domain controller (DC)
A DC is used in a Windows Server 2008 R2 domain. The DC hosts the read-write copy of the Active Directory database file, `ntds.dit`.

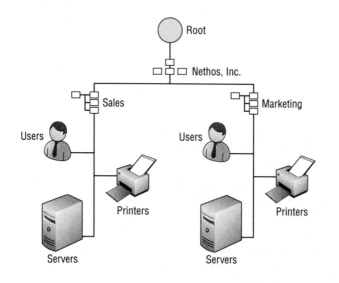

When Appropriate

For medium to large networks, this model is the most commonly deployed today. The main network operating systems—OES 2, and Windows Server 2008 and Windows Server 2008 R2—use a directory services network model.

Consider these advantages to using directory services:

◆ This model scales well to any size network.

◆ The administrator can logically group users and resources within the directory services tree.

◆ You can centralize or decentralize account and resource management as much as you wish. Administrative tasks can be delegated to other individuals without jeopardizing consistency in the directory services database.

You should also consider these disadvantages:

◆ This model is the most difficult to design and manage.

◆ This model requires a trained and experienced network administrator to install and manage it.

◆ There is added complexity when migrating from the *domain model* to a directory services model.

domain model
Logically groups computers, users, and groups into a domain. Users log on to the domain and have access to any resources within the domain to which their user account has permission.

Terms to Know

client	domain model
client-server network	Hypertext Markup Language (HTML)
directory services model	peer-to-peer network
domain controller (DC)	workstation

Review Questions

1. Define *peer-to-peer network model*.

2. What is the role of a DC?

3. What are two functions of a DC?

4. Which client-server network model does Windows Server 2008 R2 use?

5. True or false: The directory services model is always the best network model to choose.

6. Which network model is the best choice if you have a small number of users and no dedicated server hardware?

7. What is an object in the directory services model?

8. True or false: If you have an account on one server in a client-server model, you can access resources on other servers even if you do not have a user account defined.

9. True or false: In a directory services network, you must add new users and groups to each of the DCs individually.

10. Which network model provides the most scalability and is the best solution for large national or global networks?

Chapter 10

Data-Link and Network Layer Protocols

pro•to•col *n* : a set of rules that governs how communication should occur

In Chapter 8, "A Communications Framework," you learned about the OSI model. The Data-Link layer includes the physical network hardware and transmits data onto the network. The two layers of this model that are responsible for moving data over an internetwork are the Network and Transport layers.

The Network layer of the OSI model determines the best route that a packet should take when it needs to be delivered over an internetwork. The Transport layer is primarily responsible for reliable data delivery.

At both layers, protocols must be designed to fulfill the functions of packet delivery and reliability. *Protocols* are a set of rules that govern how communication should occur between upper and lower layers in addition to defining the rules for communication with other devices. Without protocols, there would not be any agreed-upon format for how to handle data. This is especially a problem in a field with many technologies and thousands of manufacturers.

Introduction to Topologies

Before you can even begin installing your networking software, you must have some type of hardware that connects all the computers. In this section, you will learn about network topologies and *Ethernet*, the most common network communication architecture for connecting network hardware. A *topology* is defined as the layout of the network. Topologies can be physical or logical:

Physical topology   Describes how the network physically looks or how the network is physically designed and connected

Logical topology   Describes how data is transmitted through the network

The concept of a topology is important because each network card is designed to work with a specific topology. Conversely, if your network cable is already installed and you want to use existing wiring, you must select your network cards based on the preexisting physical topology.

Ideally, you can design your network from scratch. Then you can choose your topology, cabling, and network cards based on what best meets your needs.

This section will review the commonly defined topologies:

◆ Bus topology

◆ Star topology

◆ Ring topology

◆ Mesh topology

Bus Topology

Physically, a bus topology uses a linear segment of cable to connect all network devices. Devices typically connect to the bus (the cable) through T-connectors. At each end of the bus are terminators. Each terminator absorbs the signal when it reaches the end of the cable. Without a terminator, a signal would bounce back and cause network errors.

The physical bus topology uses a logical bus to transmit data on the cable in both directions. In a logical bus topology, only one transmission can occur at any given moment. If two transmissions are sent at the same time, the two will collide on the cable, creating a collision and causing network errors. Termination ensures that the signal is removed from the cable when it reaches either end, which prevents possible network errors.

The benefits of a bus topology include the following:

- This is one of the least expensive topologies to install, because it uses less cable than the star topology and needs no hardware for a central device.

- It is an easy way to network a small number of computers.

The drawbacks of a bus topology include the following:

- If there is a break in the cable, the entire network will fail.

- This topology can be difficult to troubleshoot because cabling problems often cannot be isolated to one computer.

- On a medium-sized to large network, reconfiguration is more difficult than the cable management of a star topology.

In the early days of networking, the bus topology was very popular. It used less equipment than other topologies and was therefore inexpensive to set up. But now Ethernet concentrators are inexpensive. The falling cost to build a star topology–based network, combined with its fault tolerance, has made 10BASE-T with the star topology the most popular Ethernet configuration.

10BASE-T
A network communication standard that uses Ethernet on unshielded twisted-pair cable in a star topology at 10 Mbps.

Star Topology

Physically, the star topology looks like a star. A hub or switch is deployed at the center of the star, and all other devices attach to the hub or switch via cables.

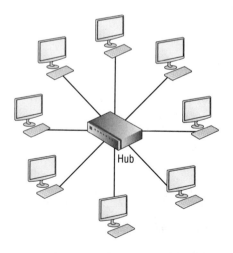

Hub

The term *hub* is used generically to specify the central device in a star topology. In a *10BASE-T* network, the hub is technically called a *concentrator*, but typically a switch device is deployed today.

Logically, the physical star topology operates just as a logical bus topology, by sending the data signal to all nodes at once. The hub or switch at the center of the star works as a signal splitter, which means the signal is split and sent to all computers at the same time, with one exception—it is not sent back to the computer from which it originated. The signal is terminated at each network card, thereby preventing the signal from accidentally reentering the network. If this were to happen, data packets would travel the network endlessly—seriously slowing down network performance.

The benefits of a star topology include the following:

◆ A star topology is fault tolerant because a cable break does not bring down the entire network.

◆ Reconfiguring the network, or adding nodes, is easy because each node connects to the central hub or switch independent of other nodes.

◆ Isolating cable failures is easy because each node connects independently to the central hub or switch.

One drawback of a star topology is that if the central device fails, the entire network becomes unavailable.

Ring Topology

Physically, the ring topology is shaped in a ring. Cables pass from computer to computer until the ring is complete. When data is transmitted, each workstation receives the signal and then passes it on when it is done with the data. Other than the Fiber Distributed Data Interface (FDDI), no current networks use a physical ring topology, because a break in the ring makes the entire network unavailable.

Logically, a ring topology works by passing the signal, traditionally called a token, from one node to another until it goes all the way around the ring. Only a single machine can utilize the token at a given time, which eliminates the possibility of collisions. Token-passing schemes use the logical ring topology.

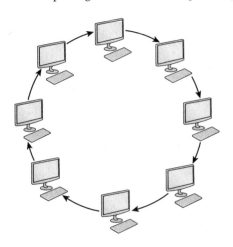

A logical ring topology ensures access to the network without the risk of *collisions*, which can occur in logical star or bus topologies.

The drawbacks of a ring topology include the following:

◆ If there is a break in the cable of a physical ring topology, the network becomes unavailable.

◆ Physical ring topologies are difficult to troubleshoot.

◆ Physical ring topologies are hard to reconfigure.

◆ There is limited support for ring networks.

◆ The costs for a ring network are significantly higher than for star or bus networks.

collision
A problem on Ethernet networks that occurs when two computers transmit on the wire simultaneously, causing an electrical spike twice the strength than is normal for the network.

Mesh Topology

Physically, a *mesh topology* is multiple devices connected in a crisscross pattern to create multiple redundant paths between devices. A mesh topology improves on the concept of the star; instead of having devices connected to a single central hub or switch, where if the central device fails no device can communicate with any other, a mesh topology lets each device connect to all others, adding a significant layer of redundancy.

Logically, the mesh topology operates just as a logical bus and the star topology, by sending the data signal to all nodes at once. The signal is terminated at each network card, thereby preventing the signal from accidentally reentering the network. If this happened, data packets would travel the network endlessly—seriously slowing down network performance.

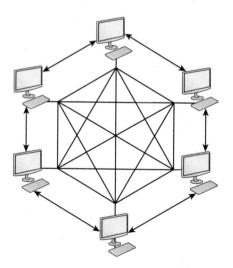

The benefits of a mesh topology include increased redundancy due to multiple paths to each device on the network.

The drawbacks of a mesh topology include the following:

◆ This topology has the most expensive configuration due to the many redundant links that are configured.

◆ Many connections may go unused or underutilized.

◆ It has increased installation and configuration complexity.

Ethernet Communication Architecture

In the preceding section, you learned that every network has a physical and logical topology. The topology can provide important information on the capabilities of the network, from its reliability to its method of communication. The bus, mesh, and star topologies are three such topologies that are used with the Ethernet standard for communication on a network.

Ethernet is one of the oldest network protocols and it is the most popular. Xerox first developed it in the 1970s, and in the 1980s, Xerox, Intel, and Digital Equipment Corporation proposed formal Ethernet specifications. In fact, Ethernet has its own standard from the *Institute of Electrical and Electronic Engineers (IEEE)*, called the IEEE 802.3 standard. The Ethernet protocol is used at the Physical and Media Access Control (MAC) layers of the OSI model (see Chapter 8, "A Communications Framework").

Ethernet works with a contention scheme (a way of accessing the network) called Carrier Sense Multiple Access with Collision Detection (CSMA/CD). CSMA/CD works by allowing any computer to transmit at any time, assuming the line is free. The steps in this process are as follows:

1. When a workstation wants to send a packet on the network, the workstation listens to see whether any other nodes are transmitting packets over the network.

2. If the network is in use, the workstation waits.

3. If the network is not in use, the workstation sends its packet.

4. If two or more workstations send packets at the same time because they both thought the line was free, a collision occurs.

5. If a collision occurs, all workstations on the network cease transmission and each implements a back-off timer that generates a random number indicating how long the workstation must wait before it retransmits.

6. After the time expires, workstations can begin transmitting again.

Institute of Electrical and Electronic Engineers (IEEE)
Pronounced I triple E, an international organization that defines computing and telecommunications standards. The local area network (LAN) standards defined by IEEE include the 802-workgroup specifications.

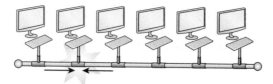

Two stations transmit at the same time—a collision occurs.

Benefits and Drawbacks of Ethernet

The benefits of Ethernet include the following:

- ◆ The protocol is fairly simple and does not have the overhead associated with Token Ring.

- ◆ As long as the network segment is not too busy, stations can transmit without any wait.

- ◆ Because Ethernet hardware is nonproprietary and less complicated than Token Ring hardware, Ethernet is less expensive.

The drawbacks of Ethernet include the following:

- ◆ As network traffic increases, so does the probability of network collisions, which degrade network performance.

- ◆ Because all stations have equal access, there is no way to establish higher priority for nodes such as servers.

Ethernet Rules

Ethernet is so popular because it is fairly easy to install and uses inexpensive hardware compared to Token Ring and FDDI. Although the latter two are well proven and reliable technologies, they are expensive and have mostly fallen out of use today.

Ethernet has the added advantage of offering higher-speed networks on the same wire. Two Ethernet technologies, Fast Ethernet and Gigabit Ethernet, perform at 100 Mbps and 1000 Mbps, respectively. That is a huge performance increase to the original standards. And considering that most new computers come with network interface cards that support Fast Ethernet, it should be no surprise that Fast Ethernet is the default choice on new network installations.

The most popular form of Ethernet is 100BASE-T. With 100BASE-T Ethernet, you connect to the network with *unshielded twisted-pair (UTP)* cable; a connector on the end of the cable looks similar to, but is larger than, a telephone connector. One end of the cable attaches to the network card and the other end connects to a central switch which is referred to as a concentrator.

unshielded twisted-pair (UTP)
A type of media that can contain four, six, or eight wires. Pairs of wires are twisted together to prevent signal interference. The wires are then wrapped in a plastic cover. UTP is identified by the category nomenclature.

Ethernet Standards

Ethernet has many standards that have developed over the years, however three primary standards still dominate:

IEEE 802.3   10 Mbps Ethernet

IEEE 802.3u   100 Mbps Fast Ethernet

IEEE 802.3z and *IEEE 802.3ab*   1000 Mbps Gigabit Ethernet

Traditionally, Ethernet was deployed as a 10 Mbps standard. However, now that standards require networks to support voice, video, and other high-capacity bandwidth items, Fast Ethernet and Gigabit Ethernet are the standards for desktop computers and servers in the enterprise. While Fast Ethernet still dominates, Gigabit Ethernet is playing an increasing role as a key technology to the desktop as well as for its support of network backbones. Just as Gigabit Ethernet has become more prevalent to the desktop, 10 Gigabit Ethernet (or 10GE) is becoming more common in datacenters today. Many industry experts agree that due to the declining cost of 10GE, it is destined to become the standard in networks everywhere.

Ethernet has many other characteristics in addition to speed. Depending on which Ethernet standard you choose, you will have flexibility in which physical topology and which cable type you use.

Ethernet can use the following cable types:

◆ Thin *coaxial* cable, also known as thinnet (RG-58AU)

◆ Thick coaxial cable, also known as thicknet (RG-8 or RG-11)

◆ Unshielded twisted-pair (UTP) cables (type depends on access speed needed)

◆ Shielded twisted-pair (STP) cable

◆ *Fiber-optic* cable

The IEEE has defined naming conventions for Ethernet standards. The standards are to be named as follows:

◆ The first part of the name specifies the speed in megabits per second (Mbps).

◆ The second part of the name specifies that the standard is using baseband (BASE) or broadband (BROAD) signaling.

◆ The last part of the name describes the type of cable being used, or an estimate of a maximum cable run for the standard.

For example, the 10BASE-T standard defines 10 Mbps speed, using baseband signaling, over twisted-pair cabling.

IEEE 802.3

The IEEE standard that is also known as Carrier Sense Multiple Access with Collision Detection (CSMA/CD) and defines how most Ethernet networks function.

IEEE 802.3u

The IEEE standard for 100 Mbps Fast Ethernet. IEEE 802.3u defines the specifications for implementing Fast Ethernet at the Physical and Data-Link layers of the OSI model.

IEEE 802.3z

The IEEE standard for 1000 Mbps Gigabit Ethernet over fiber-optic cable.

IEEE 802.3ab

The IEEE standard for 1000 Mbps Gigabit Ethernet over unshielded twisted-pair cable (UTP).

coaxial

A type of media that has a single copper wire surrounded by plastic insulation, is wrapped in metal braid or foil, and is protected by a plastic cover.

fiber-optic

A type of media that uses glass or plastic to transmit light signals. Single-mode fiber-optic cable contains a single fiber. Multimode fiber-optic cable has two individually protected fibers.

This table summarizes the Ethernet standards.

Ethernet Standard	Speed in Mbps	Physical Topology	Cable Used
10BASE2	10	Bus	Thin coaxial cable RG-58AU (50-ohm cable)
10BASE5	10	Bus	Thick coaxial cable RG-8 or RG-11 (50-ohm cable)
10BASE-T	10	Star	Unshielded twisted-pair cable (category 3 or better)
10BASE-F	10	Star	Fiber-optic
100BASE-T	100	Star	Unshielded twisted-pair cable (uses category 5 with all four pairs)
100BASE-TX	100	Star	Unshielded twisted-pair cable
100BASE-FX	100	Star	Fiber-optic cable (uses two strands of fiber as specified by *ANSI*)
1000BASE-X	1000	Star	Fiber-optic and copper cable
1000BASE-T	1000	Star	Unshielded twisted-pair (UTP)
10GBase-LR	10000	Star	Fiber-optic
10GBase-CX4	10000	Star	Copper cable

American National Standards Institute (ANSI)
An organization that seeks to develop standardization within the computing industry. ANSI is the American representative to the ISO, or International Standards Organization.

Ethernet Hardware

Depending on which Ethernet standard you choose, you can configure Ethernet as a physical bus or a physical star topology. This section provides an example of each topology and the hardware needed to support each configuration.

Ethernet Bus Topology

In the 1980s, before 10BASE-T became standardized, the most popular way of configuring Ethernet was in a physical bus topology. You might still use the bus topology in small networks, because it does not require a concentrator as the star configuration does. However, because the cost of Ethernet hardware has dropped drastically, this is often not a large concern.

The most popular configuration for the bus topology utilized the 10BASE2 standard, or thin coaxial cable. In this configuration, you connect a T-connector to the network card. You attach the cables to either side of the T-connector to form a linear bus network. At the ends of the bus, you need 50-ohm terminators. You should ground one end. This configuration has fallen almost completely out of use in modern network environments.

Ethernet Star Topology

The Ethernet star topology is by far the most commonly implemented topology for Ethernet networks. This topology is easier to set up and configure than the bus topology. It also provides more fault tolerance because a cable break does not cause the entire segment to go down.

In the star topology, you attach all your devices to the hub or switch, also known as a concentrator. You can buy concentrators with whatever number of ports you require, from 4 to well over 100 in a single unit.

When determining the hardware that you will use, you should first decide whether you will need 10 Mbps, 100 Mbps, 1000 Mbps, or 10,000 Mbps networking capabilities. This factor determines the type of hub or switch, Ethernet card, and cabling you will need. After your hardware is in place, the star will look like the following diagram.

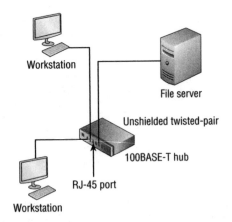

In this graphic, both the workstations and the file server are connected to the network by using a 100BASE-T hub. In a small network of 5 to 10 computers, this configuration is fine. But as the number of computers on the network grows, you will need to reconsider the design. Most network designers will select a switch that has at least a 1000BASE-T connection. The file server will connect to the 1000BASE-T to give optimum performance for multiple computers. Recently, networks have been designed with 10GE switches to provide optimal network performance.

Using TCP/IP

One of the most popular networking protocols is the Transmission Control Protocol/Internet Protocol (TCP/IP). TCP/IP was originally developed in the 1970s by the Department of Defense (DoD) as a way of connecting dissimilar networks that would be capable of withstanding a nuclear attack. Since then, TCP/IP has become a de facto industry standard and is the protocol used on the Internet today. It is important to note that although TCP and IP are the cornerstone protocols, TCP/IP is actually a collection of many protocols that are generically referred to as the TCP/IP protocol suite.

As you now know, the two main protocols that make up the TCP/IP suite of protocols are TCP and IP. These protocols fall into the Transport and Network layers of the OSI model, respectively.

IP functions at the Network layer of the OSI model. The primary function of IP is to provide each attached device with a unique address with one of the two iterations in use today: IPv4 and IPv6. Each address indicates not only the individual device, but also the network to which the device belongs. IP is also responsible for routing packets over an internetwork. The IP address is used to determine the exact location of the destination network where the device exists. For example, assume that you have three subnets (independent network segments) connected through routers, and you want to send a packet from subnet A to subnet B. IP is responsible for addressing the packet, and it is these addresses that are used to route the packet through the internetwork.

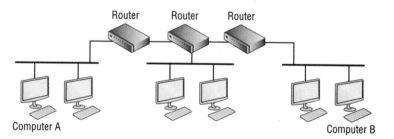

TCP is a Transport layer protocol whose primary function is to provide reliable delivery of data through a connection-oriented service. This is done by establishing a *fully duplexed*, *virtual circuit* connection. Sending data through TCP is a two-part process: The sender and receiver exchange a "handshake" to establish communication, and then acknowledgments are sent to verify that data was received. Acknowledgments are sent throughout the transmission.

If you do not need the reliability of TCP, you can send packets through the Transport layer with a protocol called User Datagram Protocol (UDP). UDP

fully duplexed
Means that simultaneous two-way communication can take place.

virtual circuit
A logical connection between two devices that transmits and receives data.

provides connectionless service and has considerably less overhead than TCP, but it does not provide reliable data transmission. As a connectionless protocol, UDP sends its packets over the network without any confirmation from the receiver that the packets were received successfully. The packets either get there or they don't. The sender doesn't worry about it.

Transport	TCP UDP
Network	IP

OSI model layers

Benefits of TCP/IP

TCP/IP is commonly used as the Transport and Network layer protocol for these reasons:

- It is supported by almost all network operating systems. It is the required protocol for communicating over the Internet; if you want to connect to the Internet, your computer has to use TCP/IP.
- TCP/IP is *scalable* in both small and large networks.
- The protocol is designed to be fault tolerant and is able to dynamically reroute packets if network links become unavailable (assuming alternate paths exist).
- Protocol companions such as *Dynamic Host Configuration Protocol (DHCP)* simplify IP address management.
- *Domain Name System (DNS)* is used with TCP/IP to *resolve* a *fully qualified domain name (FQDN)*, such as sybex.com, with its corresponding IP address.

Disadvantages of TCP/IP

Although TCP/IP and the Internet have been wildly successful, using this protocol has disadvantages. Of course, the disadvantages do not outweigh the advantages, but you should consider them when building your network. When you connect your network to the Internet, you will want to consider ways to avoid or minimize the following disadvantages:

- Managing IP addresses is complicated and cumbersome. IP address errors are usually due to administrative errors.

scalable
Capable of expanding to accommodate greater numbers of users and resources.

Dynamic Host Configuration Protocol (DHCP)
Automates the assignment of IP configuration information.

Domain Name System (DNS)
A system that resolves domain names to IP addresses by using a domain name database.

resolve
To convert from one type to another. In relationship to IP addresses and domain names, it is the conversion of an IP address to a domain name on the Internet or vice versa.

fully qualified domain name (FQDN)
The complete name registered with the Internet Network Information Center (InterNIC) that is used to identify a computer on the Internet. It includes the computer name (hostname) and the domain name; for example, mycomputer.sybex.com.

◆ To troubleshoot TCP/IP problems on your network, you need to understand how TCP/IP works and the many (more than a dozen) protocols that are included in the suite.

◆ Taking advantage of some of the best features of the TCP/IP suite requires considerable skill and knowledge. Depending on your type of business, you will need a significant amount of education to master TCP/IP or you will need to hire an expert.

IPv4 Addressing

A central concept of IP is addressing. The most widely used IP version, IPv4, requires a 32-bit network address. This address is broken down into four groups of 8 bits, with each group of 8 bits being referred to as an *octet*. Each octet consists of a number between 0 and 255, and the octets are separated by periods. IP addresses must be unique for each network device that can be reached on the Internet. You should request your IP addresses from InterNIC or from an ISP. IP addresses commonly fall within three classes: Class A, Class B, and Class C.

octet
One of four parts of an IP address. Each number in an octet is created using 8 bits.

Currently, only Class C addresses are available. The supply of IP addresses has dwindled to the point that almost all addresses are allocated. The IPv6 addressing scheme with 16 octets, 128 bits, has been developed to help address the depletion of IPv4 addresses, and is able to supply billions of new IP addresses.

NOTE

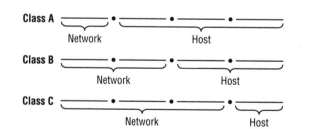

Network Class	Address Range of First Field	Number of Networks Supported	Number of Host Nodes Available
A	1–127	126	16,777,214
B	128–191	65,534	65,534
C	192–223	16,777,214	254

———— *NOTE* ————

broadcasts
Data transmitted to all devices on the same network segment.

loopback
A special function for testing a device's ability to communicate by making it communicate with itself.

The following addresses are reserved: 0 is not available because it denotes that no routing is needed; 255 is used for *broadcasts*. 127 is a special *loopback* address used for diagnostic purposes; 127.0.0.1 is the IPv4 loopback address, and ::1 is the IPv6 loopback address.

IPv4 Configuration

When you configure a network device with an IPv4 address, you typically need three pieces of information:

◆ IP address

◆ Subnet mask

◆ Default gateway, which is the IP address of a router

IP Address

As we mentioned earlier, each network device needs a unique IPv4 address. The system administrator, or someone who coordinates IPv4 address assignment and configuration, should assign this address from the pool of addresses assigned by InterNIC or your ISP. The following is an example of a IPv4 address: 192.168.1.1.

Subnet Mask

A subnet mask defines which part of the IP address is the network address and which is the host address. By defining subnet masks, you specify which network your node belongs to. With this information and the destination address for your data, TCP/IP can determine whether source and destination nodes are on the same network segment. If they are on different segments, routing will be needed.

Default Router, or Gateway

You need a default router, or gateway, configured on your workstations if you want your packets routed over an internetwork. The default router is typically the IP address of the local router that you use to connect your network to the Internet. The workstation needs to have this information if it wants to send packets out to the Internet. Without it, the workstation is clueless about where to send packets destined for networks other than its own.

These are basic IP configuration options. Depending on the complexity of your IP network, you might also specify other configuration options, such as the DNS and *Windows Internet Naming Service (WINS)* servers that will be used.

IPv6 Addressing

As the growth of the Internet boomed and reached dramatic proportions in the 1990s, the IP addresses available for use were depleted at an amazing rate. This led developers to create a new standard intended to replace the original IPv4 protocol. This newest IP addressing standard, IPv6, arrived in 1998 but has yet to be widely adopted. When it was built, one of its primary goals was to create an addressing scheme that had a larger pool of addresses than the widely deployed IPv4 so that the Internet would have a virtually unlimited number of possible addresses.

IPv6 utilizes a 128-bit network address. This address is broken down into eight groups of 4 hexadecimal bits, separated by colons. Similarly to the IPv4 addressing scheme, the IPv6 address is broken into two components: the network or subnetwork prefix and the host address.

IPv6 has quite a few feature improvements over its predecessor:

◆ Larger address space

◆ Quality of Service (QoS) improvements

◆ More efficient header

◆ Support for IPSec

IPv6 Configuration

When you configure a device for IPv6, you have two configuration methods to choose from: automatic configuration using stateless addresses and manual configuration. In both cases you need a unique address for each interface. An example of an IPv6 address is: 2001:0:4137:1fab:30b3:34fb:519f:8993. If you need routing outside of the local network, then the default gateway is still required; however, IPv6 systems are capable of discovering the default router for a network segment automatically. The final component that you can configure for IPv6 is the address information for the DNS Server. A single NIC can have both an IPv4 and an IPv6 assigned simultaneously.

NOTE

Windows Internet Naming Service (WINS)
A Microsoft proprietary protocol that runs on a Windows server. The protocol is used on Windows servers to resolve NetBIOS names, the workstation names on Windows computers, to IP addresses. WINS is similar in concept to DNS.

The Function of DHCP in an IP Network

Having a system administrator or other person manually configure IP addresses is inherently flawed and can lead to misconfiguration, causing IP address conflicts and network errors. Fortunately, one TCP/IP protocol helps automate configuration. The Dynamic Host Configuration Protocol (DHCP) uses a DHCP server to automate this process.

The DHCP server contains a range of IP addresses called the scope. As requested, the DHCP server will pull available IP addresses from the scope to lease to clients. A lease option specifies how long an IP address will be assigned to a DHCP client. As long as a client keeps using the IP address, that client is allowed to keep it. If the address is not used within the lease period, it is returned to the DHCP server scope and is available for use by other DHCP clients.

The exchange between the DHCP server and the DHCP client that results in a lease being granted consists of four steps. First, a discovery request is issued from the DHCP client. Any DHCP server in the environment that receives the request from the client responds with a DHCP lease offer. The client then responds to the DHCP server offer with a request to accept the lease offer. Finally, the DHCP server acknowledges the client's response to the lease offer. The client receives the acknowledgment from the DHCP server and begins to use the IP address assigned in the lease. An easy way to remember these steps is with the acronym DORA:

◆ Discover

◆ Offer

◆ Request

◆ Acknowledge

The follow image depicts the DHCP process used to assign addresses:

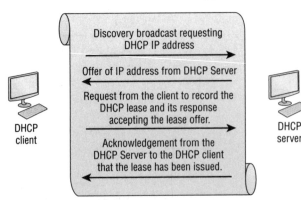

DHCP Servers in a Windows Server 2008 R2 Environment

After you have installed the DHCP server, you must configure the scope and subnet mask that the DHCP clients will use. Through DHCP, you can also configure options such as the default gateway, WINS server, and DNS server.

The Function of DNS in an IP Network

The Domain Name System (DNS) is a process that allows IP addresses to be resolved to fully qualified domain names (FQDNs). These are the easily remembered names that people use to access network resources, particularly websites. To demonstrate the usefulness of DNS, take this quiz:

1. What is the URL to access the Microsoft website?

2. What is the IP address of Microsoft's website?

If you answered microsoft.com for question 1, you are right. Most people can answer this question; however, very few people can answer the second question. This is OK, though, because this is where DNS comes into play. DNS enables you to use a name that you can remember in place of an IP address; DNS then translates the name into an address used to contact the host you wish to communicate with.

DNS uses FQDNs to logically organize resources. Domains are logically grouped by type of function into a hierarchical structure. At the top of the structure is the root. Examples of root domains include .com for business, .edu for education, and .gov for government. Domain names must be unique. InterNIC assigns and centrally manages them.

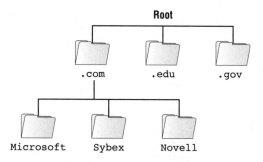

DNS domains are different conceptually from Windows domains, and you should not confuse the two terms.

NOTE

Terms to Know

10BASE-T	IEEE 802.3ab
American National Standards Institute (ANSI)	IEEE 802.3u
	IEEE 802.3z
broadcasts	Institute of Electrical and Electronic Engineers (IEEE)
coaxial	
collision	loopback
DHCP	octet
DNS	resolve
fiber-optic	scalable
FQDN	unshielded twisted-pair (UTP)
fully duplexed	virtual circuit
IEEE 802.3	WINS

Review Questions

1. What are three common IPv4 configuration requirements?
2. Which TCP/IP protocol allows you to automate IP configuration?
3. What is the protocol used on the Internet?
4. What is the primary purpose of IP?
5. At which layer of the OSI model does IP function?
6. TCP/IP uses the _____ protocol to provide connection-oriented services at the Transport layer of the OSI model.
7. Which TCP/IP address class offers the largest number of network addresses?
8. Which protocol offers the fastest service?
9. Which protocol is most widely implemented?
10. List the two most common physical topologies.
11. What is the primary function of DNS?
12. In TCP/IP configuration, what defines which part of the address is the network address and which part is the host address?
13. True or false: TCP/IP is a proprietary protocol.

Chapter 11

Network Operating Systems: A Comparison

sys•tem *n* : a collection of parts designed to function together

As you learned in Chapter 9, "Network Models," the client-server architecture uses a dedicated server. A server is a computer that provides a variety of services to clients. Services can include email and providing access to files, databases, or other applications. The factors that determine the capabilities of the server depend on the software that is selected. The network operating system is software that runs on the server and makes the centralized services just described possible.

In the world of networking, you have many operating systems to choose from. Some factors to consider when choosing a network operating system include price, function, interoperability, the skill set required to manage the software, existing applications, hardware and software requirements, and personal preference.

Introduction to an NOS

A network operating system (NOS) is the system software designed especially for servers. You may have heard *server* used in several different ways, for instance, *file server*, *print server*, and *database server*. Each type of server fits a particular need. In small businesses, it is not uncommon to find a single computer used as a file and print server. In large corporate networks, each server is configured to serve a specific task. More often than not, these large networks also will have multiple computers serving the same role (for example, multiple file servers).

The concept behind an NOS is that it is easier to manage a centralized network than it is to manage a network that has all its resources spread out. An example of a decentralized model (one without a server) is a peer-to-peer network. In order for centralized servers to be effective, they have to be designed to meet stringent performance and reliability demands. The design criteria include the following:

Reliability   If a major software error or hardware failure occurs, the server will continue to function.

Scalability   As the needs of the company grow, the NOS is able to meet the demands. This may be accomplished by supporting larger and more powerful hardware and by adding additional servers that are designed to work in tandem.

Performance   The server provides optimum performance for the task it has been configured to serve, in addition to being adapted for more demanding scenarios.

Interoperability   Now more than ever, an NOS needs to be able to integrate with other devices, systems, and software platforms. In some instances, this integration may include a single point of management for all resources on the network.

Building a system that incorporates these criteria may seem easier than it really is. You have to remember that the NOS is only software. You still have to contend with hardware and other software (such as applications) that will be running on the system. In the case of Microsoft Windows, you should be able to run on any Intel- or Itanium-based computer. Does that mean that the system will run well or is stable? Not at all. You need to consider the extent to which all of the hardware components have been tested. These include critical components such as network interface cards, tape backup drives, and special adapters (for example, Serial Attached Small Computer Systems Interface [SAS] or Serial Advanced Technology Attachment [SATA] cards).

file server
A computer that is dedicated to the task of centrally sharing files and folders for access by users.

print server
A centralized computer that manages printing of user documents for one or more printers. Print servers store documents temporarily when the printer is busy.

database server
A type of computer that maintains information records that can be added, deleted, changed, or searched. Database servers play a major role in most companies and on the Internet.

What to Look for in an NOS

Selecting the right network operating system for your company's needs is important. Although most NOSs provide some similar features, each one has unique features that you should consider. The features available in an NOS may not be the only factors you will have to examine.

All the NOSs discussed later in this chapter offer the critical features a network administrator would expect to find. These common features include the following:

Fault tolerance   Fault tolerance in a server means that it is able to recover from a hardware failure or software crash without losing any data and, ideally, without any downtime. Fault tolerant servers support SATA or SAS storage, uninterruptible power supplies, and tape or external hard drive–based backup systems.

Multiprocessing   An NOS must be able to maintain performance under demanding loads. To accomplish a consistent level of performance on a growing network, the server will need to be able to support multiple processors. An NOS that supports multiprocessing can use two or more CPUs to process an instruction simultaneously.

Multitasking   Servers, by nature, are required to complete several tasks simultaneously. If they couldn't do that effectively, they would not be of much use on a network of 1,000 users. A server capable of multitasking can juggle several actions. A powerful server can handle hundreds of tasks efficiently, and without a significant decrease in performance or stability.

Besides these features, each NOS has unique qualities that may make it a good fit for your network.

Additional features to consider include wide support for different external backup drives, antivirus software, and SAS or SATA. Compatibility with different external drives is critical. As your data storage needs grow, so does your demand for larger backup storage. The NOS must include support for the latest external drive technologies, including tape drives, SATA drives, and SAS drives. As for antivirus programs, second best doesn't cut it. With the proliferation of email and web-based viruses, a robust, networkable antivirus application needs to be supported by the NOS you select. And finally, the NOS must be able to support hardware- and software-based RAID options. Fortunately, this typically is not a problem because almost all NOSs recognize a hardware RAID solution as a hard drive.

Windows Server 2003 R2

Windows Server 2003 R2 is designed to provide support for diverse networking needs. It can be deployed in a centralized or distributed environment. Even though it is not the most current of the Microsoft Server operating systems, it is still very prevalent in network enterprises and will continue to be for some time. Here are some of the key server roles that can be performed using Windows Server 2003 R2:

- File and print server
- Web server and web application services
- Directory services
- Terminal server
- Virtual private network server and remote access server
- Mail server
- Streaming media server

When to Choose Windows Server 2003 R2

Windows Server 2003 R2 is designed to be a reliable and scalable server platform. One of the key improvements with this operating system over previous iterations is that it is optimized to be integrated with XML-based web services. Through the Windows Server 2003 R2 Framework, there is native support for web services and standards, including XML (Extensible Markup Language), SOAP (Simple Object Access Protocol), UDDI (Universal Description, Discovery, and Integration), and WSDL (Web Services Description Language). There is also integrated support for Microsoft Passport, which is used for security and secure authentication of Internet users.

In today's computing world the most common reason for deploying new Windows Server 2003 R2 systems comes back to application support. Many companies require support for application software that has not been updated to run on Windows Server 2008 or Windows 2008 R2 systems. This forces many administrators to deploy the aging NOS for application compatibility and support.

Windows Server 2008

Windows Server 2008 offers all the benefits of Windows Server 2003 R2 but with many improvements in security, a reduction in administrative overhead, and an increase in efficiency and productivity.

Beyond the major changes to the core of the software, Windows Server 2008 takes a different approach to system administration. The most significant change is the introduction of Server Manager. Unlike Windows Server 2003 R2, which contains many tools and interfaces for administration, Windows Server 2008 brings many of the existing tools together into this single, simple-to-work-with interface. Server Manager also introduces functionality that replaces some portions of the Windows Server 2003 R2 tool, such as Add or Remove Windows Components and Configure Your Server.

Additionally, a new installation mode exists with Windows Server 2008: Server Core Installation. This installation mode allows an administrator to deploy a server with a reduced set of services and capabilities. This reduces the system's network footprint, which also reduces attack possibilities on the system. A Server Core Installation doesn't have a GUI and only displays a command line for the administrator to work with. Therefore, administrators must have advanced experience working with the command line so that they can administer and configure the installation.

Windows Server 2008 also introduces additional security features such as User Account Control and BitLocker. User Account Control allows administrators to make changes during a non-administrative logon if they have the proper authorization. This means the administrator no longer needs to log off or use the Run As command before he or she executes administrative actions. BitLocker allows for hard drive encryption. Once BitLocker is enabled and the hard drive has been encrypted the system will require a password for hard drive access. These types of features allow an administrator to run a more secure network environment.

A much sought-after feature in Windows Server 2008 is support for Windows PowerShell. Windows PowerShell is a command line–based utility that allows for local and remote administration through the use of *cmdlets*. Cmdlets can be used to create rich scripts that allow for automation and present a powerful forum for system manipulation.

When to Choose Windows Server 2008

Windows Server 2008 builds on the advantages of Windows Server 2003 R2, with the added introduction of Server Manager and PowerShell as well as many other system changes and improvements.

Some clear advantages to selecting Windows Server 2008 include

- Increased security features, such as BitLocker, enhanced Encrypted File System (EFS), and a new Security Configuration Wizard

- Support for Server Core Installation

- Simplified server management and administration with Server Manager

cmdlet
A command executed within Windows PowerShell that performs an action and can be used to create powerful scripts for local or remote administration.

Here are some disadvantages to consider before you adopt Windows Server 2008 Server:

◆ Legacy applications may not be compatible.

◆ Increased hardware requirements

Windows Server 2008 R2

The Windows Server 2008 R2 operating system offers improvements over the already existing enhancements to security and performance in the Windows Server 2008 operating system. One of the changes that has had the most impact in Windows Server 2008 R2 is the lack of support for x86 systems. Windows Server 2008 R2 can only be deployed on x64-based systems. Many environments still run legacy applications that will not function on an x64-bit system. Make sure to consider this when you decide what NOS to deploy to support a specific application.

Improvements and feature-set enhancements to fundamental components such as Active Directory Domain Services (AD DS), Internet Information Services (IIS), Windows PowerShell, NTFS, and Server Manager are all included with the Windows Server 2008 R2 release. Examples include the addition of the Active Directory Recycle Bin, which allows administrators a second chance to recover deleted items, much like the Recycle Bin on a user's desktop, and the introduction of AppLocker, which allows administrators to control the way users utilize and access applications.

When to Choose Windows Server 2008 R2

Windows Server 2008 R2 is the most current of the Microsoft Windows Server platforms and has proven itself to be a reliable and robust operating system. Windows Server 2008 R2 continues the trend of improvements to features, functionality, scalability, security, and performance within the Windows Server family of operating systems.

There are some clear advantages to selecting Windows Server 2008 R2:

◆ The x64 architecture offers robust performance and scalability.

◆ It is the most current Microsoft operating system; therefore it currently holds the longest possible support cycle.

◆ It has advanced and enhanced features and functionality.

Here are the disadvantages to consider before you adopt Windows Server 2008 R2:

◆ It has x64 support only, so existing hardware may not support it.

◆ It may not be compatible with legacy applications.

Unix Servers

Just like Windows Server 2008 or Windows Server 2008 R2, Unix is an operating system that can be used for workstations or servers. As a server, Unix is often considered the workhorse of the Internet and is used for high-demand applications on large corporate networks. Unix has acquired this role because of its reliability and performance that has taken decades to develop.

Unix has had a long history. Its roots began in the 1960s at Bell Telephone Laboratories at AT&T, where it was first developed. After that, Unix rapidly grew into several versions. The most notable achievement was the development of BSD Unix by students at the University of California at Berkeley. In those hallowed halls of UC Berkeley rose an operating system that was the basis for the development of other versions of Unix, from Sun Microsystems and Hewlett-Packard to Apple Computer.

When to Choose Unix

The reasons to choose Unix are as varied as the versions of Unix in existence today. The reasons for selecting Unix as your NOS include these:

- It is one of the most stable and fastest operating systems available.
- It is the best choice for supporting critical applications because of its rock-solid performance and proven reliability.
- It is the undisputed king of the Internet.
- There are hundreds, if not thousands, of tools for managing your Unix server.

There are disadvantages to consider, including these:

- Unix is a complex system that requires the administrator to learn hundreds of archaic commands.
- Proprietary versions of it are expensive.
- Some proprietary versions will run only on that company's hardware.

Linux

Linux is a version of Unix that has been written from the ground up. What makes Linux unique is that it offers comparable performance to other network operating systems, with one interesting twist: It's free!

When Linux was first released in 1991 by Linus Torvalds, a student at the University of Helsinki, it wasn't much of an operating system. In an effort to spawn rapid development of Linux, Torvalds made the source code free so that other programmers from around the world could assist him. The only condition

open source
The free distribution of source code (software) for the purpose of improving the software by the programming community. Regardless of modifications or adaptations of open source software, the code is still protected by the Open Source Definition.

was that anyone who developed Linux had to agree that the source code remain free as required by the *open source* license. Since the early 1990s, Linux has grown into a popular operating system that has generated a lot of excitement in the computer industry.

When to Choose Linux

You may have already downloaded or purchased one of the available distributions, but before you completely jump on board, make one final review of the following benefits and shortcomings.

These are some of the benefits of Linux:

◆ It provides Unix performance without the cost.

◆ It's free.

◆ It runs on almost every known platform, including PCs and Macintosh.

It might fall short of your expectations in these areas:

◆ Like Unix, Linux can be complex to learn, with hundreds of archaic commands.

◆ It has limited technical support from just a few companies.

Terms to Know

cmdlets

database server

file server

open source

print server

Review Questions

1. What are two criteria for evaluating network operating system software?
2. How does multiprocessing improve NOS performance?
3. How does the Recycle Bin in Windows Server 2008 R2 Active Directory help reduce administration?
4. What is one disadvantage of Windows Server 2008 that may result in application problems?
5. What significant improvement did Microsoft make to Windows Server 2003 R2?
6. True or false: Windows Server 2003 R2 Active Directory Domain Services supports the NT domain model.
7. Why is Unix typically the first choice for Internet servers?
8. What is a disadvantage of both Unix and Linux?
9. Why might Linux be a poor selection for someone new to Linux and Unix?
10. What is one major reason why Linux has become so popular?

Chapter 12

Windows Server 2008 R2 Origins and Platforms

or•i•gin *n* : the source from which something is derived

Windows Server 2008 R2, Microsoft's latest server operating system, has come a long way from its ancestor, Windows NT. The first version of NT to be released was NT 3.1, in July 1993. NT 3.5 followed in September 1994, and NT 4 was released in July 1996. The current release of Microsoft's business class workstation is called Windows 7 and the server operating system is called Windows Server 2008 R2. This chapter covers NT 4.0, Windows 2000/Windows Server 2003, and Windows Server 2008/2008 R2 and the differences between them.

Understanding the Origins of Windows Server

During the 1980s and early 1990s, Novell cornered the network operating system market. Microsoft offered networking software—OS/2 (which was originally developed by IBM) and LAN Manager—but these operating systems never really caught on.

Microsoft decided to create a new operating system from the ground up. By designing a new operating system, they would eliminate the inherent limitations of older software. In late 1988, Microsoft hired Dave Cutler from Digital Equipment Corporation, a veteran of minicomputer systems architecture, to design the new network operating system. This "New Technology" was to become Windows NT.

Before the programmers could begin creating this new operating system, the design team had to come up with the software design goals that would define what the NT operating system should do. The following subsections describe these goals.

Provide Flexibility in OS Code

The operating system code had to be written so that it could easily be modified to accommodate market demands.

In this sense, NT was fairly flexible—new software components could be added and deleted as current software and hardware standards dictated. New services and drivers could be written as standards changed, and they did not affect the core operating system. Also, you could configure each server or workstation to use only the services and drivers that each unique configuration required.

Offer High Performance

A major design goal of NT was that it had to be a high-performance operating system. Each component of NT had to be optimized to provide the highest performance for individual use and on a network, including large networks with thousands of users.

Be Reliable

The operating system had to be able to handle errors in a reliable and fault tolerant manner. This means that NT would shield itself from most hardware and software errors so that the system would continue to operate.

Memory is one area where reliability is critical. NT would manage memory through virtual memory. *Virtual memory* is the combination of physical RAM and the page file—a special file on the hard drive that is used to supplement physical RAM. Whenever you would launch an application in NT (with the exception of older Windows 16-bit applications), the memory manager would allocate the application its own separate memory space in RAM. The allocated portion could not be used by any other program until the first application closed. This technique kept a failed application from crashing or interfering with the operation of other applications or with the operating system.

The *New Technology File System (NTFS)* was also designed so that it was able to recover from many types of file errors.

Use Portable Code

As hardware standards changed, NT had to be able to be moved from one processor type to another. For example, NT should run on an Intel processor or an Alpha processor.

Be Compatible with Existing Standards

Another goal was that NT needed to be compatible with existing standards. This compatibility would make NT a better choice for computer networks with several types of operating systems coexisting (not just Microsoft operating systems). In addition, NT needed to be able to support existing applications that were written to run under other operating systems, particularly older Windows applications.

NT was to be compatible with existing network standards of the time. For example, NT would support networking transport protocols such as TCP/IP, IPX/SPX, and NetBEUI. (TCP/IP is covered in Chapter 10, "Data-Link and Network Layer Protocols.") NT would also be compatible with other network operating systems, such as NetWare, Systems Network Architecture (SNA), Unix, and AppleTalk networks.

In addition, NT was to support applications by providing modular subsystems for DOS, OS/2, and POSIX applications. As new standards emerged, new subsystems could be developed. Each configuration loaded only the necessary subsystems. This level of modularity meant that only parts of the operating system needed to be changed; the entire software code for NT did not have to be rewritten.

Understanding NT 4

The most obvious change that occurred with the release of NT 4 was that it adopted the Windows 95 user interface. Although the interface had changed, administrators who were familiar with the previous iterations of NT quickly learned that many of the built-in utilities had not.

New Technology File System (NTFS) Developed by Microsoft for the NT operating systems, this feature added better file management, larger disk compatibility, and file-level security on the local computer.

NT Server 4 had two versions:

- NT Server 4 (Standard version)
- NT Server/E 4 (Enterprise version)

NT Server 4

Several enhancements were included in the NT 4 version release:

- Performance improved over previous versions of NT. On a single-processor computer, NT 4 ran up to 66 percent faster in file and print tests than its predecessors.
- More drivers were supported during installation than ever before. NT 4 increased support to more than 1,000 hardware devices. This made installation and setup much easier, because the driver software for network interface cards and video adapters was likely to be available through the NT installation media.
- Hardware profile support was a feature added for mobile users who used their laptops on the road and when the laptops were connected to additional hardware in the office.
- Critical error messages were rewritten to provide clearer information and possible solutions.
- Administrative wizards were added to step administrators through common configuration tasks.
- Improvements to Task Manager included the added feature of Performance Monitor, which enabled administrators to easily and quickly view memory and resource use.
- New services, such as Internet Information Server (IIS) and Index Server, were added. Internet Information Server 2.0 was Microsoft's first introduction of a World Wide Web server as a part of the operating system. Index Server added the capability to search directories on an NT server by using a web browser.
- A new protocol was added for *Remote Access Service (RAS)*. Point-to-Point Tunneling Protocol (PPTP) enabled you to create encrypted communications between a Windows 95/98 or compatible client computer and an NT 4 server running RAS.

Remote Access Service (RAS)
Allows computers to access the network remotely; for example, through a phone, ISDN, or Internet connection.

clustering
Connecting two or more computers to make them appear as one system. Clustering is used to take advantage of the processing power of multiple computers.

load balancing
Distributing similar tasks (such as accessing an application or assigning an IP address) equally across multiple computers.

NT Server/E 4

This Enterprise version of NT Server added greater support for larger networks with higher performance demands by including many features and services:

- *Clustering* services were supported for two-server clusters. These services provided fault tolerance and *load balancing*. Clustering services were able to monitor server health and reliability, and recover applications and data in the event of system failure by using the second server in the cluster.

♦ The user was licensed to run more than four *symmetric processors* without special *original equipment manufacturer (OEM)* versions of NT Server. Windows NT Server/E 4 could support up to 32 Symmetric Multiprocessing (SMP) processors.

♦ Better memory tuning existed for applications with high memory requirements. This version could also use up to 4 GB of RAM per application as opposed to previous versions of NT, which supported only 2 GB of RAM.

♦ NT Server/E 4 also shipped with these services: Service Pack 2, Internet Information Server 3, Microsoft Transaction Server (MTS), Microsoft Message Queue Server (MSMQ), and FrontPage 97. Each of these services addressed specific needs of large companies that needed to take advantage of Enterprise's powerful features for Internet-based applications such as IIS.

Microsoft periodically releases service packs for its operating systems and various products. Service packs traditionally only contained fixes to known problems, but now they may also include new features and functionality for the target system. Microsoft recommends that you always install the latest service pack.

symmetric processors
Two or more processors in a computer that are capable of completing processes simultaneously, which maximizes performance.

original equipment manufacturer (OEM)
A term used to describe the device or software that is sold to a reseller who then passes the product on to a consumer. OEM versions of software can sometimes be altered by the reseller in an effort to make the product integrate with the reseller's hardware.

NOTE

Understanding Windows 2000/Windows Server 2003

Just when most people thought they had NT under their belt, Microsoft announced the release of Windows 2000. Originally, Windows 2000 was named NT 5. It was supposed to ship in 1998 but was delayed. After many beta releases and an incredible level of input from the Windows community, Microsoft released Windows 2000 to manufacturers on February 17, 2000. Windows 2000 built on all of the core principles that were established as a part of the NT operating system release.

Windows 2000 had four *platforms*:

♦ Windows 2000 Professional was the business desktop operating system that offered the superior performance of NT Workstation but with several significant enhancements.

♦ Windows 2000 Server.

♦ Windows 2000 Advanced Server replaced the Enterprise edition of NT 4 as the next-generation Windows cluster server.

♦ Windows 2000 Datacenter Server was designed for the most demanding server environments found in large companies or high-demand websites.

All versions of Windows 2000 include several major changes from Windows NT 4:

♦ A 64-bit operating system that supported Intel's 64-bit Itanium processor.

♦ Plug-and-Play capability was included. This capability enabled the operating system to recognize hardware additions or changes to the system and automatically load the necessary software if available or prompt the user for the software.

platform
The hardware or software that supports any given system. The term platform can be used, for example, to reference an x64-based system or Windows Server 2008 R2.

◆ Microsoft Management Console (MMC) was extended as the central management interface for all administrative tools. With MMC, administrators could customize the console they were using.

◆ FAT32 disk partitions were supported. FAT32 is a way of formatting your logical drives to store data more efficiently than by using FAT16. This had been supported by Windows 95/98 but not by previous versions of NT.

◆ Windows 2000 had no Alpha processor support.

Just a few short years after the release of Windows 2000, Microsoft went through a paradigm shift in their operating system strategy and announced that the server and client versions of the operating system would follow different naming conventions as well as individual release dates. The client operating system release that followed is still one of the most commonly deployed and run client operating systems today: Windows XP. Windows XP was released in October 2001 in a 32-bit format.

The next iteration of the Microsoft core server operating system took another year and a half to complete and was subsequently released as Windows Server 2003 in March 2003. March 2003 also yielded the first 64-bit version of the Windows XP operating system.

The Windows Server 2003 release provided improvements over its Windows Server 2000 predecessor in both performance and quality while it was still able to provide value to the organizations that committed to deploying it.

A summary comparison of the Windows NT and Windows Server 2003 operating systems displays the leaps and bounds made across the platform releases through the years:

	Windows NT 4	**Windows Server 2003**
Network Model	Domain	Directory services
Plug-and-Play support	No	Yes
Management Tool format	Multiple	Microsoft Management Console
Performance	Baseline performance	100 times more scalable
Disk formats supported	FAT16, NTFS	FAT16, FAT32, NTFS
Ease of use	Minimal wizards	Improved and expanded wizards and much improved installer
Recovery options	Use of repair disk or reinstall	Safe mode and capability to repair damage

	Windows NT 4	Windows Server 2003
Reliability	Reboots for every device change, service installation, and some configuration changes	No reboots for device configuration, most software installations, and for configuring and starting services

The Windows Server 2003 product family offered four editions, each catering to particular consumer and business segments and their needs and budgets:

- Windows Server 2003 Standard Edition, designed for the most common server environments

- Windows Server 2003 Enterprise Edition, designed for larger enterprise environments or businesses that required higher reliability and performance

- Windows Server 2003 Datacenter Edition, designed for businesses that used mission-critical applications and also needed a higher level of scalability and reliability

- Windows Server 2003 Web Edition, designed to be optimized for hosting web servers

Windows Server 2003 System Requirements

The system requirements and support for the Windows Server 2003 platforms are specified in the following table:

Windows Server 2003	Web Edition	Standard Edition	Enterprise Edition	Datacenter Edition
Minimum RAM	128 MB	128 MB	128 MB	512 MB
Recommended RAM	256 MB	256 MB	256 MB	1 GB
Maximum RAM	2 GB	4 GB	32 GB for x86-based computers, 1024 GB for Itanium-based computers	128 GB for x86-based computers, 1024 GB for Itanium-based computers
Minimum CPU speed	133 MHz	133 MHz	133MHz for x86-based computers, 733 MHz for Itanium-based computers	400 MHz for x86-based computers, 733 MHz for Itanium-based computers

Windows Server 2003	Web Edition	Standard Edition	Enterprise Edition	Datacenter Edition
Recommended CPU speed	550 MHz	550 MHz	550 MHz	733 MHz
Multiprocessor support	1–2	1–2	Up to 8	Minimum of 8, maximum of 32
Disk storage for setup	1.5 GB	1.5 GB	1.5 GB for x86-based computers, 2 GB for Itanium-based computers	1.5 GB for x86-based computers, 2 GB for Itanium-based computers
Cluster nodes	No	No	Up to 8	Up to 8

NOTE System requirements are subject to change, and you should check Microsoft's website for the most current specifications.

Windows Server 2003 Family Features

The following table summarizes the features found in the different Windows Server 2003 families:

Feature	Web Edition	Standard Edition	Enterprise Edition	Datacenter Edition
.NET Framework	Yes	Yes	Yes	Yes
Active Directory	Limited	Yes	Yes	Yes
Metadirectory Services (MMS) support	No	No	Yes	No
Internet Information Services (IIS) 6.0	Yes	Yes	Yes	Yes
ASP .NET	Yes	Yes	Yes	Yes

Feature	Web Edition	Standard Edition	Enterprise Edition	Datacenter Edition
Enterprise UDDI services	No	Yes	Yes	Yes
Network load balancing	Yes	Yes	Yes	Yes
Server clusters	No	No	Yes	Yes
Virtual Private Network (VPN) support	Limited	Yes	Yes	Yes
Internet Authentication Services (IAS)	No	Yes	Yes	Yes
IPv6	Yes	Yes	Yes	Yes
Distributed File System (DFS)	Yes	Yes	Yes	Yes
Encrypting File System (EFS)	Yes	Yes	Yes	Yes
Shadow Copy Restore	Yes	Yes	Yes	Yes
Removable and remote storage	No	Yes	Yes	Yes
Fax services	No	Yes	Yes	Yes
Services for Macintosh	No	Yes	Yes	Yes
Print services for Macintosh	Yes	Yes	Yes	Yes
Terminal services	No	Yes	Yes	Yes
IntelliMirror	Yes	Yes	Yes	Yes
Remote OS Installation (RIS)	No	Yes	Yes	Yes
64-bit support for Itanium-based computers	No	No	Yes	Yes
Datacenter Program	No	No	No	Yes

Understanding Windows Server 2008/ Windows Server 2008 R2

Windows Server 2008 and Windows Server 2008 R2 are the latest additions to the Windows Server family. Windows Server 2008 was released in February 2008. Windows Server 2008 R2 is an update to Windows Server 2008 and it was released to manufacturing in July of 2009 and became generally available in October 2009. Windows Server 2008 R2 is Microsoft's first 64-bit-only operating system release. The Windows Server 2008 R2 product family offers seven editions to choose from:

Windows Server 2008 R2 Foundation Edition, designed as a cost effective and simple environment for small businesses

Windows Server 2008 R2 Standard Edition, designed for the most common server environments

Windows Server 2008 R2 Enterprise, designed for businesses that use mission critical applications and require more support and reliability than the Standard edition

Windows Server 2008 R2 Datacenter, designed for the largest scale enterprise deployments with the highest level of scalability and availability

Windows Web Server 2008 R2, designed as a web server exclusively

Windows HPC Server 2008 R2 Suite, designed for high-performance computing and able to support large clusters spanning thousands of nodes

Windows Server 2008 R2 for Itanium-based systems, designed for the Intel Itanium processor

The different editions cater to the different customer needs by offering a group of features and capabilities that appeal to specific budgets and roles.

Windows Server 2008 R2 System Requirements

Microsoft provides system requirements guidance for their operating systems as part of each release. Windows Server 2008 R2 is no different, with the one key difference being that this release is only available in a 64-bit platform. The system requirements for Windows Server 2008 R2 are as follows:

Windows Server 2008 R2	Web Edition	Standard Edition	Enterprise Edition	Datacenter Edition
Minimum RAM	512 MB	512 MB	512 MB	512 MB
Maximum RAM	32 GB	32 GB	2 TB	2 TB
Minimum CPU speed	x64-based 1.4 GHz	x64-based 1.4 GHz	x64-based 1.4 GHz	x64-based 1.4 GHz
Multiprocessor support	Up to 4	Up to 4	Up to 8	Up to 64
Minimum Disk space	32 GB	32 GB	32 GB	32 GB

An Intel Itanium 2 processor is required for Windows Server 2008 R2 Itanium-based systems.

——————————————
——————   ***NOTE***   ——————

   This chart depicts the recommended specifications, but as any administrator will tell you, typically more is better. This is especially true when it comes to disk space. The minimum disk space allocations shown in the chart allow you to install the operating system, but they do not accommodate any additional files.

   Depending on the intended usage of the server, you may need to allocate additional disk space. Examples of additional content that may require disk space include print spooling, application installations, or application source files. Now that you are familiar with the minimum requirements, it is time to look at the features for each edition so you can better understand each edition and its role.

Windows Server 2008 R2 Family Features

The seven editions of the Windows Server 2008 R2 all have a variety of features that differentiate them from each other. By looking at what the primary editions include, it is easier to understand what the intended purpose is for each of the specific editions. A summary of these features is outlined for easy reference in the following table:

Feature	Web Edition	Standard Edition	Enterprise Edition	Datacenter Edition
Hyper-V Virtualization	No	Yes	Yes	Yes
Windows PowerShell (MMS) support	Yes	Yes	Yes	Yes
Internet Information Services (IIS) 7.5	Yes	Yes	Yes	Yes
ASP .NET	Yes	Yes	Yes	Yes
Network load balancing	Yes	Yes	Yes	Yes
Server clusters	No	No	Yes	Yes
Virtual Private Network (VPN) support	Limited	Yes	Yes	Yes

Feature	Web Edition	Standard Edition	Enterprise Edition	Datacenter Edition
Network Access Protection	No	Yes	Yes	Yes
IPv6	Yes	Yes	Yes	Yes
Distributed File System (DFS)	Yes	Yes	Yes	Yes
Encrypting File System (EFS)	Yes	Yes	Yes	Yes
Shadow Copy Restore	Yes	Yes	Yes	Yes
Remote desk-top services	No	Yes	Yes	Yes
IntelliMirror	Yes	Yes	Yes	Yes
Windows deployment services	No	Yes	Yes	Yes

As you can see, each edition has its strong points, with the Enterprise-oriented editions being more robust and having more features. Microsoft Windows Server 2008 R2 includes new virtualization features, new Active Directory Domain Services features, and Internet Information Server 7.5.

As the latest step in the evolutionary process of the server operating system, Microsoft Windows Server 2008 R2 is powerful, secure, and reliable. It has come a long way from Microsoft Windows NT, and just like its ancestor, it will some-day be replaced by something more advanced and even more powerful, secure, and reliable.

Terms to Know

clustering

load balancing

NTFS

OEM

platform

RAS

symmetric processor

Review Questions

1. List the five major design goals of the NT operating system.
2. What are four of the seven platforms available with Windows Server 2008 R2?
3. Which version of NT first used the Windows 95 Desktop interface?
4. Which edition of Windows Server 2008 R2 will support a system with 32 processors?
5. What is the minimum RAM that can be used to install Windows Server 2003 Standard Edition?
6. What does EFS stand for?
7. What is the first version of NT to support 64-bit processing?
8. What is the purpose of MMC?
9. What is the first version of the server operating system to support FAT32?
10. What is clustering?

Chapter 13

Windows Server 2008/2008 R2 Active Directory Domain Services

di•rec•to•ry ser•vice *n*: the format used by an operating system to identify and organize objects on the network

Before Windows Server 2008 and Windows Server 2008 R2 were released, Windows Server 2003 was the operating system of choice for businesses of many sizes. Microsoft included Active Directory in Windows Server 2003, and it is still used in conjunction with Active Directory Domain Services running on Windows Server 2008 and Windows Server 2008 R2 in many environments today.

Features of the Active Directory Domain Services

One of the major tasks of any network operating system is keeping track of users and regulating resource access. In Windows Server 2003 this was performed by using Active Directory. With the release of Windows Server 2008 and Windows Server 2008 R2, Active Directory was renamed Windows *Active Directory Domain Services (AD DS)*. AD DS is a directory service that consists of forests and domains; these utilize a database structure to house directory objects that are replicated between the servers that host the directory database.

NOTE — **For a review of the directory service model, refer back to Chapter 9, "Network Models."**

In Windows Server 2008 and Windows Server 2008 R2, the directory service provides a way to keep track of users, machines, groups, and other network- and user-related information. The AD DS provides services more efficiently and with more features than previous iterations of Active Directory.

One of the most interesting things about both Active Directory and AD DS is that the location of a resource—its *physical location*—is transparent to users. With AD DS, users can access shared directories and printers just by knowing the name of the share. The directory does the rest, by finding and connecting users to the resource they have requested.

Another interesting characteristic of the AD DS is that it is tightly tied to the Transmission Control Protocol/Internet Protocol (TCP/IP) and the Internet Domain Name System (DNS). All Windows Server 2008 and Windows Server 2008 R2 domain names are structured like Internet domains. If your company's name is FOO, your Windows Server 2008/2008 R2 domain might be foo.com. The short version of the domain name is called a NetBIOS name and is written FOO. (Windows Server 2008 R2 domains still receive a NetBIOS name for backward compatibility.) The NetBIOS name is understood only by other Microsoft-compatible machines; the domain name (foo.com) can be understood and referenced by any machine that can use TCP/IP. This is just one of many ways in which the AD DS tightly integrates with and complies with Internet standards.

physical location
The actual location of a resource. Each resource must be homed on a server somewhere on the network. Windows Server 2008/Windows Server 2008 R2 enable you to organize resources logically rather than physically.

TIP — **Because of this level of integration, Windows AD DS is dependent on the presence of the TCP/IP protocol suite, and more specifically DNS. TCP/IP and DNS must be installed in order for AD DS domains to be used.**

The following table shows other Internet specifications that are supported by AD DS. Note that each of the specifications listed is in actuality a TCP/IP protocol. The TCP/IP protocol suite is made up of a number of protocols that work together to provide network functionality. Each of the items in this list is therefore a separate Internet protocol, with its specific function listed to its right.

Specification	Purpose
DHCP	Stands for Domain Host Configuration Protocol. Internet Protocol (IP) addresses must be unique for each machine on a network, and DHCP automates the process of assigning addresses and other TCP/IP information.
NTP	The Network Time Protocol provides timekeeping and time synchronization functions, which allow machines to check their internal clocks and make certain that the entire network knows the proper time.
LDAP	The Lightweight Directory Access Protocol provides a way to query Active Directory to request email addresses, usernames, and other data.
LDIF	The LDAP Data Interchange Format is used for bulk import and export operations on a directory.
Kerberos	This advanced authentication protocol provides enhanced security during logon and resource access.
X.509 certificates	Certificates are used to prove who you are. They can be used for functions such as digital signatures, for sending secure messages by encrypting them for transmission, and for authentication.

Last, AD DS object naming is based on a structure known as *X.500*. This is an industry-standard naming structure that allows millions of objects to be uniquely named easily and logically. Within AD DS, every object is assigned a distinguished name (DN). The DN of an object consists of naming components that are hierarchical in nature, that uniquely identify the object within the directory, and that also can be interpreted to identify the location of the object within the directory. The DN for a user named Humphrey Bogart within an AD DS domain named foo.com would look like this:

X.500

An industry-standard directory structure used by Windows Server 2008 and Windows Server 2008 R2 to organize and name network elements. Other network operating systems, such as Novell's NetWare Directory Services, also use X.500.

```
CN=Humphrey Bogart,CN=Users,DC=foo,DC=com
```

In this example DC is the abbreviation for domain component. DC is used to represent each portion of the domain name in which the user account exists. CN is the abbreviation for common name and is used to indicate the name of an object within the directory. In this case, CN=Users is referencing an AD DS container called Users that is typically used to store user and group objects. CN=Humphrey Bogart represents the user object itself.

Structure of the Active Directory Domain Services

In Windows NT 4, Microsoft used a flat directory model for its domains. The resulting structure was simple and straightforward on small and medium-sized networks but could become confusing and difficult to manage on an enterprise scale.

As a result, the NT 4 successor, Active Directory, was developed based on multiple industry standards, such as LDAP and X.500, to be hierarchical in nature. This hierarchical structure was brought forward into Windows Server 2008 and its Active Directory Domain Services (AD DS). The hierarchical structure is established by creating multiple object types within AD DS, such as organizational units (OUs), domains, trees, and forests. Each type is explained in the following sections.

TIP

If you are familiar with the Windows Server 2003 Active Directory structure, think of the Windows Server 2008 and Windows Server 2008 R2 AD DS environments as being the same, with OUs as subdivisions of domains, and trees and forests as better ways of organizing and connecting domains.

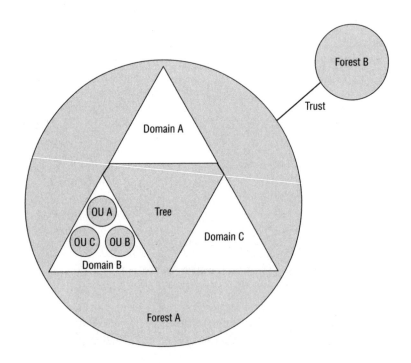

Windows Server 2008 and Windows Server 2008 R2 Domains

The most basic Windows Server 2008 and Windows Server 2008 R2 security structure is the *domain*. Domains are independent administrative units with their own security boundaries and administrative policies. All domain controllers (DCs) within a domain replicate their information to each other automatically and all host a read/write copy of the directory database. This is known as a *multimaster replication model*. Any domain controller can receive changes and then replicate these out to other servers in the domain.

The one exception to the multimaster replication model is the *Read-Only Domain Controller (RODC)*. An RODC is a type of domain controller that was introduced with Windows Server 2008. RODCs host read-only copies of the AD DS database and cannot write any changes to the directory.

In small branch offices where a single server may perform multiple functions or in locations where a local administrator is not present, RODCs make it possible for directory services to exist while reducing the level of risk associated with deploying a standard domain controller under the same circumstances. They can be useful in locations that lack physical security, but they can be deployed anywhere in the enterprise. Since the database is read-only, if the server is compromised or even stolen, the level of possible damage to the directory is greatly reduced.

To allow for an orderly migration from Windows Server 2003 Active Directory, Windows Server 2008 and Windows 2008 R2 AD DS supports coexistence with Active Directory domain structures and security through the use of a Windows Server 2003 domain functional level. Then, after you upgrade all your domain controllers to Windows Server 2008, you can perform a one-time conversion to the Windows Server 2008 functional level. If all your domain controllers have been upgraded to Windows Server 2008 R2, you can then convert the domain environment to run at the Windows Server 2008 R2 functional level. Each incremental domain level has additional features that are unavailable to the previous levels. The following is a Windows Server 2008 R2 Raise Domain Functional Level screen, from which you can switch domain levels.

replicate
The process by which a machine sends a copy of its databases to another machine. This usually occurs on a scheduled basis.

child domain
A domain created under the namespace of an existing tree within a forest.

global catalog
A fast-access copy of the full directory representing all objects within a forest that includes only those attributes that are commonly searched, such as usernames and logon names.

schema
The set of configuration elements that defines a particular directory. The schema contains information about all objects and attributes in the directory.

TIP

Since Windows Server 2008 and Windows Server 2008 R2 share the same directory services model, the upgrade from Windows Server 2008 to Windows Server 2008 R2 requires no special configuration.

As new domains are added, you have three choices:

◆ Create the new domain as a *child domain* in the existing tree. If you simply create the new domain as a child domain, permissions and other configuration information are shared automatically between the domains.

◆ Create the new domain as a new tree in the existing forest. Configuration data—the *schema* and *global catalog*—will be shared, but the domains will be separate administrative entities.

◆ Create the new domain as a new tree in a new forest. This provides the greatest degree of administrative separation and makes interaction between the domains more difficult. No configuration data is shared, and trusts must be set up to share resources between forests.

You do not have to upgrade clients or member servers to use higher domain levels.

Organizational Units

organizational units (OUs)
Organizational units break the directory into subdivisions and are used to group and store directory objects such as groups, user accounts, and resources.

Within Active Directory, you can arrange the objects in the domain by using *organizational units (OUs)*. This allows for administrative flexibility and presents multiple possibilities for permissions assignments and modeling within the directory. Here are some administrative examples:

Limiting administrative authority within the domain   If your domain has three campuses, you can create an OU for each and assign a different administrator access to each.

Organizing users by function   You can create OUs for Sales, Accounting, Manufacturing, and so on. You can then add users and resources to these and manage them as a group. Here users and resources have been arranged using OUs.

TIP

Trusts, which you will learn about later in this chapter, have multiple types: Parent-Child, Tree-Root, External, Forest, Shortcut, and Realm.

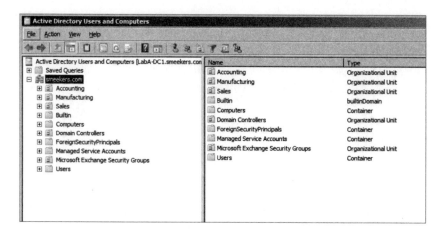

The beauty of combining Active Directory's capability to support millions of objects and its capability to subdivide domains into OUs is that a single domain will be all that many companies ever need.

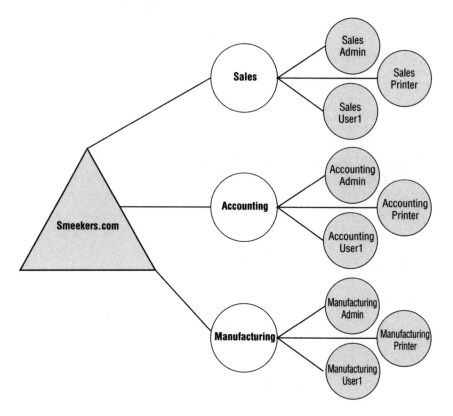

Forests and Trees

Microsoft's use of the words *tree* and *forest* can be confusing. You do not, for instance, need a bunch of trees to make a forest. A tree is simply a single domain or a set of domains that all have a similar DNS naming structure, and a forest consists of all the trees within a single organization.

When the first server is installed in a new domain (foo.com), it becomes a domain controller within that domain and also is the *parent domain* of a new tree. If you are not joining an existing forest, this tree also becomes the root domain of a new forest, or the forest root domain. Although you have installed only one server, you now have a domain, a tree, and a forest.

The real difference between a tree and a forest is not in the numbers. Within a single tree, all the domains must fall under a contiguous *namespace*. Assume that you have created the domain foo.com in your New York office, and now you want to create additional geographically based domains in Hong Kong, Rome, and Fargo. If you want to use a subdomain of the parent namespace, you need to put the new domains into the same tree. To do this, the new domains will need to incorporate the existing DNS name, such as apac.foo.com or europe.foo.com. We will explore the concept of forests and trees more in the next sections.

Forests

A *forest* is created when the first domain controller in an environment is installed, thereby establishing the first domain. The first domain in a forest also represents the first tree in the forest. The first domain in a forest is referred to as the *forest root domain*.

However, if an enterprise contains multiple naming conventions, it is important to understand that these varied naming conventions can be supported in a single forest by using multiple trees. Different namespaces are incompatible and can't be used in a single tree, but they can still remain within the same forest, since a single forest can contain multiple trees.

A forest allows the administrator to create multiple domains organized into multiple trees while still retaining a distinct security boundary and remaining within the same enterprise.

Thinking of a forest in terms of an organization helps to better define it. In most cases, all domains in a single company will be placed into a single forest. Domains are grouped into trees within the forest based on namespace delineation, and additional domains will be created based on geographic or administrative need. Additional domains can be added to existing trees at any time as security or administrative circumstances dictate.

TIP

Remember that Windows Server 2008's and Windows Server 2008 R2's AD DS will support millions of users and other objects. You should begin by assuming a single domain/tree/forest is best and only modify this plan based on particular requirements of your company or client. The major reasons for creating multiple domains in AD DS are based on administrative models and bandwidth limitations.

---

parent domain

The domain from which all other domains in a tree take their name.

tree root

The top domain within a newly created namespace. All other domains in the tree must fall within the tree root domain tree's namespace.

namespace

The part of the naming structure occupied by a certain domain or tree. If the domain is foo.com, all machines and subdomains of foo.com exist within its namespace: www.foo.com, accounting.atlanta.foo.com, and so on.

Trees

Each tree within a forest can be used to establish multiple domains within the same naming context. The first domain in a new tree is referred to as the *tree root*. Note the following two graphics. In the graphic on the top, notice how the DNS namespaces are in different branches. These, therefore, are not within a single tree. In the bottom graphic, the three new domains nest under the foo.com parent domain and share its DNS namespace. They are incorporated into a single tree within the forest.

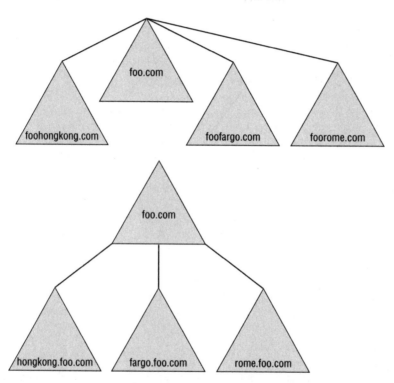

What all of this means is that if you have a company with four offices, you may want to split up network administration by using four domains in a single tree. As long as the naming structure is not an issue, this is the easiest and most integrated approach to adding domains. If Aathe namespaces within the organization are non-contiguous, you can also add new domains into a forest with their distinct namespace to form additional trees. Each tree in a forest has a distinct naming convention. Multiple trees, each with its own distinct namespace, are depicted in the top graphic above.

Windows Server 2008 and Windows Server 2008 R2 Trusts

Trusts allow domains within a forest and domains between forests to communicate and exchange authentication information so that users can access resources across

trust
A trust is configured to allow two Windows domains to share user authentication information and to allow users from one domain to access resources in another domain.

the enterprise regardless of their account location in the AD DS. In a Windows Server 2008 and Windows Server 2008 R2 forest, trust relationships are automatically created between all domains. This occurs in one of two ways: A trust may be formed due to a parent-child relationship that occurs between domains within the same tree, or there may be a tree-root trust, which is established between a tree root and the forest root upon installation of the first domain in the new tree.

All of these trusts are transitive in nature, therefore, if Domain A trusts Domain B, and Domain B trusts Domain C, then Domain A transitively trusts Domain C. The transitive nature of these trusts allows all domains within a forest to trust all other domains within the forest without administrator intervention. This allows a domain to act as a security boundary while authentication of security principals flows throughout the forest. A security principal is an object that is assigned a security identifier (SID) and is typically used for granting resource access within the environment.

In addition to the two trust types that are natively set up, there are four types of trusts that can be manually configured by the administrator: External, Forest, Shortcut, and Realm.

External Trusts

transitive

Trusts that are transitive allow a domain to act as an intermediary for two other domains. If A trusts B, and B trusts C, there is an implied trust between A and C. Directory information will pass from A to C only if B acts as a transitive link.

An *External trust* is used to connect a single domain within a forest to a single domain that exists outside the forest. External trusts are not *transitive*. External trusts are unidirectional in nature, and in order for a two-way relationship to exist between two domains in different forests, two External trusts need to be established, one in each direction. Because of this, if five domains all needed to trust each other—referred to as a complete trust—20 trusts must be created and maintained. As you might suspect, this could quickly become an administrative nightmare, as shown in the following graphic. Note that each arrow represents the directionality of a single External trust.

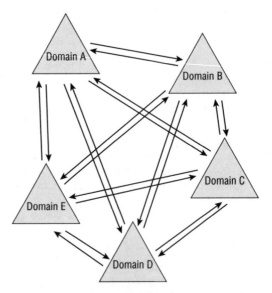

Even though this model is still available in Windows Server 2008/Windows Server 2008 R2, it is intended only for the purpose of backward compatibility or for short-term or emergency connections between otherwise separate domains. Here is the Trusts tab on a Windows Server 2008 R2 DC; it shows the two fields where External trusts can be established. Note how the trust is configured in each direction individually.

Forest Trusts

Take a look at the preceding example. If you created five Windows Server 2008/ Windows Server 2008 R2 domains within a single tree and needed to connect all of these domains to all of the domains in an external forest containing two domains, doing so using External trusts would mean that you would have a very large number of trusts that needed to be configured.

A better option in a situation like this is to create a *Forest trust*. A Forest trust establishes either a one-way or a two-way transitive trust relationship between all the domains in each forest. The trust is established between the forest root domains in each forest. This saves the administrator from creating endless numbers of trusts and getting endless headaches!

Although External trusts can be used between forest roots, the nontransitive nature of the trust relationship means that the other domains in each forest do not trust each other and will not allow resource sharing. Only the forest roots in each forest will be able to resource share with each other as a result of this External trust configuration.

NOTE

Shortcut Trusts

By default, within a forest, trust relationships already exist between domains. However, trust relationships are only directly established between parent-child domains and tree-root domains. Due to the transitive nature of these trusts, all domains indirectly trust each other, but when authentication takes place within the forest, the established trust paths must be followed.

The authentication request is passed along trust paths until it reaches the appropriate domain. One way to reduce the transit time for authentication is to manually create Shortcut trusts between domains that frequently need to pass authentication traffic back and forth. Shortcut trusts can only be created between domains within a forest and are always automatically transitive.

For instance, let's assume that Darien has a user account that resides in Domain C, which is the third domain within a tree, and has a DNS namespace of `sed.us.foo.com`. Domain C is a child domain of Domain B with a namespace of `us.foo.com`, which is a child domain of Domain A with the namespace of `foo.com`.

An application that Darien uses every day has been deployed into Domain A and he has been granted access to the application. When Darien tries to access the application, the domain controllers in Domain A will receive the authentication request for the application. Since Darien's user account resides in Domain C, the Domain A domain controllers must pass the authentication request down the trust path to Domain B to request authentication.

Since Darien's account doesn't reside in Domain B, the Domain B domain controllers must pass the authentication request down the tree again to Domain C to request authentication. Authentication is granted by the Domain C domain controllers, and it then has to be passed back up the trust path from Domain C to Domain B and then from Domain B to Domain A. This process must complete before Darien is allowed access to the resource!

By manually establishing a Shortcut trust from Domain A to Domain C, the domain controllers in these domains are able to directly pass authentication requests, removing Domain B from functioning as a middleman. This streamlines the authentication requests and allows quicker access to applications and resources for users accessing content across domain boundaries within a forest.

Realm Trusts

Realm trusts are used to establish trust relationships between non-Windows Kerberos realms and an AD DS domain in a Windows Server 2008/Windows 2008 R2 forest. Realm trusts can be one-way or two-way and can be configured to be either transitive or nontransitive.

The Physical Network

In addition to the logical structure of domains, trees, and forests discussed earlier, there are other things you should consider when you're planning an AD DS environment. One of these is the layout and configuration of the actual physical network. This impacts two primary AD DS considerations:

◆ Geographical placement of domain controllers

◆ Bandwidth availability and management between sites

Sites

A *site* is defined as a part of the network that is typically connected by a high-speed *local area network (LAN)*. The advantage of defining multiple sites within AD DS is that replication traffic between domain controllers and other server-to-server communications can occur at scheduled times or at certain frequencies by configuring a *Site Link*.

In the following example, your company has established headquarters in Fargo and has branch office locations in Los Angeles, Atlanta, and New York. Each of the sites has a 512 Kbps connection back to headquarters. To be able to control bandwidth utilization during the day, you may create separate sites representing each of the offices. You would then use Site Links to connect the sites, which can then be configured to replicate directory content only in the evenings. Also, in the following image, the central site will pass the configuration changes on to all sites, so connectors do not need to be created between Atlanta and Los Angeles or any of the other branch offices.

local area network (LAN)
A LAN is contained within a single building or campus and can operate independently of any outside connection.

Site Link
A logical connection that links two sites and controls the flow of traffic over wide area network (WAN) links. Just as a trust regulates the flow of permissions and resources, a Site Link regulates the speed and type of traffic that is allowed across the WAN. Site Links therefore enable an administrator to optimize bandwidth usage.

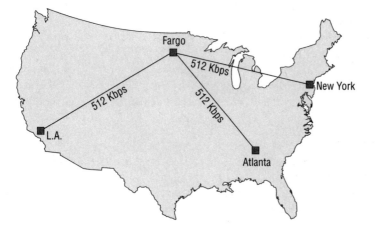

——————————
TIP
——————————
Remember that the logical and physical structures of the network do not have to be the same. A network with a physical connection structure like this one can still easily use a single Windows Server 2008/Windows Server 2008 R2 domain.

Domain Controllers

Domain controllers are servers that have Active Directory Domain Services installed and contain information about users and the security structure of the network.

Windows Server 2008/Windows Server 2008 R2 allows for a multimaster domain controller model. Most domain controllers contain a read-write copy of the entire domain's AD DS database. Most domain controllers are peers and therefore essentially equal, with the one exception being domain controllers deployed as RODCs. Also, there are a few special roles that are assigned to domain controllers at the forest or domain level called Operations Master roles, which are explained in more detail momentarily. These are the basic functions of a Windows Server 2008/Windows Server 2008 R2 domain controller:

◆ Keep a copy of the directory database.

◆ Process changes to the directory database.

◆ Alert other domain controllers of changes through replication.

◆ Perform authentication for users and computers within the domain.

——————————
NOTE
——————————
If you have a network with 10 Windows Server 2008/Windows Server 2008 R2 servers in a single office, you probably do not want to make them all DCs. You'll need at least one DC to create a domain, and a second is recommended for fault tolerance. You may need more than two in a location if the load generated by applications or user/computer authentication requests is large. It is important to monitor DC usage to ensure that adequate processing power is made available to the network environment.

Specialized Domain Controllers

Besides the purposes listed earlier, some Windows Server 2008/Windows Server 2008 R2 domain controllers can be assigned specific roles to play on the network. Domain controllers can take on the following roles:

◆ Global Catalog server

◆ Schema Master

◆ Domain Naming Master

◆ Relative Identifier (RID) Master

◆ PDC Emulator

◆ Infrastructure Master

Global Catalogs

One of the primary functions of a domain controller is the authentication of users, which could be accomplished by any domain controller on the network. In Windows Server 2008/Windows Server 2008 R2 AD DS environments, domain controllers that have been designated Global Catalog servers (GCs) also perform this task, but they have a more specialized function. Every GC in the forest stores all objects from all domains in the forest, but with a limited subset of attributes. This allows the GC to be used as a search repository for all objects that exist within the forest. The first domain controller in any domain is always a GC, but additional domain controllers have to be specifically configured if you want them to provide this functionality.

GCs also play a very specific role during user logon. If a user logs on to their domain using their User Principal Name (UPN), a GC is utilized to determine which domain in the forest should be utilized to authenticate the user's logon request. GCs are also queried by domain controllers for Universal Group memberships. Since Universal Groups can exist in any domain in the forest and can contain members from any domain in the forest, DCs must query a GC to ensure that a user has the appropriate Universal Groups added to their access token during logon.

The Global Catalog has a representation of all objects in the entire forest, not from only one domain. On large networks, the Global Catalog can significantly speed up the process of finding resources in other parts of the forest.

NOTE

Operations Master Roles

Besides GCs, several other domain controller roles are assigned to specific machines. Each of these functions must be performed by one—and only one—server, either within the forest or the domain. There are five types of specialized domain controllers, collectively known as Operations Master roles, which were once referred to as Flexible Single Master Operation (FSMO) roles. Initially, all these roles are given to the first server in the forest and some are also assigned to the first server in each domain, but they may be reassigned to other domain controllers later.

> **Schema Master**   Holds the master reference as to the objects in the forest and the way objects are organized. Also manages all updates to the schema by hosting the only writable copy of the schema. Only a single Schema Master exists within a forest.

Domain Naming Master   Manages the addition or deletion of domains and directory partitions within the forest. Only a single Domain Naming Master exists within a forest.

security identifier (SID)
A unique number used by Windows Server 2008 and Windows Server 2008 R2 AD DS to represent a user or a computer on the network.

Relative Identifier (RID) Master   In Windows Server 2008/Windows Server 2008 R2 domains, an object's security identification number is referred to as a *security identifier (SID)*, just as in previous versions of Active Directory. The SID consists of a domain identifier (which uniquely identifies the domain) and a relative identifier (RID) that uniquely identifies the object in the domain. Together, these two numbers distinguish an object from all other objects in the forest. The RID Master in a domain manages and tracks the pool of available RIDs and assigns groups of RIDs to other domain controllers in the domain so they can be used for assignment during object creation.

PDC Emulator   The PDC Emulator has a misleading name. When Windows NT 4 domain controllers existed within an Active Directory domain environment, the PDC Emulator did manage replication to NT 4 Backup Domain Controllers (BCDs). In Windows Server 2008 and Windows Server 2008 R2 domains, BDCs cannot exist but the PDC Emulator is still utilized. It serves as the master for all password changes and as the source time server for all machines in the domain.

Infrastructure Master   This domain controller manages and tracks security principles from other domains in the forest that are members of groups within its own domain. In a multidomain forest, the Infrastructure Master should not be homed on a DC that also serves as a Global Catalog server.

Terms to Know

child domain	schema
global catalog	security identifier (SID)
LAN	Site Link
organizational unit (OU)	transitive
namespace	tree root
parent domain	trust
physical location	X.500
replicate	

Review Questions

1. The Active Directory Domain Services (AD DS) is based on the _____ directory standard.

2. NTP is used for _____.

3. Which specialized type of domain controller is used by Windows Server 2008/Windows Server 2008 R2 domains to ensure that all machines in the forest have their time in sync?

4. What is the purpose of an External trust?

5. True or false: All clients on the network must be upgraded from Windows XP to Windows 7 before you can use higher domain levels.

6. Which protocol must be installed with the operating system in order for a Windows Server 2008/Windows Server 2008 R2 domain to be created?

7. Which contains more objects, a domain controller or a Global Catalog server?

8. Two considerations when planning where to place sites on the physical network are geographical location and _____.

9. True or false: In Windows Server 2008/Windows Server 2008 R2, all domain controllers can authenticate users.

10. The _____ ensures that new objects in a domain receive a unique ID to identify them on the network by generating a pool of RIDs for the domain controllers to use.

11. True or false: If five domains in a forest all need to access each other through trusts, only one PDC Emulator is needed in the forest to accomplish this.

12. The connector used to manage traffic between two geographical locations or two poorly connected subnets is a _____.

13. The first domain you create in a new forest also creates a new tree, known as the _____ of the forest.

14. True or false: If you have a domain called `foo.com` and a domain called `foofoo.com`, they can reside in the same tree, since they share the `foo.com` namespace.

Chapter 14

Account Management

group *n* : an object created to represent a number of users that is used in assigning rights and permissions

Account management is the process by which an administrator configures the network to allow users to access what they need and to prevent them from accessing what they shouldn't. Sounds simple, right? Actually, it pretty much is. Each user is represented on the network by an object (their user account) that has membership in one or more groups. An administrator assigns these group objects permissions to use other objects, files and printers, for example.

This chapter explains the first part of that process—creating the users and groups that enable you to identify and organize users on the network. Chapter 15, "File and Print Management," then finishes the process by showing you how to give permissions to network resources.

Structuring the Active Directory

An old saying warns us, "A stitch in time saves nine," and the basic premise underlying the statement still holds true: A bit of extra work in the planning stages of any job is the best way to save you trouble and embarrassment later. Planning a network is no different, and when you are setting up your new Active Directory, you should resist the urge to simply start adding users and other *object*s immediately. Active Directory Domain Services (AD DS) is very forgiving of this—moving objects from place to place is extremely easy. Still, why make an account and move it, when you can just wait a bit and put it in the right place to start with?

You should try to have two organizational elements in place before adding other objects: organizational units and groups. These objects will be created based on an analysis of the network, its resources, and its users, and will provide the foundation on which all other permissions rest.

object
Every element of the network—from people to machines—is represented in the Active Directory by an object. These objects each represent one specific element of the network and have their own properties and configuration elements.

Organizational Units

An *organizational unit (OU)*, as shown in Chapter 13, "Windows Server 2008/2008 R2 Active Directory Domain Services," provides a way of organizing resources logically within the domain. There are two primary reasons to create an organizational unit: for administrative delegation or for policy management. To determine your OU structure, first identify any groupings of users or resources within your organization that need to be kept separate from other areas for one of these two reasons.

Good examples of areas that are often given their own organizational units are accounting and personnel departments. Rather than allow all administrators of the domain to have *admin access* to accounting and personnel resources, you may find it preferable to assign a specific user the role of personnel administrator or accounting administrator. To do this, you create organizational units, and then create users and assign them administrative *rights*. This is a good example of how to create OUs for administrative delegation.

A real-world example of this is shown in the following exercise.

organizational unit (OU)
Organizational units break the directory into subdivisions and are used to group and store directory objects such as groups, user accounts, and resources.

admin access
What is granted as a result of having membership in the Administrators group.

rights
A right is different from a permission. Rights allow you to do a task, whereas permissions concern a particular resource. For instance, in order to access a particular file, a user must have permission to use that file, whereas changing the system time is considered a right.

TIP

Remember that you can divide a domain in two ways—physically and logically. A physical division uses sites and Site Links. It is generally used to control traffic over wide area network (WAN) links and user logon traffic. A logical division uses organizational units and is used to organize objects and break up administrative authority.

Test It Out: Designing a Directory

A company with 400 employees wishes to deploy AD DS. The company has four locations: Los Angeles, Chicago, New York, and a Fargo headquarters. Fargo has 175 users, and each of the branches has about 75. There are four major divisions within the company as well: manufacturing, personnel, accounting, and sales. Each division requires distinct policies to be applied to their user accounts. In addition, each division is active at all sites.

1. How many domains would you recommend?

2. Would you use organizational units? If so, would you make them geographic or administrative?

3. How would you break up administrative control?

Answer: Any of a number of options may be acceptable, but one answer is closest to the spirit of how Active Directory is intended to be configured. This option would create only a single domain with four organizational units based on company departments. There is no reason why the domain would have to be split up, and organizational units based on the company divisions will provide administrative separation between the divisions and allow for a simple model of policy application to their user accounts.

To create a new organizational unit, open *Active Directory Users and Computers*, which is located in the Administrative Tools group on the Start menu under All Programs. Right-click the domain in which you wish to create the new organizational unit and select New ➢ Organizational Unit. You will be asked to supply a name for the new *container*. When you have finished, the new name will appear under the domain and will be ready to have resources such as users, printers, computers, and even groups added to it.

Active Directory Users and Computers

This tool, found in the Administrative Tools, enables you to manage users, groups, and other elements of Active Directory and is based on the Microsoft Management Console model.

container

Any object in the directory into which other objects can be placed. Objects that do not have this capability are called leaf objects.

Groups

Creating groups also requires planning. Groups are objects that enable a number of users to be administered as a single account. Whereas users are created to identify individuals on the network, groups are created for the purpose of grouping users and assigning permissions to the group for a particular task or role. Users can be given permissions to resources directly, but this is not recommended; groups are the standard mechanism for granting access. Therefore, you will want to create a number of groups, some of which may even have only one member!

TIP Creating a group of one may seem like a lot of unnecessary work, but this process has a number of advantages over simply giving that user permissions to resources directly. For instance, if the user who performs backups goes on vacation, you can simply put the user who is covering for that person into the backup group temporarily. If you did not have a group, you would have to assign the temporary backup user rights and permissions equal to those of the original backup user. This would take time and be confusing to administer. Once again, plan early and avoid trouble later!

Using and Creating Groups

AD DS allows for four types of groups: global, domain local, universal, and local. Each of these has a particular scope (area of use), and AD DS is stocked by default with a number of built-in groups of each type.

In general, the use of groups in AD DS is similar to the use of groups on local machines, and indeed many of the built-in groups listed in this section are identical in name to the groups found locally on every Windows operating system.

global groups
Groups that hold users in the domain and that are placed into universal, domain local, or local groups. Global groups are primarily used to group users with similar network roles.

The recommended method of utilizing groups consists of several steps. First, you need to create *global groups* in the environment. These are used for assigning permissions and typically map to a job function. Next, create user accounts and then place them into one or more global groups. These global groups are then placed into domain *local groups*, and the domain local groups are given permissions to resources.

If you are looking for a process to remember this by, Microsoft has two acronyms it recommends:

local groups
Groups that are created on Windows 7 workstations and Windows Server 2008/2008 R2 servers and allow for local administration of resources. Global groups or domain users could be placed into these groups to give them permissions on the machine.

AGDLP   This stands for Accounts placed into Global groups, which are placed into Domain Local groups, which are given Permissions to resources.

UGDLR   Users are placed into Global groups, which are placed into Domain Local groups, which are given permissions to Resources.

TIP Neither of the "official" acronyms is especially catchy, and you might find this works better: Remember that setting permissions is one of the U-G-DL-ie-R tasks you will need to perform!

Types of Groups

Besides the standard built-in groups, there are also five other default system groups that are not based on who the user is, but on how they are connected to a resource. These are the Everyone, Authenticated Users, Creator Owner, Network, and Interactive groups. The Interactive group, for instance, includes only those users who are logged on locally to a machine. If the same user accesses a share across the network, they are considered to be in the Network group. These last five groups cannot have their membership configured through the Active Directory Users and Computers tool, but they can be used while setting permissions on resources.

Global Group

Only users from the same domain in which the global group is created can be added to this group, but the group can be used to access resources in any domain in the forest. Global groups are generally used to organize users with similar roles in the organization. One user may be in any number of global groups.

Built-in Global Group	Description
Domain Users	Includes all users created in the domain.
Domain Admins	Accounts added to this group gain full administrative power of the domain.
Domain Guests	The only default member in this group is the Guest user, which is disabled by default. Users can be added to this group to allow them temporary, low-level access to the network.
Enterprise Admins	Administrators on the domain who need to administer other domains in the forest as well can be added to this group, which must then be given rights in the other domains (usually by being added to the domain local Administrators group in those domains).

Domain Local Group

This group type allows users, universal groups, and global groups from any domain in the forest to be members and should be used to apply permissions for resource access, but only within the domain in which the group has been created. These groups are generally used to identify resources that have a similar function on the network.

Built-in Domain Local Group	Description
Account Operators	Allows members to create and configure user and group information, but not network resources.
Server Operators	Allows members to create, configure, and delete network resources such as printers, files, and shares. Members can also set permissions on these resources but cannot create or modify users or groups.

Built-in Domain Local Group	Description
Administrators	The Domain Admins global group is placed into this group, and it is this Administrators domain local group that wields power on the domain. Members can add users and groups as well as create and configure resources.
Guests	The Domain Guests global group is a member of this domain local group. Any permissions granted to Guests will be available to all Guest users (if Guest access is enabled).
Backup Operators	Allows members to perform backup and restore procedures
Users	Contains the Domain Users global group and, by extension, all users on the domain

Universal Group

Users and global groups from any domain in the forest can be members of this group, and they can be given permissions to resources in any domain. This group is generally used in large multidomain networks. Universal groups and their entire membership are stored on all Global Catalog servers (GCs) in the environment. This means that when changes are made to Universal groups, such as adding or removing members, more replication results between GCs in the forest. In order to reduce the amount of replication traffic whenever possible, you can choose to place global groups into universal groups. This way, if universal group membership needs to be changed, it is performed by adjusting the membership of the global group that is nested in the universal group. Since this is not a direct change to the universal group membership, this does not result in Global Catalog replication. There are no built-in universal groups, however, in an environment that is running Microsoft's email software, Microsoft Exchange Server; groups that are used for sending and receiving email messages are required to be universal groups.

Local Group

A local group is created locally and exists only on a single machine. It is used to assign permissions only to resources that are on the machine that the group was created on. These groups are available on Windows 7 and Windows Vista workstations and on Windows Server 2008/ 2008 R2 servers that do not have Active Directory installed on them. For the most part, the built-in groups mirror the domain groups that are named similarly, but their scope does not extend past the machine they are created on.

Built-in Local Group	Description
Administrators	Allows full access to all machine configurations and resources
Power Users	Allows users to install software and hardware and do some admin tasks
Backup Operators	Allows access to file resources for backup
Users	Includes accounts that need non-admin access to the machine
Guests	Can be used to grant low-level guest access to the machine

Power Users

Intended to allow Windows users greater authority over their workstations. Power Users are not as powerful as the Administrator, but they can do far more than just Users, in that they can install software and configure more workstation options.

Creating a Group

Although the built-in groups can help get you started, you will likely want to create groups of your own. Creating a group is relatively straightforward. Within the Active Directory Users and Computers tool, select a container for the new group and create the group by right-clicking the container and selecting New ➤ Group. This allows you to then use the New Object – Group window shown here to name the group and set its Type and Scope. After you have created a group, you can add users to it as they are created. You can also add users from the group's Properties window later.

Configuring a Group

After you have created a group, you can configure a number of elements concerning that group, including adding users to the group. To do this, right-click the group in Active Directory Users and Computers and select Properties. Using the Members tab, you can select users and add them to the list of members. You can also add the group to other groups, select a manager for the group, and add other information regarding the group object.

Reasons for Using Groups

Organizing permissions that are assigned to groups is easier than organizing them on an individual user-by-user basis. Here are two other reasons for getting used to using groups:

- ◆ If you create a network by using standard Microsoft techniques (remember A-G-DL-P?), another administrator who knows the same techniques can easily manage the network when you go on vacation—or when you take a more lucrative position elsewhere!

- ◆ Microsoft certification exams expect you to assign permissions the "right" way, meaning by utilizing the recommended Microsoft method.

User Accounts

After you have created your organizational units and groups, it is time to add user accounts and begin matching users with the resources that they need to do their jobs. The first factor that you should consider at this point is, *just what is a user account, and what is it good for?* This is a slightly more difficult question than it may seem at first.

When you create a new account for Ulysses Grant in your accounting department and another for Teddy Roosevelt in the sales department, you will likely put each of them into separate groups, with permissions to various resources that reflect the access required by their departmental membership. Remember, though, that in truth you are not assigning *them* access, but rather you are assigning *their role in the company* access. A user account, in other words, represents a particular job in the company—not an individual. If Teddy decided to leave the company and run for president, all you would have to do is rename the account and give it to the person hired to replace him. That person would then fill the role and would have all the rights necessary to do their work.

The other point to remember is that in a well-implemented network, user accounts actually do not have permissions to resources at all. This is not to say that users should not be able to access files or printers! A user account is created, given particular configuration options and rights based on its network role, and is then placed into groups that provide access to the resources needed. In other words, groups, not individual users, should have permissions granted.

You should never have to give a user *explicit permission* to a resource (file, directory, or printer). Doing so can cause significant confusion and raise questions such as, "Why can that user print to the color printer? None of the groups she is in has rights to it." The answer may be that another administrator gave the user explicit permission to the printer for a particular task and then forgot to take it away. Although it is certainly possible to give users permissions directly, in general you should remember to use the groups. That's what they're there for.

explicit permission
Occurs when a user is given permissions to a resource without any groups involved.

Other than the users you create, two built-in users are created with the domain:

Administrator   The most powerful account on the domain, the Administrator account cannot be deleted, only disabled, and effectively has access to all resources and configuration options on the domain. Access to the Administrator account password should be kept to a small number of people. Oh, and don't forget the password.

Guest   The Guest account is used to provide anonymous access to certain resources on the network. This is obviously a low-security option, and the

Guest account is disabled by default. It can be useful for visitor access in a kiosk or for allowing read-only access to certain materials on the network.

Creating User Accounts

If possible, a user account should be created for every individual on the network. Shared accounts (for example, Interns) can certainly be created, but if all interns use the same username and password to log on to the network, it is difficult to maintain any real distinction between them in a security context. It would be far better to create separate accounts—Intern1, Intern2, and so on.

To create a new user, simply go to Active Directory Users and Computers and select the container you wish to create the user in. The default is the *Users folder*, but you can also place the user in an organizational unit. Right-click the container and select New ➢ User. When you create a new user, you will be able to configure the following information.

Users folder
One of a number of default containers in the Active Directory. In most cases, using this default location is fine for storing user accounts. User accounts in this folder can later be placed into groups that exist in other folders or organizational units.

Data	Description
First Name	User's first name
Initials	User's initials
Last Name	User's last name
Full Name	Full name
User Logon Name	Unique name within the Active Directory forest
Password	Authentication information used to log on the user.
Confirm Password	The initial password, assigned by the administrator, is retyped here to ensure it is correct.
User Must Change Password at Next Logon	If the user is assigned an initial password by the administrator, this option ensures that the user will create their own password when they first use the account.
User Cannot Change Password	Prevents a user from changing a password. Good for shared accounts.
Password Never Expires	Overrides password expiration options.

You can require specific password lengths, expiration times, and password reuse policies. Although these provide greater security, don't make the policy so draconian that users can't remember their passwords. Users writing their passwords on sticky notes and leaving them on their monitors is usually a good clue you have gone too far!

TIP

Before you start creating users, make sure that you have worked out an acceptable naming convention, or policy. For instance, will you use first initial last name, such as ugrant **and** trooseve1t, **or first name last initial, such as** u1yssesg **and** teddyr? **If the company is small enough, perhaps just** U1ysses **and** Teddy **will do. Regardless, make sure you create a naming strategy that works for the organization and can expand. What happens when a second Ulysses Grant is hired, for instance?**

Configuring User Accounts

After you have created an account, you will be given a number of additional options that will add to or restrict the power of the account on the network. To access an account's configuration information, select the account in Active Directory Users and Computers and right-click it. Select the Properties option. The User Properties window has a number of tabs, including those shown here.

Tab	Configuration Options
General	Name, display name, description, office, phone, email, web page
Address	Full mailing address
Account	Logon name, logon hours, workstation restrictions, account options, account expiration
Profile	*Profile* path, logon script, and home folder locations
Telephones	Additional phone numbers and comments
Organization	Job title, department, company, manager, and direct reports
Member of	Group and Primary group memberships
Dial-in	Remote access, callback, and IP address info

profile
A record of the user's personal configuration data and preferences. You can store a profile locally or you can store all user profiles on the server and allow them to roam, which means a user could log on to any machine in the domain and get their own profile.

Many of these fields are simply informational, such as the Address and Telephones fields. Others serve specific network security or organizational purposes. The Account and Profile tabs are extremely important to understand, because they allow an administrator to set network locations and user options, including:

- Through the use of a logon script, an administrator can map drives for a user, attach printers, and set system or user variables. However, this is typically performed with Group Policies in most networks today.

- Profiles can be used to standardize the Windows Desktop and to restrict which programs or options a user can access.

- Home folders can be set up to ensure that all users have their own place on the network to store files. Home folders are secured so that only the user who owns the folder can access its information. Be aware that these days, it is also common and easier to manage if you redirect a user's Documents folder to a network location using Group Policy instead of assigning them a home folder.

◆ Logon Hours and Workstation Restrictions options enable the administrator to specify the times that a user can use the network, as well as the
machines that they are allowed to use.

◆ Account options enable the administrator to set password options, such
as how the password is saved for the user, and when it expires.

These options give you a great deal of power over the way that users access
and use the network. Thus, the end of this chapter returns us to the same idea
that we started with: Taking extra stitches here means taking enough time to
figure out what your users need, and how you can best configure the network
to make their job easier and their work secure. You will therefore want to think
carefully about the consequences of implementing any of these options. Using
home folders, for instance, allows for easier network backup of user files, but
it also means that if the home folder server ever fails, users will not be able to
access their files until the server is available again.

**Depending on which options you have installed, you may see more than just the
eight tabs described here.** *Remote Desktop Services,* **for instance, adds multiple
tabs to the User Properties page when installed.**

Terms to Know

Active Directory Users
and Computers

admin access

container

explicit permission

global groups

local groups

object

organizational unit (OU)

Power Users

profile

rights

Remote Desktop Services
(RDS)

user account

Users folder

Review Questions

1. Each user on the network is represented in Active Directory by a user _____ object.

2. Windows Server 2008 R2 user accounts are created and managed by using which tool?

3. An object that can hold other objects is known as a _____.

4. _____ are used to logically group objects within a domain.

5. True or false: A user may be in only one group other than the default Domain Users group.

6. A user who needs to administer multiple domains may be made a member of the _____ group.

7. Users who need to set permissions on files but do not need to modify user accounts should be placed into the _____ group.

8. In general, should users be placed into global groups or domain local groups?

9. Which type of group usually is assigned access to resources?

10. Groups created in Active Directory to allow membership from any domain in the forest are known as _____ groups.

11. True or false: A user account in Windows Server 2008 R2 should be thought of as representing a role in the organization, not an individual employee.

12. The hours when a user may log on to the network can be configured from the _____ tab in the User Properties window.

13. Permissions give you access to resources, whereas _____ let you perform tasks.

14. True or false: Users can be prevented from changing their own password in Windows Server 2008 R2.

15. If you wish to share files from your Windows 7 machine but have no server to provide Active Directory services, you can use only _____ groups to provide this access.

Chapter 15

File and Print Management

share *n*: an access point to a resource or set of resources on the network

In Chapter 14, "Account Management," you looked at one half of the process of allowing users to access resources—creating users and groups. The other half of the process, covered here, is creating and making network resources available for these users to access. Numerous hardware and software components can be made available on the network, but by far the most commonly shared resources are printers and data directories.

In general, this second half of the process requires two steps. First, you need to create the resource and prepare it for use by network users. Second, you need to make it available through the process of sharing. This chapter takes you through both steps. You will also examine the creation and sharing of a printer in Windows 7/Server 2008 R2. You can use printers locally or share them through the network. Just as you can apply permissions to folders, you also can apply security to printers.

Sharing Folders

If more than one user needs access to the same data, the easiest way to provide access is to create a network share. In Windows 7/Server 2008 R2, you create a directory on the computer and then place the information you wish to share into the directory. The next step is to make the directory available to other users by creating a network share. The information is stored on the *local drive* of the machine that is sharing it but is then accessible by all users to whom you choose to give permissions to the network share or shared folder.

By applying security to shared folders, you can control how users access the folders. For example, assume you have a folder called DATA on a server that stores information for users in the sales department. You might assign members of the Sales group *Full Control* access to the share, assign members of the Accountants group *Read* access to the share, and not allow any other users any access to the share.

Local users can see which folders are shared on their computer through Windows Explorer or Computer Management with the Shared Folders Microsoft Management Console snap-in. Both of these tools are accessible from the Start menu and can be located easily with the Search Programs and Files feature. In the Computer Management console, under the Shared Folders section, a double-headed icon is displayed on the bottom left-hand corner of all shared folders. Details of the shared folder are also displayed in Windows Explorer in the details pane at the bottom of the screen, including information such as the shared state and who the folder has been shared with.

local drive
Storage that is physically located on the user's own machine. Often the only local drives are the primary hard drive (C: drive) and the CD-ROM (D: drive).

full control access
General term meaning that the user has Full Control permissions on the resource.

read access
Permissions that allow a user to view a resource but not modify it.

The term *server* is usually used to describe a *dedicated server*—a powerful machine reserved for use by administrators. In this chapter, though, *server* simply means a machine that shares resources. All Windows 7/Server 2008 R2 machines have the capability to share resources, and if the Windows 7 workstation at your desk is sharing a directory, then it is acting as a server.

NOTE

After a folder is shared, network users access the share through the Network utility (assuming the user has been given sufficient permission). Additional methods of access include mapping network drives and using a universal naming convention (UNC), such as \\server1\data.

Creating a New Share

To share a folder in Windows 7/Server 2008 R2, you must be a member of the Administrators group or have group membership in one of these groups:

- ◆ Server Operators (only on a Windows Server 2008 R2 member server)
- ◆ Power Users (only on a Windows Server 2008 R2 member server)

There are multiple methods available to create a share. In Windows 7/Server 2008 R2 the Create a Shared Folder wizard available in Computer Management simplifies the task greatly. To launch the wizard, open Computer Management, select Shared Folders, and then right-click on the Shares node in the tree pane and select New Share. The wizard will then walk you through selecting the file path to the folder that you would like to share, as well as the details of the share such as share name, description, and the offline settings for the share.

The final screen of the wizard allows you to select the initial permissions that will be configured on the share. You can choose to accept one of the three default configurations, or instead, choose to customize the permissions applied. Once the wizard is completed, the folder will be shared with all of the configurations, settings, and permissions specified.

In addition to the Create a Shared Folder wizard on Windows Server 2008 R2, a more complex wizard is available from within the Server Manager toolset—the Provision a Shared Folder wizard. The basic concept is the same with both wizards; however, the Provision a Shared Folder wizard supports advanced server concepts in addition to basic folder sharing.

For instance, if a network has Unix-based systems installed that must access shared resources from the Unix system that resides on a Windows Server 2008 R2 machine, then the administrator can choose to install the Network File System (NFS) protocol on the Windows server. NFS allows file sharing with Unix-based systems, and within the wizard, the administrator can choose to enable this sharing type for a particular folder.

Additional server-specific settings include the ability to enable access-based enumeration, configure quotas for the file share, configure a file screening policy that restricts the file types that can be stored in the share, and publish the share to Distributed File System (DFS).

If the administrator finds that directly browsing to the folder to be shared is easier than using Server Manager or Computer Management, he or she will find that the new Share With menu option makes it simpler to configure the share. To create a network share using this method, right-click any folder and select the Share With option. The menu items displayed on the Share With menu will vary depending on the configuration of the machine.

If the machine is a member of a HomeGroup, then the options will include the ability to share with the HomeGroup. If the machine is only a member of a domain or a workgroup, the options will be limited to sharing with either Specific People or Nobody. When you select Specific People, it launches the File Sharing wizard, which is used to select individuals to share the folder with; the wizard allows you to select their corresponding permissions.

The traditional mechanism of folder sharing still exists within Windows 7/ Server 2008 R2. Someone with appropriate permissions can launch Computer or Windows Explorer, select a folder, click Properties, and use the Sharing tab to manually share the folder with either the Share button or the Advanced Sharing button.

The Share button launches the same File Sharing wizard as the Share With option that displays when you right-click a folder. If an administrator is accustomed to the traditional, more customizable method of adding users to a share, then the Advanced Sharing button provides the familiar options to do so. The Advanced Sharing options are outlined in the following table.

Option	Purpose
Share This Folder	Indicates whether the folder will be available for network access. You must check the box to share the folder.
Share Name	Specifies the name to be displayed that users will see when they access the share.
Comments	Enables you to provide a description of the folder. Users will see this description when accessing the share.
Limit the Number of Simultaneous Users to	Specifies how many concurrent users can access the share. In Windows 7, the maximum number is 20. In Windows Server 2008 R2, the number of connections is unlimited, but you must have sufficient Client Access Licenses to legally support the number of connections you set.
Permissions	This button displays the Share Permissions screen that allows permissions to be assigned; users and groups will have these permissions when they access the folder over a network share.
Caching	Configures offline access settings for the folder.

caching
A process whereby information is retrieved from the network and is then stored locally for use later, when the network is not available.

Applying Permissions for Accessing Folders

When a folder is shared, the method used to share the folder dictates what permissions the administrator will be able to select and where they will display on the share properties. When you're using the File Sharing wizard, only two options are available for assigning permissions to users or groups:

◆ Read

◆ Read/Write

You can select either of these permissions from a drop-down that appears for each of the users or groups having their permissions assigned in the File Sharing wizard. When you are using this wizard, only the groups or users specified are granted permissions and the permissions assigned are only visible within the wizard. If you desire, you can also use the wizard to remove users or groups and their permissions.

Share Permission	Description
Read	Allows a user to read the files within the folder.
Read/Write	Allows a user to read and make changes to files within the folder.

If you use the Advanced Sharing button to assign permissions, then the Everyone group is granted Read permissions to the share by default. You have the option of changing share permissions to restrict access to the folder for specific users and/or groups, but be aware that permissions you assign through the Advanced Sharing button are not displayed within the File Share wizard.

If the Create a Shared Folder wizard or the Provision a Shared Folder wizard is used to assign the permission, then the permissions granted are visible when you go to the shared folder's Data Properties dialog, select the Sharing tab, and click the Advanced Sharing button. When the Advanced Sharing dialog opens, click Permissions.

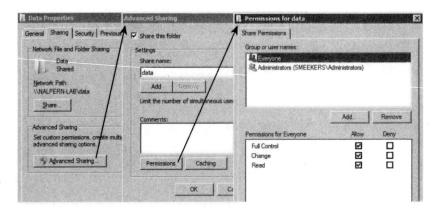

Advanced share permissions include

◆ Full Control

◆ Change

◆ Read

For each of these three permission options, you have two choices when assigning permissions to a share: You can allow a group access, or you can explicitly *deny* it access at any of the permission levels. Most commonly an administrator will only add groups to the access control list (ACL) that need to be granted permissions or explicitly denied permissions; therefore, all other groups in the environment will be left off the ACL. In this case, even though the other groups are neither allowed nor denied access on the share, this configuration functions as an implicit, or implied, deny to the share.

deny
To prevent a user from using other permissions to access a resource. It is far more powerful to deny than simply to not give users permissions.

Share Permission	Description
Full Control	Allows a user to read and make changes to files within the folder. In addition, a user can change the permissions for other users and groups and *take ownership* of files on New Technology File System (NTFS) partitions.
Change	Allows a user to read files, add files and subfolders, edit the data within existing files, delete files and subfolders, and edit file attributes within the shared folder.
Read	Allows a user to display files, read the contents of a file, execute program files, copy files to other folders, and display file attributes.

take ownership
Each file on an NTFS drive has an "owner"—a user account or group that is given complete access to that file. Taking ownership is the process of becoming the owner of a resource.

Be extremely careful when explicitly using the Deny permission. Deny not only prevents a group from using the resource, but it also keeps all members of the group out even if they are members of another group that has been granted permissions!

WARNING

Assigning Permissions to Users and Groups

You can apply share permissions to folders either to individual users or to groups. As noted in Chapter 14, it is recommended that you use the group strategy, but either way the processes are similar. When a user attempts to access a shared resource, the operating system must determine what access the user should have.

access token

A set of credentials that represents the user on the network and that contains information about who you are and what groups you belong to.

effective permission

A user's effective permission is the permission that they are actually able to use on an object after all permission elements have been added together (or denied, as the case may be).

Windows 7/Server 2008 R2 creates an *access token* each time users log on to a Windows 7 workstation or a Server 2008 R2 domain, and this token is the key to determining whether users can access network resources. The token specifies their unique user identification and any groups that they belong to. This information is used by the network to verify that users have share access permissions to the share that they are attempting to access.

If users have access permissions applied through user and group permissions, or if they belong to multiple groups that have access permissions assigned, their *effective permission* will be the most permissive permission that has been assigned. The exception to this rule is if users have a Deny permission through user or group assignment. If Deny has been assigned, users have no access to the resource at the level they have been denied, even if they have been granted that permission through other assignments.

For example, assume that you have two users, Kate and Magda. Kate and Magda are both members of the group Sales, while Kate is also a member of the group Execs, and Magda is also a member of the group Temps. These permissions have been assigned:

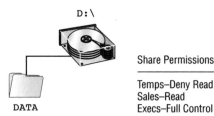

In this case,

- Kate is granted Read and Full Control. Her applicable permissions are Full Control, because it is most permissive.

- Magda is granted Read and also is denied Read. The resulting permissions is denied access, because Deny permissions will always take precedence over any allow permissions.

In the following exercise, you will experiment with setting share permissions. Make certain that you are logged on to a Windows 7/Server 2008 R2 computer with sufficient permissions to share folders. Note that in this section, you will first see the exact steps for sharing a folder, and then you will create test users and experiment with permissions levels.

1. From Windows Explorer, right-click the folder that is or will be shared.

2. Click Properties and then select the Sharing tab.

3. Click the Advanced Sharing option.

4. In the Advanced Sharing dialog box, click the Permissions button. You will see the following dialog box:

5. If you do not want to leave group Everyone with Read permission, highlight this group and click the Remove button.

6. To add new share permission assignments, click the Add button.

7. You add groups by typing in the group names, resolving them with the Check Names button, and then clicking OK. After the groups are added, select them in the Permissions dialog box list and add the proper permissions levels. To add user assignments, complete the same steps that you used to assign the group permission.

It is important that you use Network for this test, because this accesses the resource over the network and as a share. If you use Windows Explorer or Computer, you are accessing the resource locally, and no share permissions are applied.

TIP

Besides folders that you share, Windows 7/Server 2008 R2 also makes a number of administrative shares, and some applications also create shares. Be sure to research these and to account for them in your security planning.

TIP

logging on
The process of authenticating to the network and gaining access to the network as a particular user.

Test It Out: Sharing and Securing a Folder

1. Start by creating two users on which you can test share permissions. To do so, first make sure you are logged on as Administrator, and open Active Directory Users and Computers. Create a user named Kate and a user named Magda.

2. Next, create a folder that the users will share. Right-click Computer and click Open. Browse to a location on your local hard drive and create a folder. Name your new folder SHAREME.

3. To share the folder, right-click the SHAREME folder. Select Share With and then select Specific People.

4. In the File Sharing wizard, click the drop-down arrow and select Find People. Use the Select Users or Groups windows to add Kate and Magda and then click OK.

5. On the Choose People on Your Network to Share With screen, select Kate and use the drop-down to the right of her name to grant her Read/Write permissions. Repeat the same steps to grant Magda Read permissions. Then click the Share button at the bottom of the screen to complete the wizard and grant the permissions.

6. You can test share permissions by *logging on* as Magda and accessing the share through Network. If you try to create a file in the shared folder, you should be denied access, because Magda has only Read permission to the share.

7. Log on as Kate and repeat the test. Kate should be allowed to create a file in the shared folder since she has been granted Read/Write permissions.

Using NTFS

There are two independent mechanisms that can be employed to protect the files on your Windows 7 or Windows Server 2008 R2 system. You have already seen security applied at the share level, and now we will explore NTFS security. The basic differences between these are listed here:

Share	NTFS
Only takes effect if the user accesses the resource using the share path from the network	In effect regardless of how the user connects to the resource, either across the network or locally

Share	NTFS
Permissions include Full Control, Change, Read, and Deny in the Advanced Sharing model, or Read and Read/Write through the File Sharing wizard.	Has more complex permissions, including Read, Write, List Folder Contents, Read and Execute, Modify, Take Ownership, and Full Control.
Security can only be applied at the folder level and applies to all folder content.	Security may be applied to individual files and folders.

NTFS is more than just a security system, though. It is a file system that offers enhancements over the traditional File Allocation Table (FAT) system used by very early versions of Microsoft platforms. It is also significantly different from the FAT32 system that can be utilized by some versions of Windows. This section examines what NTFS is and the services and options it gives you when you are configuring your system.

FAT32 support was introduced with the release of Windows 2000. Windows 2003 and newer systems support FAT, FAT32, and NTFS file systems.

NOTE

To determine the type of file system that is configured on an existing drive, launch Computer and then right-click the drive and select Properties. Information is presented about the drive, including its file system and size.

Selecting a File System

Each local drive on a Windows server must be formatted with a file system before it can be used to store data. A *file system* defines how information is stored on the disk and defines the properties that can be applied to files. Windows servers support four file systems:

- ◆ FAT (File Allocation Table)
- ◆ FAT32 (File Allocation Table, 32-bit edition)
- ◆ NTFS (New Technology File System)
- ◆ CDFS (Compact Disc File System)

When you format your disk partitions, you may choose to utilize FAT/FAT32 or NTFS. This table describes some of the major differences between them.

FAT/FAT32	NTFS
Operating systems such as DOS, OS/2, Windows 3.x, Windows 95/98/Me, Windows 2000/XP, Windows Server 2003, Windows Vista, Windows 7, and Windows Server 2008 and 2008 R2 all support FAT. Windows 95/98/Me and Windows 2000, Windows XP, Windows Server 2003, Windows Vista, Windows 7, and Windows Server 2008 and 2008 R2 all support FAT32.	Windows NT, 2000, and XP, Windows Server 2003, Windows Vista, Windows 7, and Windows Server 2008 and 2008 R2 are the only operating systems that can access an NTFS partition.
If you require dual-boot capability to an operating system that cannot support NTFS or FAT32, you must use FAT.	If you wish to dual-boot to any other operating system than the ones listed above, you may not use NTFS for the system or boot partitions.
FAT/FAT32 offers no local security. This means that if multiple users share the same computer, all data stored on the FAT partition is available to all users.	One of the main advantages of NTFS is that you can specify local security. Because logon is mandatory, you can specify what rights users and groups have to NTFS folders and files.
No native file compression or encryption is available.	File compression and encryption is supported, although you can only use either file compression or encryption on a folder, not both at the same time.
You can convert FAT/FAT32 to NTFS at any time (except to the partition with the system files; for this partition, the actual conversion will take place during the next restart).	The only way you can go from NTFS back to FAT is if you reformat your partition. This means that you will lose all data and you must restore it from backup.

Understanding the Basics of NTFS

NTFS is the native file system of the Windows Server 2008 R2 and Windows 7 operating systems. You can format a disk partition to use NTFS by installing utilities or with the *Computer Management utility.*To convert an existing FAT disk partition to NTFS, you can also choose to use the CONVERT command-line utility as seen here:

    CONVERT [*drive letter*]: /fs:NTFS

For example, if you want to convert the C drive, you use this syntax:

    CONVERT C: /fs:NTFS

The main advantage of the NTFS file system is that you can apply *local security*, also referred to as local permissions. For example, assume that you have two users, Terry and Ron, who share the same computer. Each user has a folder at the root of C:\ called TERRY and RON, respectively. With NTFS permissions, you can specify that only user Terry has permission to the TERRY folder and that only user Ron has permission to the RON folder. This is possible only with NTFS and cannot be defined on FAT partitions.

When you format a partition as NTFS, permissions are applied in two ways:

◆ To any user who accesses the computer locally, meaning that user is logged on to the computer where the resource is located

◆ To any user who accesses an NTFS folder that has been shared over the network

NTFS permissions are different from share permissions in that you can apply them individually to both folders and files.

NOTE

Unlike Advanced sharing for shared folders, the Everyone group is not granted permissions by default.

WARNING

Computer Management utility
Used to monitor and configure the Windows 7 and Windows Server 2008 R2 computer systems. System tools, system drives, and services can all be accessed from here. To launch the Computer Management utility you must right-click Computer in the Start Menu and select Manage.

local security
Permissions settings that take effect even if the user is working locally on the machine where the resource is located.

Assigning NTFS Permissions

NTFS permissions allow for many more specific permission assignments than do share permissions.

NTFS permissions can be set at two levels: the file level and the folder level. As you have seen, share permissions are set only on folders.

Folder level   Setting permissions at the folder level changes the attribute for the folder object and also changes the default permissions of any new files or subfolders created in the folder. Existing files in the folder may also be set to the new permissions. Folder-level permissions include the following:

Permission	Allows
Read	View folder and files within it.
Write	Create new files and subfolders.
List Folder Contents	See the contents of the folder.
Read and Execute	View and run programs from the directory.
Modify	Change properties or delete the folder.
Full Control	Change permissions and ownership. Can create, modify, or delete folder and files.

File level Permissions set at the file level are generally best left the same as those of the folder they reside within, but this does not have to be the case. Each file has the capability to support security on its own. The following permissions can be set at the file level:

Permission	Allows
Read	View the file and its attributes.
Write	Change the content of the file.
Read and Execute	Used on a program file, it allows the user to run the program.
Modify	Includes Read as well as Read and Execute, but also allows the file to be deleted.
Full Control	Change permissions and ownership. Can modify or delete the file.

Special permissions are also available for configuration at both the folder and file levels. All available permissions are included as part of Full Control, however it is possible to allow permissions to be granted on a more granular level. The permissions available within the granular breakdown are referred to as *special permissions*.

Special permissions include capabilities such as the ability to take ownership as well as additional granular breakdowns of the more generalized permissions just described, such as Write. For instance, instead of applying the Write permission to a folder or file for a group, an administrator may choose to apply only the ability to Write Extended Attributes.

You apply NTFS permissions in a similar fashion to share permissions. One difference is that you can only apply share permissions to folders, and you can choose to apply NTFS permissions at both the folder and file levels. NTFS permissions are configured from the Security tab of a file or folder, which is accessed through the item's Properties.

Combining NTFS and Share Permissions

NTFS is similar to share permissions in the sense that if a user belongs to multiple groups that have been granted access to the same resource, the least restrictive access permission is applied. The exception to this rule is if the Deny permission has been specified. A user given Deny through any user assignment or group membership has no access to the specified resource for the permission type that has been denied.

If a user has a different set of permissions for a folder and the files within the folder, the file permissions are applied.

As an example, assume this directory structure:

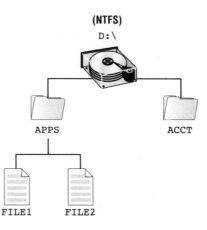

These assignments have been made:

Resource	Assignment	Permission
D:\APPS	Everyone	Read
D:\APPS\FILE2	Everyone	Modify
D:\ACCT	Temps	Deny Read, Deny Modify
	Accountants	Modify
	Managers	Full Control

These assignments mean:

◆ When accessing the D:\APPS folder locally, all users have Read permissions to the files in the folder except for FILE2, which has been explicitly assigned a different permission.

◆ A user belonging to Temps and Accountants would still have no local access to D:\ACCT, because Deny overwrites any other permission assignments.

Applying NTFS Permissions

To implement NTFS permissions, you must first format the disk partition as NTFS. If you have an existing partition, you use the CONVERT command to convert the drive and retain existing data.

To access the Security tab, which you use to assign NTFS security, complete these steps:

1. From Windows Explorer, single-click the folder to which you want to apply permissions.

2. Right-click the folder and select Properties.

3. Select the Security tab to view the Permissions area, shown here:

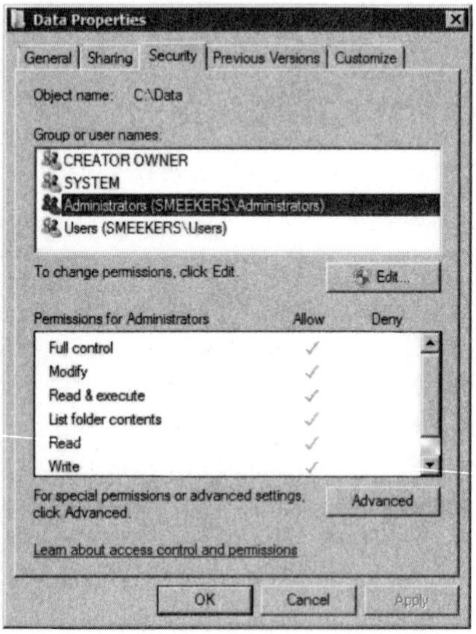

4. You will notice that the group Administrators has Full Control permissions. To change the existing permissions, click the Edit button. This displays the Permissions screen for the file or folder.

5. To make a new assignment, click the Add button to see the Select Users, Computers, Service Accounts, or Groups dialog box.

6. For each group to which you want to assign permissions, type the name of the group in the Enter the Object Names to Select box and click the Check Names button to resolve the groups. Click the OK button.

7. Back at the main permissions window, select each group in the Group or User Names section of the screen and set the permissions required.

NOTE

To manipulate NTFS permissions, you must be logged on as a user who has Full Control of the folder whose permissions you want to manipulate.

Understanding Share and NTFS Permission Interaction

Remember that by default the permissions on NTFS and share resources are set differently. If you leave these permissions as is, any folder you share may not have the appropriate NTFS-level permissions required for users to access the content from the network.

To prevent this, you must apply local security to the files (using NTFS permissions) and you must ensure that you use compatible share-level security on the shared folder itself. In deciding how you should approach this, you will need to take a few key elements into account:

♦ When you access files locally, only NTFS permissions are considered.

♦ When you access resources across a share, share permissions and NTFS permissions are combined and the more restrictive of the two are applied. For instance, if users have only read access to a shared file, they cannot modify it, even if they have Full Control of the file at the NTFS level.

♦ If NTFS permissions are more restrictive than permissions across the share, the more restrictive NTFS permissions will be used.

If you are concerned about providing maximum security for your shared resources, you will usually want to use NTFS permissions because they are more powerful and flexible than share permissions.

Consider this example:

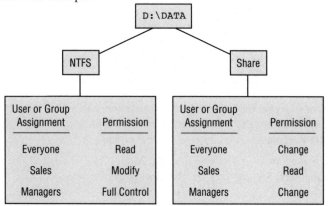

Scenario 1: Lars is a member of the Sales group and wants to access the DATA folder. If he accesses the folder locally, he will have only NTFS security applied and will have Modify access. If Lars accesses the DATA folder over a network share, the system will look at his NTFS access, which is Modify, and his share permission, which is Read. Because Read is more restrictive, this is the permission that will be applied over the share.

Scenario 2: Peter is a member of the Everyone group and the Managers group and wants to access the DATA folder. If he accesses the folder locally, he will have only NTFS security applied and will have Full Control access. If Peter accesses the DATA folder over a network share, the system will look at his NTFS access, which is Full Control, and his share permission, which is Change. Because Change is more restrictive, this permission will be applied over the share.

Accessing Resources

Resource access is what happens when a user tries to access any Windows Server 2008 R2 or Windows 7 object. The object can be a share, a file, or a network printer. By understanding resource access, you can more effectively troubleshoot access problems.

As stated earlier, when a user logs on to a computer, an access token is created. The access token is created only at logon. The access token identifies the user and any groups that the user belongs to. If the user is added to a group after they have already logged on, the user has to log off and log on again for the access token to be updated.

When the user attempts to access a resource, Windows checks the *Access Control List (ACL)* of the object, which identifies the users and groups that can access the resource. The ACL is part of the object and determines whether the user has permission to access the resource from a user or group permission assignment.

Access Control List (ACL)
List of users with permissions to a specific resource.

If the user or a group that the user is a member of is on the ACL, the system checks the *Access Control Entries (ACE)* for the user or group to see which permissions the user should be granted based on user and group assignments. If the user has a Read-Deny listed in the ACE, Windows will not even check for other Read permissions.

Access Control Entry (ACE)
List of permissions a specific user or group has to a specific resource.

TIP

A common error in access assignment occurs when a user fails to log off and then log on again before they try to access a resource for which they have been granted access via a new group membership. Whenever you make new group assignments, you should advise users to log off and then log on again. Many users do not realize that this is required to update their access token with the new group assignment.

Sharing Printers

In addition to files, printers are another common resource that users share over a network. If printer sharing didn't exist, any user who needed to print hard copies of information would have to have a printer attached directly to their own machine—a significant expense for companies and an administrative problem as well. With Windows Server 2008 R2, you can install a single printer on a machine on the network (usually referred to as a print server) and then allow numerous users to access it for printing services. This section covers how to install and share printers on a Windows Server 2008 R2 machine.

Understanding Network Printing Basics

To understand how network printing works, you should first contrast network printing with local printing. With local printing, you attach a physical printer to your computer (usually through a USB port) and install the software that comes with the printer. This process is generally straightforward. But, as noted before, in a large computing environment, this can be an expensive way to manage printing because each computer would require its own printer.

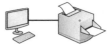

The next evolutionary step in shared printing is to allow multiple computers to access a single printer through some kind of device such as a *switch box*. With an A/B/C switch box, three users can share a printer. The first user is assigned port A, the second user is assigned port B, and the third user gets port C. In order to print, a user must walk over to the switch box and turn the dial to their port. This also is an inefficient way to manage printing for a large number of users.

switch box
A device that enables multiple machines to share a single device, such as a printer or a monitor. The disadvantage is that only one machine at a time can use the device.

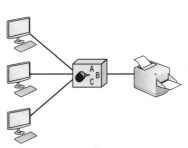

Network printing works in a different fashion. In this case, a special computer is designated as a print server. The print server runs a service called a print spooler that stores print jobs in a queue until they can be printed.

An analogy for network printing is that the print spooler is like the air traffic controller of printing. The spooler processes all jobs and determines which print jobs are printed and when. The print queue is like the gates and runways and serves as a place where print jobs can wait before they are actually printed. The print queue is a special directory on the print server, so you need to make sure that your print server has enough disk space to accommodate all the print jobs that potentially could be submitted at any one time. After a print job has completed, it is deleted from the print queue.

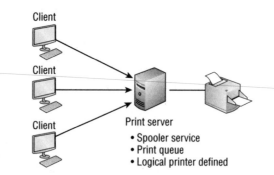

Here are some important terms that you should know for Windows Server 2008 R2 printing:

Printer   The software installed on the computer that enables it to format and manage information that needs to be printed. The printer is specific to a particular print device.

Print device   The actual physical printer or hardware device to which you print.

Print server   The computer on which the printer has been defined. Print jobs are sent to print servers before they are sent to the print device.

Print spooler   The service on the print server responsible for managing incoming print jobs and passing the print jobs to the print device.

Print queues   Special directories that reside on print servers and store print jobs until they are sent to the print device.

Creating a Printer

To create a printer, you must be logged on as an Administrator, Server Operator, or Print Operator. The Windows Server 2008 R2 software provides an Add a Printer wizard to help facilitate the creation of printers. To access the Add a Printer wizard, click Start, Devices and Printers. After you are in the Devices and Printers view, click the Add a Printer button at the top of the Devices and Printers screen.

This table describes the printer configuration options.

Configuration Option	Description
Local Printer or Network, Wireless Or Bluetooth Printer	Specifies whether you will create a new local printer (local) or connect to an existing printer on the network, across a Wireless network, or through a Bluetooth connection (network).
Find A Printer By Name Or TCP/IP Address (network only)	Enables you to find the printer in the directory, to browse to the printer, or to find it at a TCP/IP URL.
Choose A Printer Port (local only)	Specifies whether the print device will be connected to a local computer port (a parallel or serial port) or whether the printer has a network card and will be directly attached to the network.
Install The Printer Driver (local only)	Defines the printer so that the correct printer driver will be installed. You can use a default driver provided with Windows Server 2008 R2, a driver provided by the manufacturer, or a driver obtained over the Internet by using *Windows Update*.
Type A Printer Name (local only)	Enables you to define a name that will be used for the printer locally and to determine whether this will be the default local printer.
Printer Sharing (local only)	Specifies whether the print device will be configured as a local printer or a network printer. If it will be shared, you should provide a friendly name to identify it on the network.
Location and Comment (local only)	Used to help further identify the printer.
Print Test Page	Prints a sample page so that you can verify that you properly installed and configured the printer.

Windows Update
A set of online updates and drivers provided by Microsoft that allow users to locate current files for their system and for new devices.

Configuring Printer Properties

After you have created a printer, you can change the settings of the printer through its Properties sheet. To access a printer's Properties sheet, highlight the printer you want to manipulate, right-click it, and select Printer Properties.

This table shows some options you can configure. Because different printers may have specific options not available on other models, you might find that not all printers have the same Property tabs. One good example is the Color Management tab, which appears only on color-capable printers.

Configuration Option	Purpose
General	Specifies the general properties of the printer and includes comment information, location information, the driver that the printer will use, whether a *separator page* will be used, and the *print processor* that will be used. It also gives you the option of printing a test page.
Sharing	Configures the printer as a local printer or a network printer.
Ports	Configures the port that the printer is attached to. Ports can be local ports or network ports.
Advanced	Configures many options. You can specify which hours the printer is available, set the priority of the printer, specify whether jobs must be completely spooled before they are printed, and bypass network printing and print directly to the printer.
Security	Configures the printer's permissions.
Device Settings	Enables you to configure properties that are unique to your printer (based on the print driver you select). Device settings include options such as form assignments to paper trays and font cartridges used by the printer.

separator page
A page that is used to show where one print job stops and another one starts.

print processor
The print processor and the default data type determine how much of the formatting of a document is done by the printer, as opposed to the application.

Sharing a Printer

One option available in the Printer Properties window is the Sharing tab. To share a printer on the network, simply click this tab and check the box labeled Share This Printer. Accept the default or type a new share name for the printer—something people can easily identify. For instance, "3rd-Floor Color Printer" is easily distinguishable, whereas "Printer_02" is a bit vague.

The last sharing option is an important one. Unlike files, printers are not accessed in the same way by every operating system. Some operating systems may share *drivers*, such as Windows Vista and Windows 7, but other Windows operating systems may require a different driver type. Because of this, the Additional Drivers button enables you to install drivers for other operating systems, such as Windows XP, so that when users on those systems print, the server can offer them the correct driver and make sure they are able to print properly.

drivers
Software that allows a particular operating system (Windows 7, for instance) to access and interact properly with a specific device (an HP Color LaserJet 9000, for instance). Each piece of hardware may require a different driver for every operating system in which it is installed.

TIP

The sharing state of a printer that has been shared is viewable from within the Devices and Printers screen within the Details pane.

Establishing Print Permissions

In Windows Server 2008 R2, a printer is an object, like a share or an NTFS folder. Because printers are objects, you can assign permissions to printers as you do to shares. For example, if you have an expensive printer that is intended for the marketing department, you can share the printer as a network printer but allow only the Marketing group to have Print permission. As with files, you can either grant or deny any of the permissions levels shown momentarily. Files have two sets of permissions, Share permissions and NTFS permissions, printers do not. Printers use the Security tab to set the permissions for local use of the printer and for use through the network share.

This table defines the print permissions.

Print Permission	Description
Manage This Printer	Enables you to create, manage, and delete printers. Equivalent to Full Control file permissions.
Manage Documents	Enables you to manage documents that are submitted to the printer. With this permission, you can pause, restart, resume, and delete print jobs.
Print	Enables you to submit print jobs to a network printer and to manage your own jobs.

Special permissions are also available, just as in NTFS-based file and folder permissions assignments. To manipulate printer permissions, you highlight the printer in Devices and Printers, right-click the printer, select Printer Properties, and then select the Security tab. The following graphic shows a printer to which a number of groups have been given permissions.

Terms to Know

access token	local drive
ACE	local security
ACL	logging on
caching	print processor
Computer Management utility	read access
deny	separator page
drivers	switch box
effective permission	take ownership
full control access	Windows Update

Review Questions

1. Which groups can share folders on Windows 7 and Windows Server 2008 R2?

2. What is the default permission assigned when a folder is shared utilizing Advanced Sharing?

3. Sam is a member of the Sales and Managers groups. These share permissions have been assigned to the \\SALES\DATA share:

Sales	Change
Managers	Full Control
Peons	Deny Full Control

   The NTFS permissions on the folder are Everyone – Full Control. What permission will Sam have when he accesses this share?

4. Dianne is a member of the Sales, Peons, and Managers groups. These share permissions have been assigned to the \\SALES\DATA share:

Sales	Deny Change
Managers	Full Control
Peons	Deny Full Control

   The NTFS permissions on the folder are Everyone – Full Control. Which permission will Dianne have when she accesses this share?

5. True or false: You can apply local NTFS permissions to a FAT partition.

6. Which command do you use to change a FAT partition to NTFS while preserving existing folders and files?

7. True or false: When you apply NTFS permissions to a folder, they are applied to the folder's subfolders by default.

8. What minimum NTFS permission would you assign to a user who needed to create, edit, and delete files within a folder?

9. If a user's combined share permissions to a resource are Change and their combined NTFS permissions to the resource are Read, what access will the user have to the resource when it is accessed over the share?

10. If a user's combined share permissions to a resource are Read and their combined NTFS permissions to the resource are Full Control, what access will the user have to the resource when it is accessed locally?

11. The _____ is used to store print jobs before they are sent to the printer.

12. Which default permissions are assigned when a printer is created?

13. True or false: A Windows Server 2008 R2 print server can provide print drivers for Windows XP and Windows 7 clients.

14. In Microsoft terminology, a _____ is the actual physical printer.

Appendix A

Review Question Answers

Chapter 1

1. 8088

2. 8086 was a true 16-bit path.

3. The number of operations that are processed in one second

4. SDRAM is much faster

5. A DIMM is a Dual In-line Memory Module—a form factor used for RAM.

6. The internal speed of a computer or processor expressed in megahertz (MHz) or gigahertz (GHz)

7. Electrically eErasable pProgrammable ROM (EEPROM) typically maintains the BIOS code, which can be updated either with a downloadable file or with a disk that the BIOS manufacturer supplies

8. Programmable Read Only Memory - A chip used to hold specific code. Typically used with the system's BIOS

9. PCIe is a new computer expansion card standard that will eventually replace PCI and AGP PCIe standard offers a faster bus throughput and a smaller physical connector footprint and supports hardware I/O virtualization 10. 3.1 million

11. In the asymmetric multiprocessing (ASMP) model, one CPU is dedicated to managing tasks (which usually involves managing the other CPUs) for the computer system. The remaining CPUs process user tasks. In symmetric multiprocessing (SMP), additional CPUs can be added to boost performance.

12. A secondary processor that speeds operations by taking over math calculations of decimal numbers

13. 512 MB

14. RAM is volatile and will lose stored information if the power is shut off. In ROM, the content is stored, even if the power is turned off.

15. Faster bus speed

Chapter 2

1. SATA and SCSI
2. True
3. 7
4. 50, 68, or 80
5. SATA
6. A logical drive is one you create on a physical drive.
7. Volume set is created on a dynamic disk and allows you to create other redundant and fault-tolerant drives.
8. RAID 1, 5, 6, 10
9. Mirroring uses one disk controller and two drives. Duplexing uses two drives and two controllers.
10. False
11. True
12. You do not need to be connected to the offline storage to have access.
13. 25 GB
14. Capacity
15. Higher capacity, support for HDTV
16. True, just to be safe

Chapter 3

1. Serial communication is the process of transmitting and processing data one bit at a time.
2. In serial communication, data is transmitted and processed one bit at a time, whereas in parallel communication, data is transmitted and processed one *byte* at a time (or 8 bits).
3. False. The refresh rate signifies the number of times the beam of electrons shot from the electron gun redraws the screen in one second.
4. WUXGA, 1920 × 1200
5. DB-9 (oldest and rarely found any more), DIN-type, PS-2, USB (still most popular), and wireless (gaining popularity very quickly)
6. False
7. Modems convert digital signals from a computer into analog signals that can be transmitted over phone lines and convert incoming analog into digital signals. Cable modems allow high-speed access to the Internet over cable TV (CATV) lines.
8. Modems are limited to an FCC-mandated limit of 53 Kbps, whereas cable modems are not and can reach speeds in excess of 10 MBs.

9. True

10. False

11. This allows many users to use a single printer.

Chapter 4

1. Plug the hardware into the appropriate slot on the motherboard and connect any required cables. Configure the device through DIP switches, command-line or GUI.with cables or both.

2. IRQ, DMA, Base memory, I/O memory

3. The hardware device tells the processor that it needs attention through an interrupt request.

4. 5

5. False

6. 3F0-3F7

7. DMA enables a device to transfer data directly to RAM without using the attention of the processor for the entire transfer period.

8. 2

9. A software driver is the bridge between a piece of hardware and a specific operating system's software.

10. False

11. False

12. Direct Memory Access

13. Input/Output memory

14. Interrupt request

Chapter 5

1. Disk Operating System

2. graphical user interface

3. Windows 7

4. 6.2.2

5. Windows 98

6. X Window

7. V Unix, BSD

8. Ubuntu

9. True

10. X-Window System

Chapter 6

1. CD\

2. DEL C:\TEST\TEST.DOC

3. REN

4. You use ? to represent a single character, while * can represent any number of characters.

5. With MAKE DIRECTORY, you create a new directory. With REMOVE DIRECTORY, you delete the specified directory.

6. ATTRIB TEST.DOC +H

7. A PowerShell module is a collection of providers, functions, and cmdlets that can be utilized to extend the functionality of PowerShell.

8. Get-Help

9. Get-Module

10. Get-ExecutionPolicy

Chapter 7

1. The Recycle Bin

2. Network And Internet

3. Computer

4. The Taskbar

5. The Start button

6. Devices And Printers

7. Right-click on the Start menu and select Properties.

8. Help And Support

9. Shut Down, Switch User, Log Off, Lock, Restart, Sleep, and Hibernate.

10. False. The most direct way is by choosing Start ➢ Control Panel. These three examples do not have a direct route to the Control Panel.

11. They enable you to create a pointer that you can use to quickly and easily access another object.

12. A wizard is a program that steps you through the installation of a particular item.

Chapter 8

1. It makes networking easier to understand. It makes it easier to replace modular components as technology changes.

2. Session

3. Data-Link

4. Application

5. Network

6. Physical

7. Presentation

8. Transport

9. Logical Link Control (LLC) and Media Access Control (MAC)

10. Router

11. Connection-oriented services establish a connection between the sender and the receiver and are more reliable. Connectionless services send data without establishing a connection and are more efficient.

12. A physical address is identified at the Data-Link layer of the OSI model and is hard-coded on the network interface card. A network address is associated with the Network layer of the OSI model and is a logical address that the network administrator assigns.

13. Physical

    Data-Link

    Network

    Transport

    Session

    Presentation

    Application

Chapter 9

1. Peer-to-peer networks do not use dedicated network servers for authenticating users and providing secure access to network resources. In this model, clients share resources, and other clients have access to whatever has been shared.

2. The role of the domain controller, or DC, is to store the directory services database, which contains all of the objects in the domain environment. The DC also sends updates of the database to all other DCs within the domain.

3. DCs process logon authentication. They also provide fault tolerance if another DC were to go offline.

4. Directory services model

5. False. Each network model has its own strengths and drawbacks. No one network model meets the needs of every network.

6. Peer-to-peer network

7. An object is a logical representation of anything that can be managed on the network, including user accounts, servers, and printers.

8. False. In a client-server model, you need an account on each server on which you want to access resources.

9. False. You can add users to any single DC and the account information is automatically replicated to the other servers in the environment.

10. The directory services network model

Chapter 10

1. IP address; subnet mask; default router or gateway

2. DHCP

3. TCP/IP

4. Providing each attached device with a unique address

5. Network layer

6. TCP

7. Class C networks

8. TCP/IP

9. TCP/IP

10. Bus, Star

11. DNS resolves domain names to IP addresses, which makes accessing resources easier for people.

12. The subnet mask

13. False

Chapter 11

1. Reliability, scalability, performance, interoperability

2. Two or more CPUs can be used to simultaneously process a single instruction.

3. If an administrator accidently deletes an object, the object is recoverable within Active Directory, which often removes the need for a restore.

4. Configuration changes often require the server to reboot.

5. Windows Server 2003 R2 offers enhanced performance and reliability.

6. True

7. Unix is the most reliable, stable, and fastest NOS.

8. Both can be difficult to learn because of the vast number of commands.

9. In addition to the effort involved in learning commands, they will find very limited support for Linux.

10. It has characteristics similar, and in some cases, equal to Unix. And it is free.

Chapter 12

1. Provide flexibility in OS code

   Be reliable

   Offer high performance

   Use portable code

   Be compatible with existing standards

2. Windows Server 2008 R2 Standard Edition, Windows Server 2008 R2 Enterprise Edition, Windows Server 2008 R2 Datacenter Edition, Windows Server 2008 R2 Web Edition, Windows Server 2008 R2 Foundations Edition, Windows Server 2008 R2 for Itanium-based systems, and Windows HPC Server 2008 R2 Suite

3. NT 4

4. Windows Server 2008 R2 Datacenter Edition

5. 128 MB

6. Encrypting File System

7. Windows 2000

8. MMC, or Microsoft Management Console, provides a common interface and utility for all administrative tasks. The administrator can customize this utility.

9. Windows 2000

10. A group of computers running together that appear as if they are one system to clients and applications. Clustering improves performance by distributing tasks across multiple computers. It also provides reliability by allowing a computer in the cluster to be removed for maintenance without stopping service.

Chapter 13

1. X.500

2. Timekeeping and time synchronization

3. PDC Emulator

4. An external trust is used to connect a single domain within the forest to a single domain outside the forest.

5. False

6. TCP/IP

7. Global Catalog server

8. Bandwidth

9. False

10. Relative Identifier (RID) Master

11. False

12. Site Link

13. Root tree

14. False

Chapter 14

1. account

2. Active Directory Users And Computers

3. container

4. Organizational units

5. False

6. Enterprise Admins

7. Server Operators

8. Global groups

9. Domain local group

10. Universal groups

11. True

12. Account

13. Rights

14. True

15. Local

Chapter 15

1. Administrators, Server Operators, Power Users

2. Everyone—Read

3. Full Control

4. No access

5. False

6. CONVERT

7. True

8. Modify

9. Read

10. Full Control

11. Print queue

12. Everyone – Print

13. True

14. Print device

Appendix B

Common Acronyms

Acronym	Meaning
10GE	10 Gigabit Ethernet
ACE	Access Control Entry
ACK	Acknowledgment
ACL	Access Control List
AD DS	Active Directory Domain Services
AGP	Accelerated Graphics Port
AMD	Advanced Micro Devices
ANSI	American National Standards Institute
API	Application Programming Interface
ARP	Address Resolution Protocol
ARPA	Advanced Research Projects Agency
ARPANET	Advanced Research Projects Agency Network
ASCII	American Standard Code for Information Interchange
ASMP	Asymmetric Multiprocessing
ATA	Advanced Technology Attachment
BIOS	Basic Input/Output System
bps	bits per second
Bps	bytes per second
CD	Change Directory
CD	compact disc
CDFS	Compact Disc File System
CD-R	Compact Disc-Recordable
CD-ROM	Compact Disc Read-Only Memory

Acronym	Meaning
CD-RW	Compact Disc-Rewritable
CMOS	Complementary Metal-Oxide Semiconductor
CN	Common Name
CPU	central processing unit
CRC	cyclic redundancy check
CSMA/CD	Carrier Sense Multiple Access with Collision Detection
CSS	Content Scrambling System
DC	Domain Controller
DEC	Digital Equipment Corporation
DFS	Distributed File System
DHCP	Dynamic Host Configuration Protocol
DMA	Direct Memory Access
DN	Distinguished Name
DNS	Domain Name System
DoD	Department of Defense
DOS	Disk Operating System
DSL	Digital Subscriber Line
EBCDIC	Extended Binary Coded Decimal Interchange Code
ECP	Extended Capabilities Port
EDO	Extended Data Out
EEPROM	Electrically Erasable Programmable Read-Only Memory
EFS	Encrypting File System
EIDE	Enhanced IDE
EISA	Extended Industry Standard Architecture
EPP	Enhanced Parallel Port
EPROM	Erasable Programmable Read-Only Memory
FAT	File Allocation Table
FDDI	Fiber Distributed Data Interface
FQDN	Fully Qualified Domain Name
FSMO	Flexible Single Master Operations

Acronym	Meaning
GB	gigabyte
Gbps	gigabits per second
GBps	gigabytes per second
GC	Global Catalog or Global Catalog Server
GUI	graphical user interface
HCL	Hardware Compatibility List
HDD	Hard Disk Drive
HDMI	High Definition Multimedia interface
HTML	Hypertext Markup Language
IAS	Internet Authentication Services
IC	integrated circuit
ICMP	Internet Control Message Protocol
IDE	Integrated Drive Electronics
IEEE	Institute of Electrical and Electronic Engineers
IIS	Internet Information Services
I/O	input/output
IP	Internet Protocol
IPX/SPX	Interwork Packet Exchange/Sequenced Packet Exchange
IRQ	interrupt request
ISDN	Integrated Services Digital Network
ISO	International Standards Organization
ISP	Internet service provider
Kb	kilobit
KB	kilobyte
Kbps	kilobits per second
KBps	kilobytes per second
LAN	local area network
LDAP	Lightweight Directory Access Protocol
LDIF	Lightweight Directory Interchange Format
LLC	Logical Link Control

Acronym	Meaning
MAC	Media Access Control
MAN	Metropolitan Area Network
Mb	megabit
MB	megabyte
Mbps	megabits per second
MBps	megabytes per second
MCA	Micro-Channel Architecture
MD	Make Directory
MHz	megahertz
MMC	Microsoft Management Console
MMS	Microsoft Metadirectory Services
MODEM	Modulator/Demodulator
MSMQ	Microsoft Message Queue Server
MTBF	Mean time between failures
MTS	Microsoft Transaction Server
NetBEUI	NetBIOS Extended User Interface
NetBIOS	Network Basic Input/Output System
NFS	Network File System
NIC	network interface card
NOS	network operating system
NTFS	New Technology File System
NTP	Network Time Protocol
NUMA	Non-Uniform Memory Access
OEM	original equipment manufacturer
OS	operating system
OSI	Open Systems Interconnection
OU	Organizational Unit
PC	personal computer
PCI	Peripheral Component Interconnect
PCMCIA	Personal Computer Memory Card International Association

Acronym	Meaning
POST	Power-On Self Test
PPTP	Point-to-Point Tunneling Protocol
PROM	Programmable Read-Only Memory
PSTN	Public Switched Telephone Network
QoS	Quality of Service
RAID	Redundant Array of Inexpensive (or Independent) Disks
RAS	Remote Access Service
RD	Remove Directory
RFC	Request for Comments
RIP	Router Information Protocol
RIS	Remote Installation Service
RJ	Registered Jack
RODC	Read-Only Domain Controller
SAS	Serial Attached Small Computer System Interface
SATA	Serial Advanced Technology Attachment
SCSI	Small Computer System Interface
SDRAM	Synchronous Dynamic RAM (SDRAM)
SID	Security Identifier
SMP	symmetric multiprocessing
SNA	Systems Network Architecture
SNMP	Simple Network Management Protocol
SOAP	Simple Object Access Protocol
SOI	Silicon-on-Insulator
SQL	Structured Query Language
SSD	Solid State Drive
STP	Shielded Twisted Pair
Tb	Terabit
TB	Terabyte
Tbps	terabits per second
TBps	terabytes per second

Acronym	Meaning
TCP	Transmission Control Protocol
TCP/IP	Transmission Control Protocol/Internet Protocol
THz	Terahertz
UAC	User Account Control
UDDI	Universal Description Discovery and Integration
UDP	User Datagram Protocol
UMA	Upper Memory Area
UNC	Universal Naming Convention
UPN	User Principal Name
URL	Uniform Resource Locator
UTP	Unshielded Twisted-Pair
VAX	Virtual Address Extension
VPN	Virtual Private Network
WAN	wide area network
WINS	Windows Internet Naming Service
WORM	Write Once—Read Many
WSDL	Web Services Description Language
WHQL	Windows Hardware Quality Labs
XML	Extensible Markup Language

Glossary

10BASE-T A signal capable of transmitting at 10 Mbps over unshielded twisted-pair cable by using baseband signaling in a star topology. It is the IEEE 802.3 standard for unshielded twisted-pair Ethernet.

100BASE-T A standard used for Ethernet over twisted-pair cabling. The 100 is the speed in Mbps, Base is for Baseband transmission, and the T denotes twisted-pair cabling.

Access Control Entry (ACE) List of permissions a specific user or group has to a specific resource.

Access Control List (ACL) List of users with permissions to a specific resource.

access token A set of credentials that represent you on the network and that contain information about who a user is and what groups they are in.

Active Directory Users and Computers This tool, found in Administrative Tools, enables you to manage users, groups, and other elements of the Active Directory and is based on the Microsoft Management Console (MMC) model.

active matrix Sometimes referred to as Thin Film Transistor (TFT), active matrix LCD displays offer superior clarity and color. This is due mostly to faster refresh rates and more powerful LCD cells.

active partition The partition that the computer identifies as the one that will be used to boot up the computer and load the operating system.

admin access What is granted as a result of having membership in the Administrators group.

American National Standards Institute (ANSI) An organization that seeks to develop standardization within the computing industry. ANSI is the American representative to the ISO, or International Standards Organization.

American Standard Code for Information Interchange (ASCII) A 7-bit coding scheme that translates symbolic characters into the ones and zeros that are stored as data on a computer. Extended ASCII uses an 8-bit coding scheme.

array A set of objects, all of which are the same size and type.

asymmetric multiprocessing (ASMP) A computer architecture that uses multiple CPUs to improve the performance of the computer. In the ASMP model, one CPU is dedicated to managing tasks (which usually involves managing the other CPUs) for the computer system. The remaining CPUs process user tasks.

asynchronous communication Begins transmission of each character with a start bit and ends transmission of each character with a stop bit. This method is not as efficient as synchronous communication, but it is less expensive.

Asynchronous Transfer Mode (ATM) A network technology that uses fixed-size cells to transfer data. The fixed-size cells enable it to provide better performance.

authentication A process that requires a user to enter an ID and a password and then be verified by the software to gain access to resources.

B channel Stands for bearer channel and is a 64 Kbps circuit-switched channel. Used to carry voice and data.

backup The copying of all your data to a secondary storage option. If your primary storage option becomes unavailable, you can use backups to restore the operating system, application, and data files.

bandwidth   The capacity of a network line to carry information. Bandwidth is best thought of as a highway; four lanes support more traffic than two and have fewer slowdowns. One of the few basic rules of modern networking is that more bandwidth is always better.

base memory   Memory addresses that are reserved and used to store low-level control software that is required by an add-on device.

baseband   A technology that permits a single transmission of data at a fixed frequency on a wire at any given moment.

Basic Input/Output System (BIOS)   Software located in a ROM chip that is responsible for communicating directly between the computer hardware and the operating system.

Basic Rate Interface (BRI)   The basic ISDN service offered by telecommunication companies. BRI consists of two B channels and a single D channel.

batch file   A file that contains a set of commands to be executed by the operating system. All batch files end in .BAT.

baud   A measurement of the number of signals that are transmitted each second.

bit   A binary digit. The digit is the smallest unit of information and represents either an off state (zero) or an on state (one).

bit depth   A value for the number of bits that are used to make up a pixel. The higher the number of bits, the more colors that can be displayed.

bits per second (bps)   The number of bits, or ones and zeros, transmitted each second.

boot partition   Synonymous with the active partition on a disk. The boot partition contains the necessary files to start the operating system on the computer.

bridge   A Layer 2 device that enables networks using different Layer 2 protocols to communicate with one another. A bridge can also minimize traffic between two networks by passing through only those packets that are addressed to the other network.

broadband   A type of transmission that can use a single wire to transmit multiple streams of data simultaneously using different frequencies. This method is similar to the method used by radio stations all sharing the airwaves to send their signals.

broadcasts   Data transmitted to all devices on the same network segment.

burst mode   The temporary increase in data transmission speeds beyond what is normal. The increase is not sustainable and usually prevents other devices from transmitting.

bus architecture   Any linear pathway on which electrical signals travel and carry data from a source to a destination.

byte   A single binary character, or 8 bits.

Cable Modem Termination System (CMTS) device   A device used to forward user data to the Internet. Downstream data from the Internet is forwarded to the cable television equipment in that neighborhood, where it is then forwarded to the home user.

caching   A process whereby information is retrieved from the network and is then stored locally for use later, when the network is not available.

central office (CO)   A building in a given neighborhood where all local phone lines terminate.

central processing unit (CPU)   The microprocessor, or brain, of the computer. It uses logic to perform mathematical operations that are used to manipulate data.

child domain   A domain created under the namespace of an existing tree within a forest.

client   A computer on the network that requests network services.

client-server network   Uses a dedicated server to centralize user and group account management. Users at a client, or workstation, log on to a server where they have user accounts and access resources on the server to which their user account has permission.

clock signal   Controls the rate at which synchronous data is transmitted.

clustering   Connecting two or more computers to make them appear as one system. Clustering is used to take advantage of the processing power of multiple computers.

cmd.exe   Microsoft command-line interpreter used to issue commands that are executed by the operating system.

cmdlet   A command executed within Windows PowerShell that performs an action and can be used to create powerful scripts for local or remote administration. The command is issued in a verb-noun format.

coaxial   A type of media that has a single copper wire surrounded by plastic insulation, is wrapped in metal braid or foil, and is protected by a plastic cover.

collisions   A problem on Ethernet networks that occurs when two computers transmit on the wire simultaneously, causing an electrical spike twice the strength than is normal for the network.

command line   The prompt in a command shell screen from which a command is executed by typing letters and characters.

compact discs (CDs, DVDs, and Blu-ray)   Plastic or optical disks that can be read using lasers. Compact discs have a maximum storage capacity of 700 MB or more. A DVD has a capacity of 4.7 or 8.5 GB for dual-layer. A dual-layer Blu-ray disc can hold 50 GB.

compact disc-recordable (CD-R)   A compact disc that can have data recorded on it once using a laser and can be read many times.

compact disc-rewritable (CD-RW)   A compact disc that can have data rewritten to it several times using lasers. Lasers record data to the disc like a CD-R, but slightly less powerful lasers are used to erase the data. Even weaker lasers are used to read the data.

Complex Instruction Set Computing (CISC)   A full complement of instructions used by a processor to complete tasks such as mathematical calculations. Used in the most common type of processors produced; Intel processors are currently based on this standard.

compression   A method of reducing the size of data by using a mathematical calculation.

Computer Management utility   Used to monitor and configure the Windows 7 and Windows Server 2008 R2 computer systems. System tools, system drives, and services can all be accessed from here.

connection-oriented   A method of communication that is considered reliable because the sender is notified when data is not received or is unrecognizable.

container   Any object in the directory into which other objects can be placed. Objects that do not have this capability are called leaf objects.

cyclic redundancy check (CRC)   A form of error detection that performs a mathematical calculation on data at both the sender's end and the receiver's end to ensure that the data is received reliably.

D channel   Stands for delta channel and is a 16 Kbps circuit-switched channel. Used to manage control signals.

daisy chain   To connect a series of devices, one after the other. When signals are transmitted on a daisy chain, they go to the first device, then to the second, and so on, until termination is reached.

database server   A type of computer that maintains information records that can be added, deleted, changed, or searched. Database servers play a major role in most companies and on the Internet.

defragmentation   The reorganization of data on a hard disk to optimize performance.

demodulate   To convert an analog signal back to digital data. This is typically done on the receiving end of a computer transmission using standard phone service.

deny   To prevent a user from using other permissions to access a resource. It is far stronger in its effects than simply not giving them permissions.

dialog control   Manages the dialog between the sender and receiver. It consists of managing the transfer of data, determining whether an acknowledgment is required, and determining the appropriate responses to the sender.

differential backup   Uses the archive bit to determine which files have changed since the last normal backup. Files that have changed are backed up. The archive bit is not reset until the next normal backup. If you have to restore data, you need only your last full backup and your last differential tape.

Digital Subscriber Line (DSL)   A digital signaling method used to transmit data over regular phone lines at speeds up to 6 Mbps. DSL uses Asynchronous Transfer Mode (ATM) to pass data in fixed-size cells.

digital video disc or digital versatile disc (DVD) Based on the same technology as the CD-ROM, DVDs use a much smaller laser and are able to copy many times more the amount of data. DVDs can hold at least 4.7 GB of data and as much as 8.5 GB when they are double-sided.

DIN   Deutsch Industrie Norm—a German standards organization.

direct memory access (DMA)   DMA enables a device to transfer data directly to RAM without using the attention of the processor for the entire transfer period. The result is a faster and more direct method of data transfer.

directory services model   Uses a hierarchical database to logically organize the network resources. This model scales well to small, medium, or large enterprise networks.

disk controller   Manages floppy and hard disks. It can be a separate piece of hardware, or it can be integrated with the hard drive.

distributed processing   Sharing the task of processing instructions between a server and a client central processing unit (CPU).

domain controller (DC)   A DC is used in a Windows 2008 R2 domain. The DC hosts the read-write copy of the Active Directory database file, `ntds.dit`.

domain model   Logically groups computers, users, and groups into a domain. Users log on to the domain and have access to any resources within the domain to which their user account has permission.

Domain Name System (DNS)   A system that resolves domain names to IP addresses by using a domain name database.

DOS   An operating system developed by Microsoft. DOS predominantly uses command lines to manage the operating system, applications, and files.

dot pitch   Measures the distance, in millimeters, between two dots of the same color on the monitor.

drivers   Software that allows a particular operating system (Windows 7, for instance) to access and interact properly with a specific device (an HP Color LaserJet 9000, for instance). Each piece of hardware, therefore, may require a different driver for every operating system in which it is installed.

dual in-line package (DIP) switches   A set of tiny switches attached to a circuit board that are manually configured to alter the function of a chip for a specific computer or application.

dual-boot   To have two or more operating systems on your computer. At system startup, you can select which operating system you will boot.

Dynamic Host Configuration Protocol (DHCP)
Automates the assignment of IP configuration
information.

effective permission   A user's effective permission
is the permission that they are actually able to use
on an object after all permission elements have been
added together (or denied, as the case may be).

electron gun   The device that shoots electrically
charged particles called electrons toward the back
of the monitor screen.

encryption   The process of encoding data to prevent unauthorized access.

Enhanced IDE (EIDE)   An extended version of
the IDE standard. The benefits of EIDE include the
support of hard drives over 528 MB, the capability to chain devices other than drives (for example,
CD-ROM drives and tape drives), faster access time,
and the capability to chain up to four devices.

Enhanced Parallel Port (EPP)   The standard developed for parallel communication by Intel, Xircom,
and Zenith Data Systems to allow for data-transfer
rates of more than 2 MBps. It supports bidirectional
operation of attached devices and an addressing
scheme.

error control   A mechanism for assuring that data
received is in the same condition and format in which
it was sent.

Ethernet   A network communication technology
developed by Xerox that encloses data with a destination and source address for delivery, which is
called a frame. Additional information for Ethernet
is also added to the frame.

expansion card   An add-on device, such as a
sound or video card, that is installed directly into
an expansion slot built into a motherboard. The
card must be of the same bus architecture as the
slot on the motherboard.

explicit permission   Occurs when a user is given
permissions to a resource without any groups
involved.

**Extended Binary Coded Decimal Interchange
Code (EBCDIC)**   The 8-bit character set used by
IBM mainframes.

Extended Capabilities Port (ECP)   The standard
developed for parallel communication by Hewlett-
Packard and Microsoft to allow for data-transfer
rates of more than 2 Mbps. In addition to the
high data-transfer rates, it allows for bidirectional
operation.

extended partition   A non-bootable partition containing DOS logical drives.

FAT32   File Allocation Table 32. A 32-bit version
of the FAT file system that will recognize drives
larger than 2 GB. FAT32 can adjust the size of the
clusters (individual cells that are used to organize
the data) on a hard drive to accommodate larger-
sized drives.

fault tolerance   The use of hardware and software
to prevent the loss of data in the event of a system
or hardware failure or a power disruption.

fiber-optic   A type of media that uses glass or plastic to transmit light signals. Single-mode fiber-optic
cable contains a single fiber. Multimode fiber-optic
cable has two individually protected fibers.

File Allocation Table (FAT)   A table stored on the
outer edge of the hard drive that indicates the location and order of files on the hard drive.

file server   A computer that is dedicated to the
task of centrally sharing files and folders for access
by users.

File Transfer Protocol (FTP)   An application layer
protocol for transferring files between two computers. FTP involves the use of FTP client software and
an FTP server.

File Transfer Protocol (FTP) server   Transfers files
between the FTP server and FTP clients. Most web
browsers use FTP client software to download and
upload files to Internet servers running the FTP
service.

flow control   A feature of the Transport layer that manages the amount of data being transmitted between sender and receiver. If the receiving computer is unable to accept more data, it notifies the sending computer to pause transmission.

frame   Data that has been encapsulated by the Data-Link layer protocol before being transmitted on the wire.

freeware   Software that you can use without payment.

full control access   General term meaning that the user has Full Control permissions on the resource.

fully duplexed   Means that simultaneous two-way communication can take place.

fully qualified domain name (FQDN)   The complete name registered with InterNIC that is used to identify a computer on the Internet. It includes the computer name (hostname) and the domain name; for example, mycomputer.sybex.com.

function   A block of code that performs an action or operation. A function may or may not require parameters.

gigahertz (GHz)   One billion cycles per second. The internal clock speed of a microprocessor is expressed in GHz.

global catalog   A fast-access copy of the full directory representing all objects within a forest that includes only those attributes that are commonly searched, such as usernames and logon names.

global groups   Groups that hold users in the domain and that are placed into universal, domain local, or local groups. Global groups are primarily used to group users with similar network roles.

graphical user interface (GUI)   An application that provides intuitive controls (such as icons, buttons, menus, and dialog boxes) for configuring, manipulating, and accessing applications and files.

H0   Another ISDN channel that includes 6 B channels. Other H channel definitions include H-10 and H-11, which are just another way of identifying the 23 B channels of the Primary Rate Interface.

hard drive   Stores data as a series of ones and zeros on a series of magnetically coated disks. A positive charge indicates a one, and the absence of a charge indicates a zero.

Hardware Compatibility List (HCL)   Provided by Microsoft, the HCL lists all hardware that has been tested by Microsoft and has proved to work with a particular operating system. Hardware not on the HCL might work, but it is not certain to.

hexadecimal   A numbering system that uses 16 instead of 10 as its base; it uses the digits 0–9 and the letters A–F to represent the decimal numbers 0–15.

hidden file   A file that is not viewable using the DIR command or in a folder. The hidden file attribute can be set to on or off using the attribute command or by setting the file properties in Windows.

hop   The number of foreign gateways (routers other than your own) that a packet must pass through between the source and destination computers.

hub   A Physical layer device that connects computers and other devices to make a network. A hub regenerates an incoming signal from one device and broadcasts the signal out all other ports.

Hypertext Markup Language (HTML)   A text-based scripting language that is used in the creation of web pages to control the presentation of text and graphics. It can also be used to add functionality to the web page for navigation or for interfacing with other technologies like databases and multimedia.

IEEE 802.3   The IEEE standard that is also known as Carrier Sense Multiple Access with Collision Detection (CSMA/CD) and defines how most Ethernet networks function.

IEEE 802.3ab   The IEEE standard for 1000 Mbps Gigabit Ethernet over unshielded twisted-pair (UTP) cable.

IEEE 802.3u The IEEE standard for 100 Mbps Fast Ethernet. Defines the specifications for implementing Fast Ethernet at the Physical and Data-Link layers of the OSI model.

IEEE 802.3z The IEEE standard for 1000 Mbps Gigabit Ethernet over fiber-optic cable.

incremental backup Uses the archive bit to determine which files have changed since the last incremental backup. After the incremental backup is complete, the archive bit is cleared. Incremental backups occur between normal full backups.

Input/Output (I/O) Refers to any device or operation that enters data into or extracts data from a computer.

Input/Output (I/O) channel A circuit that provides a path for an input or output device to communicate with the processor.

Input/Output (I/O) memory Memory addresses that are reserved and assigned to add-on devices. Each assignment tells the CPU about the location of a specific device.

Institute of Electrical and Electronic Engineers (IEEE) Pronounced *I triple E*, an international organization that defines computing and telecommunications standards. The LAN standards defined by IEEE include the 802-workgroup specifications.

Integrated Drive Electronics (IDE) A drive technology that integrates the drive and controller into a single piece of hardware. IDE drives are an inexpensive data-storage solution.

Integrated Services Digital Network (ISDN) A technology that combines digital and voice transmission onto a single wire.

International Standards Organization (ISO) An organization dedicated to defining global communication and informational exchange standards. The American National Standards Institute (ANSI) is the American representative to the ISO.

Internet Explorer (IE) If your computer has access to the Internet, Internet Explorer is one of the main applications for accessing Internet resources.

Internet service provider (ISP) A company or organization that provides the user with access to the Internet, typically for a fee. Users may gain access by using any one of many remote connection technologies, including modems, DSL, ISDN, cable modems, and others.

internetwork Two or more networks that are connected using a router.

interrupt A type of signal that is used to get the attention of the CPU when I/O is required. An interrupt tells the CPU that the operating system is requesting that a specific action be taken. Interrupts are prioritized; higher-numbered interrupts are serviced first.

interrupt request (IRQ) The method used by a device to inform the microprocessor (CPU) that the device needs attention. Through this method of interruption, the microprocessor can function without needing to poll each device to see whether it needs service.

IP Security (IPSec) A protocol standard for encrypting IP packets.

jumpers Plastic-covered metal clips that are used to connect two pins on a motherboard. The connection creates a circuit that turns the setting to "on."

load balancing Distributing similar tasks (such as accessing an application or assigning an IP address) equally across multiple computers.

local area network (LAN) A LAN is contained within a single building or campus and can operate independently of any outside connection.

local drive Storage that is physically located on the user's own machine. Often the only local drives are the primary hard drive (C drive) and the CD-ROM (D drive).

local groups Groups that are created on Windows 7 workstations and Windows 2008/2008 R2 servers and allow for local administration of resources. Global groups or domain users could be placed into these groups to give them permissions on the machine.

local loop The two-wire copper telephone cable that runs from a home or office to the central office of the telephone company.

local security Permissions settings that take effect even if the user is working locally on the machine where the resource is located.

logging on The process of authenticating to the network and gaining access to the network as a particular user.

logical drive Based on how you partition your physical drive, the area of the extended partition can be organized into multiple drives. Each drive is assigned a DOS identifier from D to Z.

Logical Link Control (LLC) A Data-Link sublayer that establishes whether communication with another device is going to be connectionless or connection-oriented.

loopback A special function for testing a device's ability to communicate by making it communicate with itself.

managed hubs Similar to hubs but with the exception that the device can be managed using software to monitor and control network communication.

Manchester encoding A method of identifying the beginning and end of a bit signal (one or zero) when it is transmitted on the network.

master A device that is responsible for controlling one or more directly connected devices.

Media Access Control (MAC) address A hexadecimal number that is allocated by an international organization and is burned into the network interface card (NIC) by the NIC manufacturer.

Media Access Control is a sublayer of the Data-Link layer.

megabits per second (Mbps) A measurement of the amount of data, in the millions of bits per second, is being transferred.

megabytes per second (MBps) A measurement of the transfer speed of a device in terms of millions of bytes per second.

megahertz (MHz) One million cycles per second. The internal clock speed of a microprocessor is expressed in MHz.

microcode The smallest form of an instruction in a CPU.

Microsoft Management Console (MMC) A Microsoft application framework for accessing administrative tools, called consoles.

millions of instructions per second (MIPS) A measurement of the number of microcode instructions that a CPU or microprocessor can complete in one second, or cycle.

modulate To convert digital data into analog signals. Modulation enables digital computer data to be transferred over standard telephone lines.

motherboard The main board in a computer that manages communication between devices internally and externally.

Multimedia Extension (MMX) A processor technology that dramatically improves the response time of games and multimedia-based applications. The technology was introduced through the MMX-equipped line of Intel Pentium chips.

multitask To perform several operations concurrently.

namespace The part of the naming structure occupied by a certain domain or tree. If the domain is foo.com, all machines and subdomains of foo.com exist within its namespace: www.foo.com, accounting .atlanta.foo.com, and so on.

network   Two or more computers connected for the purpose of sharing resources such as files or printers.

network drive   A mapping to a network path that appears to the user as a drive letter. You access it the same way that you access a local drive.

network interface card (NIC)   A device that connects a computer to the physical cable media and produces signals for transferring data.

New Technology File System (NTFS)   Developed by Microsoft for the NT operating systems, this feature added better file management, larger disk compatibility, and file-level security on the local computer.

node   A connection point on a network. Nodes include computers, servers, and printers.

Non-Uniform Memory Access (NUMA) multiprocessing   Each processor is provided with separate memory. This helps to avoid the problem where several processors attempt to use the same memory.

object   Every element of the network—from people to machines—is represented in the Active Directory by an object. These objects each represent one specific element of the network and have their own properties and configuration elements.

object linking and embedding (OLE)   A technology that enables applications to share data. Each document is stored as an object, and one object can be embedded within another object. For example, an Excel spreadsheet can be embedded within a Word document. Because the object is linked, changes through Excel or Word will be updated through the single linked object.

octet   One of four parts of an IP address. Each number in an octet is created using 8 bits.

offline storage   Holds data that is currently unavailable. You use offline storage to store large amounts of infrequently accessed data or to store computer backups.

online data storage   Holds data that is immediately available and can be quickly accessed, as is the case with hard disks.

open source   The free distribution of source code (software) for the purpose of improvement of the software by the programming community. Regardless of modifications or adaptations of open source software, the code is still protected by the Open Source Definition.

organizational units (OUs)   Organizational units break the directory into subdivisions and are used to group and store directory objects such as groups, user accounts, and resources.

original equipment manufacturer (OEM)   A term used to describe the device or software that is sold to a reseller, who then passes the product on to a consumer. OEM versions of software can sometimes be altered by the reseller in an effort to make the product integrate with the reseller's hardware.

OS/2   A 32-bit operating system originally developed by Microsoft and IBM. OS/2 can support DOS, Windows, and OS/2 applications. Since Microsoft's abandonment of the program in the late 1980s, OS/2 has been produced and sold exclusively by IBM.

packet   Data that has been encapsulated with information from the Transport and Network layers of the OSI model.

parallel communication   The process of transmitting and processing data one byte (8 bits) at a time.

parent domain   The domain from which all other domains in a tree take their name.

Parity (memory)   An extra bit found on some memory modules. Non-parity memory has 8 bits. Parity adds an extra bit that is used to keep track of the other 8 bits. This can help prevent memory errors and is recommended for use in servers.

Parity (disk)   In the context of a stripe set, a series of mathematical calculations based on the data stored. If a disk fails, the stored parity information can be used to rebuild the data.

passive matrix   A flat-panel LCD display technology that uses horizontal and vertical wires with LCD cells at each intersection to create a video image. Passive matrix is considered inferior to active matrix but is less expensive to produce.

PC card   A small, thin device the size of a credit card. PC cards follow the PCMCIA (Personal Computer Memory Card International Association) standard and can be of three types. Type 1 supports RAM or ROM expansions for mobile computing devices. Type 2 is slightly thicker to accommodate modems and network cards. Type 3 is the thickest and is designed for mobile storage.

peer-to-peer network   This type of network does not use dedicated network servers for logging in users or providing secure access to network resources. Instead, clients simply share resources, and other clients have access to whatever has been shared.

Peripheral Component Interconnect (PCI)   A bus standard for the transfer of data between the central processing unit (CPU), expansion cards, and random access memory (RAM). PCI communicates at 33 MHz.

physical hard drive   The physical (or real, as opposed to conceptual) drive; for example, drive 0 or drive 1 in a two-drive configuration.

physical location   The actual location of a resource. Each resource must be homed on a server somewhere on the network. Windows Server 2008/Windows Server 2008 R2 enable you to organize resources logically, rather than physically.

pipeline   A place in the processor where operations occur in a series of stages. The operation is not complete until it has passed through all stages.

pixel   Short for picture element. A pixel is one dot in an image.

platforms   The hardware or software that supports any given system. The term platform can be used, for example, to reference an x64-based system or Windows Server 2008 R2.

plotter   A special type of print device that draws high-resolution diagrams, charts, graphs, and other layouts.

port address   An address used by the computer to access devices such as expansion cards and printers.

POSIX   A standard originally developed for Unix that defines the interface between applications and the operating system. It was widely used for the development of other operating systems, including Windows 2000.

PostScript   A page description language used to convert and move data from an application to a laser printer.

PowerShell   A robust command-line shell built on the .Net Framework that includes an associated scripting language. PowerShell generally utilizes cmdlets to interact with the operating system.

PowerShell script   A file that contains a set of cmdlets to be executed by PowerShell. All PowerShell scripts end in .ps1.

Power Users   Intended to allow Windows users greater authority over their workstations. Power Users are not as powerful as the Administrator, but they can do far more than just users, in that they can install software and configure more workstation options.

power-on self-test (POST)   A set of diagnostic tests that are used to determine the state of hardware installed in the computer. Some components that fail the POST, such as bad RAM or a disconnected keyboard, will prevent the computer from booting up properly.

primary partition The first and bootable partition you create on a hard drive.

Primary Rate Interface (PRI) The high-end ISDN service offered by telecommunication companies. PRI provides 23 B channels and one D channel. This is equivalent to the 24 channels of a T1 line.

print processor The print processor and the default data type determine how much of the formatting of a document is done by the printer, as opposed to the application.

print server A centralized computer that manages printing of user documents to one or more printers. Print servers store documents temporarily when the printer is busy.

profile A record of the user's personal configuration data and preferences. You can store a profile locally or you can store all user profiles on the server and allow them to roam, which means a user could log on to any machine in the domain and get their own profile.

Program Information Files (PIFs) Files for a non-Windows application that includes settings for running applications in Windows 3.x.

protocol A set of rules for communication between two devices.

PS/2 Also known as the mouse port and DIN 6, PS/2 was developed by IBM for connecting a mouse to the computer. PS/2 ports are supported for mice and keyboards alike.

random access memory (RAM) A temporary memory location that stores the operating system, applications, and files that are currently in use. The content in this type of memory is constantly changing. When you shut down the computer, all information in this type of memory is lost.

read access Permissions that allow a user to view a resource but not modify it.

read-only memory (ROM) A type of memory that has data pre-copied onto it. The data can only be read from and cannot be overwritten. ROM is used to store the BIOS software.

Reduced Instruction Set Computing (RISC) A reduced set of instructions used by a processor. PowerPC and Alpha processors are manufactured using this standard. The reduced instruction set enables a microprocessor to operate at higher speeds.

Redundant Array of Inexpensive (or Independent) Disks (RAID) A method of using a series of hard disks as an array of drives. Some RAID implementations improve performance. Others improve performance and provide fault tolerance.

refresh rate A measurement of the number of times that an image is redrawn to the screen per second. Measured in Hertz, a higher number is better.

Remote Access Service (RAS) Allows computers to access the network remotely; for example, through a phone, ISDN, or Internet connection.

Remote Desktop Service (RDS) Whereas normal servers provide file or printer access, a terminal server provides full desktop access. Terminal services allow a single machine to be used by multiple users at once. Each individual uses their own keyboard, mouse, and monitor, and is presented with a Windows Desktop, but all programs run locally on the terminal server.

repeater A network device, similar to a hub but with only two or three ports, that can be used to extend the transmission distance of a network signal or to join two networks.

replicate The process by which a machine sends a copy of its databases to another machine. This usually occurs on a scheduled basis.

replication cycle The means by which a group of machines synchronize their information; replication is usually done on a preconfigured schedule that can be adjusted due to network or organizational need.

resolve   To convert from one type to another. In relation to IP addresses and domain names, it is the conversion of an IP address to a domain name on the Internet or vice versa.

rights   A right is different from a permission. Rights allow you to do a task, whereas permissions concern a particular resource. For instance, in order to access a particular file, a user must have permission to use that particular file, while changing the system time is considered a right.

routers   Devices that connect two or more networks. Routers work at the Network layer of the OSI model, receiving packets and forwarding them to their correct destinations.

routing table   A table created by a router that contains information on how to reach networks that are directly attached to the router and networks that are distant.

RS-232   An interface standard for use between data communications equipment (DCE) and data terminal equipment (DTE).

scalable   Capable of expanding to accommodate greater numbers of users and resources.

schema   The set of configuration elements that defines a particular directory. The schema defines information about all objects and attributes in the directory.

Security Accounts Manager (SAM)   A local database on Windows Server 2008 R2 servers that contains the local user accounts and local groups.

security identifier (SID)   A unique number used by Windows Server 2008 and Windows Server Active Directory to represent a user or a computer on the network.

separator page   A page that is used to show where one print job stops and another one starts.

serial communication   The transmission of data one bit at a time.

server   A computer that provides dedicated file, print, messaging, application, or other services to client computers.

share   A share is a resource, such as a directory or a printer, that is made available to network users. A share can have permissions associated with it to control which users can access its resources.

shareware   Software that is generally available for trial use. If you like the software, you should pay a small licensing fee.

Silicon-on-Insulator (SOI)   The microchip manufacturing innovation that IBM invented. It is based on the capability to enhance silicon technology by reducing the time it takes to move electricity through a conductor.

single-edge cartridge (SEC)   An advanced packaging scheme that the Intel Pentium II and later models use. The processor is encased in a cartridge module with a single edge that plugs into a 242-pin slot on the system board, much as an expansion card plugs into the system board.

Site Link   A logical connection that links two sites and controls the flow of traffic over wide area network (WAN) links. Just as a trust regulates the flow of permissions and resources, a Site Link regulates the speed and type of traffic that is allowed across the WAN. Site Links therefore enable an administrator to optimize bandwidth usage.

slave   A device that is controlled by another device called the master.

Small Computer System Interface (SCSI)   An interface that connects SCSI devices to the computer. This interface uses high-speed parallel technology to connect devices that include hard disks, CD-ROM players, tape backup devices, and other hardware peripherals.

Solid State Drive (SSD)   Storage device that uses non-volatile memory chips to retain data. Uses less energy and generates very little heat as compared to conventional hard drives. Used in mobile devices.

standard   An agreed-upon set of rules, procedures, and functions that are widely accepted.

start bit   The bit that synchronizes the clock on the computer receiving the data. In asynchronous data transmission, the start bit is a space.

stop bit   The bit that identifies the end of the character being transmitted so that the character is clearly recognized.

switch   The modern name used for a multiport bridge. Like a regular bridge, each port on a switch represents a separate network. Traffic on each port is kept isolated except when the packet is destined for another device on a different port or if the packet is a broadcast. Broadcasts must be sent out all ports.

switch box   A device that enables multiple machines to share a single device, such as a printer or a monitor. The disadvantage is that only one machine at a time can use the device.

symmetric multiprocessing (SMP)   A computer architecture that uses multiple CPUs to improve a computer's performance. As performance demands increase on an SMP-capable computer, additional CPUs can be added to boost performance. During operation, if one CPU is idle, it can be given any task to perform.

synchronous communication   Transmits data by synchronizing the data signal between the sender and receiver and sending data as a continuous stream. This is the most efficient way of sending large amounts of data but requires expensive equipment.

take ownership   Each file on an NTFS drive has an "owner"—a user account or group that is given complete access to that file. Taking ownership is the process of becoming the owner of a resource.

telecommuter   Someone who remotely connects to his or her office to work from home or a remote location.

termination   The use of a terminator at both ends of a SCSI daisy chain to keep data signals from bouncing back on the SCSI bus after they reach the end. The terminator is a small plastic connector that has a resistor (ceramic-based material that absorbs electricity) inside it.

tethering   Tethering is the process of connecting a mobile phone to allow connectivity to the Internet.

throughput   The amount of data that can be transferred in a set period of time.

Token Ring   A Data-Link layer protocol developed by IBM that uses a token-passing method for transmitting data. Each device on the ring takes turns using the token. The token can be used by only one device at a time.

transistor   A microscopic electronic device that uses positive electrons to create the binary value of one, or "on," and negative electrons to create the binary value of zero, or "off." Modern CPUs have millions of transistors.

transitive   Trusts that are transitive allow a domain to act as an intermediary for two other domains. If A trusts B, and B trusts C, there is an implied trust between A and C. Directory information will pass from A to C only if B acts as a transitive link.

tree root   The top domain within a newly created namespace. All other domains in the tree must fall within the tree root domain's namespace.

trust   A trust is configured to allow two Windows domains to share user authentication information and to allow users from one domain to access resources in another domain.

unshielded twisted-pair (UTP)   A type of media that can contain four, six, or eight wires. Pairs of wires are twisted together to prevent signal interference. The wires are then wrapped in a plastic cover. UTP is identified by the category nomenclature.

Upper Memory Area (UMA) The area of memory between 640 KB and 1 MB in an IBM-compatible computer. This area of memory was originally reserved for system and video use.

USB hub A connectivity device that provides multiple USB connections so that several USB devices can communicate with the computer.

Users container One of a number of default containers in the Active Directory. In most cases, using this default location is fine for storing user accounts. User accounts in this folder can later be placed into groups that exist in other folders or organizational units.

Virtual Address Extension (VAX) The technology built by DEC to run the VMS platform computers.

virtual circuit A logical connection between two devices that transmits and receives data.

virtual private networking (VPN) Using encrypted envelopes to securely transmit sensitive data between two points over the unsecured Internet.

virtual RAM A function of the operating system that is used to simulate RAM by breaking computer programs into small units of data called pages and storing the pages in a page file on the hard disk.

volume A part of a physical disk that is identified by a single drive label.

wide area network (WAN) A relatively low-speed data connection (typically 1.546 Mbps) that uses the telephone company to connect two locations separated by a large geographical area.

Windows Internet Naming Service (WINS) A Microsoft proprietary protocol that runs on a Windows server. The protocol is used on Windows servers to resolve NetBIOS names, the workstation names on Windows computers, to IP addresses. WINS is similar in concept to DNS.

Windows Internet Naming Service (WINS) server Maps the NetBIOS names that NT uses to identify computers with IP addresses.

Windows Update A set of online updates and drivers provided by Microsoft that allow users to locate current files for their system and for new devices.

wizard A configuration assistant that walks the user through a short series of guided steps to complete a task.

workstation Another name for a computer that is used by users. It is sometimes used to describe powerful computers that are used for completing complex mathematical, engineering, and animation tasks.

X.500 An industry-standard directory structure used by Windows Server 2008 and Windows Server 2008 R2 to organize and name network elements. Other network operating systems, such as Novell's NetWare Directory Services, also use X.500.

Index

Note to the Reader: Throughout this index **boldfaced** page numbers indicate primary discussions of a topic. *Italicized* page numbers indicate illustrations.